The Transition from Capitalism

Saeed Rahnema
Editor

The Transition from Capitalism

Marxist Perspectives

Editor
Saeed Rahnema
York University
Toronto, Ontario, Canada

ISBN 978-3-319-82921-0   ISBN 978-3-319-43835-1 (eBook)
DOI 10.1007/978-3-319-43835-1

© The Editor(s) (if applicable) and The Author(s) 2017
Softcover reprint of the hardcover 1st edition 2017
This work is subject to copyright. All rights are solely and exclusively licensed by the Publisher, whether the whole or part of the material is concerned, specifically the rights of translation, reprinting, reuse of illustrations, recitation, broadcasting, reproduction on microfilms or in any other physical way, and transmission or information storage and retrieval, electronic adaptation, computer software, or by similar or dissimilar methodology now known or hereafter developed.
The use of general descriptive names, registered names, trademarks, service marks, etc. in this publication does not imply, even in the absence of a specific statement, that such names are exempt from the relevant protective laws and regulations and therefore free for general use.
The publisher, the authors and the editors are safe to assume that the advice and information in this book are believed to be true and accurate at the date of publication. Neither the publisher nor the authors or the editors give a warranty, express or implied, with respect to the material contained herein or for any errors or omissions that may have been made.

Cover illustration: © Lee Mette / Noun Project

Printed on acid-free paper

This Palgrave Macmillan imprint is published by Springer Nature
The registered company is Springer International Publishing AG
The registered company address is: Gewerbestrasse 11, 6330 Cham, Switzerland

To the memory of Behrooz Soleimani, Heybatolla Moini (Homayun), Mehrdad Pakzad, Manoucher Shafiee (Halilrudi), Mahmoud Zakipour, Saeed Soltanpoor, Hossein Sadrai (Eghdami), Ali Sadrai, Pouran Jampour, Hadi Kianzad and thousand other revolutionaries perished in a failed revolution

Preface

Despite a litany of setbacks experienced globally by the entire spectrum of the left and labour movements over many decades—in part driven by the aggressive assault of neo-liberal agendas – and notwithstanding the dreadful rise of the new right and religious fundamentalisms, we are witnessing a resurgence of the left's discourse against inequality and injustice: a growing trend of resistance to and protest against the ever-widening income gap, unemployment and precariousness, environmental degradation, imperialist aggressions and the sufferings caused by capitalism in different parts of the world. We have observed the rise of the left in Latin America, popularity of Syriza in Greece, Podemos in Spain, Die Linke in Germany, the Left Party in Sweden and the left coalition in Portugal. Several years ago, it would have been unimaginable that in Britain, Her Majesty's official opposition would be led by a left Socialist, Jeremy Corbyn. Or that in the United States, where the term "socialist" is considered and often used as an insult, a Presidential candidate, Bernie Sanders, would claim it as his identity and gain surprising popular support.

Through a series of interviews with prominent theorists and leading political activists in different parts of the world, this book intends to explore the causes of the setbacks and failures as well as the achievements of both the reformist and revolutionary strategies of the left, address the larger questions around the agenda(s) of socialism in the era of globalization, and elaborate the role of social classes, identitarian and other social groups that could play instrumental roles in the transition beyond capitalist social formation.

The interviews, concentrating on several categories of questions that form the book's seven chapters, and arranged alphabetically, were conducted between Summer 2014 and Fall 2015. Responses are different in length, and depending on the specific areas of interest of each interviewee, other questions were also discussed. While there are similarities in the perspectives, the views expressed by the interviewees are different from each other, and from some of the points raised in my introduction. This is particularly notable in relation to the question of strategy.

The process that led to the present book started several years ago when I wrote a series of articles and exchanges criticizing the re-emergence of traditionalist socialist perspectives within a section of the Iranian left. We were all involved in the failed Iranian Revolution of 1979, where the left initially played such an important role in bringing about the uprisings against the Shah and gained unprecedented public support, but was later eliminated ruthlessly, quickly and rather easily by the brutal populist autocracy of the Islamists. The left's failures and destruction following the Revolution, the stunning collapse of the "actually existing socialism" in the Soviet bloc, and the "great leap" backward in China, seemed to have faded from the memory of some Iranian left activists. Leaving aside the Iranian experience, the fate of socialist and labour movements in other parts of the world, whether in developed industrial countries or less developed ones, has not been great either, even though generally without the bloodshed experienced by the Iranian left. Setbacks in the face of the aggressive global neoliberal offensive have been universal.

As almost all commentators in the present collection argue and agree, the road to socialism is a long and arduous one. All believe that capitalism is not sustainable, due largely to its inherent contradictions, and that a post-capitalist social world order is inevitable and attainable. It is believed that armed with the hard-earned lessons of past experiences and grounded in the specific and concrete objective and subjective realities and conditions of each society, the left around the world can radically strive and take practical steps for steady and progressive gains towards socialist goals, combining their collective efforts worldwide to challenge the global dominance of capital.

First and foremost, I am grateful to the interviewees who agreed to participate in these discussions. I extend my gratitude to Parviz Sedaghat for his keen support of the initial idea of this project and for the translation and publication of the Farsi version of the interviews in the on-line periodical *pecritique (Naghd-e eghtessad-e siassi)*. Roja Ghahari, my research assistant, a PhD. Candidate in the Department of Political science at York University helped me at different phases of the project, I am thankful for her assistance. I would like to thank the anonymous reviewer for useful remarks and suggestions. Last but not least, my thanks also go to Palgrave Macmillan and its publisher Dr. Farideh Koohi-kamali, for making the publication of this book possible.

Saeed Rahnema

Contents

1 Introduction: The Question of Transition from Capitalism   1

2 Failures and Achievements of the Past   27

3 Which Revolution?   53

4 Peaceful Transition   87

5 Globalization and Socialism in One Country   109

6 Which Socialism?   135

7 Social Classes   163

8 Practical Steps   189

Index   205

Contributors' Bios

Gilbert Achcar Grew up in Lebanon, researched and taught in Beirut, Paris and Berlin, and has been since 2007 Professor of Development Studies and International Relations at SOAS, University of London. His books include: *The Clash of Barbarisms: The Making of the New World Disorder* (New York: Monthly Review Press, 2002), published in 13 languages; *Perilous Power: The Middle East and U.S. Foreign Policy* (Boulder, CO: Paradigm Publishers, 2007), co-authored with Noam Chomsky; *The Arabs and the Holocaust: The Arab-Israeli War of Narratives* (New York: Henry Holt/Metropolitan, 2010); *The People Want: A Radical Exploration of the Arab Uprising* (Berkeley: University of California Press, 2013); and *Morbid Symptoms: Relapse in the Arab Uprising* (Stanford: Stanford University Press, 2016).

Aijaz Ahmad Literary theorist and political commentator, is currently Chancellor's Professor, Department of Comparative Literature, University of California, Irvine. He has been visiting professor in different US, Canadian, and Indian universities. Among his books mention can be made of *In Theory, Classes, Nations, Literatures* (1994), *Lineages of the Present* (1996), On Communalism and Globalization *(2002)*, and *In out Times: Empire, Politics and Culture* (2007).

Robert Albriton Professor Emeritus, York University, Canada. His writings include: *Economics Transformed: Discovering the Brilliance of Marx* (2007); *Let Them Eat Junk: How Capitalism Creates Hunger and Obesity* (2009);; A Practical Utopia for the Twenty-First Century, in Vieira and Marder eds. *Existential Utopia: New Perspectives on Utopian Thought* (2012).

Kevin Anderson Professor of Sociology, University of California, Santa Barbara; writings include *Marx at the Margins*, 2010, and several edited collections: *Karl Marx* (with Bertell Ollman), 2012; *The Dunayevskaya-Marcuse-Fromm Correspondence* (with Russell Rockwell), 2012; *The Rosa Luxemburg Reader* (with Peter Hudis), 2004.

Barbara Epstein Professor Emerita in the History of Consciousness Department at University of California Santa Cruz. She writes about social movements; her writings include; *Political Protest and Cultural Revolution; Nonviolent Direct Action in the Seventies and Eighties,* University of California Press, 1991; *The Minsk Ghetto 1941-43; Jewish Resistance and Soviet Internationalism*, University of California press, 2008. She was a member of the Editorial Board of *Monthly Review, Socialist Review*, and now with the *Socialist Register.*

Aron Etzler Secretary of the Left Party of Sweden, journalist and author of *Reinfeldteffekten: Hur Nya Moderaterna Tog över Makten i Sverige Och Skakade Socialdemokraterna i Grunden*, 2013, *Ta Det Tillbaka: Kampen Om Arbetarklassen Och Framtiden*. Linköping: Nixon, 2002, and *Trondheimsmodellen: Radikala framgångshistorier från Norge Och Nederländerna.* Stockholm: Karneval, 2007.

Sam Gindin Former was Research Director and later an Assistant to the President of the Canadian Autoworkers Union (now UNIFOR) from 1974-2000, he then became the Packer Chair in Social Justice at York University from 2001-2010. Among his publications are *The Canadian Auto Workers: the Birth and Transformation of a Union*. Toronto: J. Lorimer, 1995, (with Leo Panitch) *The Making of Global Capitalism: the Political Economy of American Empire*. London: Verso, 2012, and with (with Greg Albo and Leo Panitch), *In and out of Crisis.*

Peter Hudis Professor of Humanities and Philosophy at Oakton Community College and is a member of The International Marxist-Humanist Organization. His works include *Marx's Concept of the Alternative to Capitalism*, Haymarket Books, 2012, and *Frantz Fanon: Philosopher of the Barricades*, Pluto Press, 2015). He is also general editor of the planned 14-volume collection *The Complete Works of Rosa Luxemburg*, Verso Books; two volumes have appeared so far.

Ursula Huws Professor of Labour and Globalisation at the University of Hertfordshire and the director of Analytica Social and Economic Research

Ltd in the UK. She is also the editor of *Work Organisation, Labour and Globalisation;* Her latest book, is *Labor in the Global Digital Economy: the Cybertariat Comes of Age*, Monthly Review Press, 2014.

Michael A. Lebowitz Professor Emeritus of Economics, Simon Fraser University, Canada. His latest book, *The Socialist Imperative: from Gotha to Now* was published in 2015. Earlier books include *Beyond Capital: Marx's Political Economy of the Working Class* (2003), *Build it Now: Socialism for the Twenty-first Century* (2006), *The Socialist Alternative: Real Human Development* (2010). He worked between 2004 and 2010 as an adviser in Venezuela and as Director of the programme, Transformative Practice and Human Development at Centro Internacional Miranda in Caracas.

Leo Panitch The Canada Research Chair in Comparative Political Economy, and Distinguished Research Professor of Political Science at York University, Toronto. For the past three decades he has been the co-editor of the annual *Socialist Register*. His recent book with Sam Gindin entitled *The Making of Global Capitalism: The Political Economy of American Empire* (Verso 2012) has been awarded the Deutscher book prize in the UK and the Davidson book prize in Canada.

Saeed Rahnema Former Director of School of Public Policy and Administration at York University, Canada and Professor of Political Science, Public Policy and Equity Studies. He has also served as an officer of the UNDP, and as a Director of the Middle East Economic Association (MEEA). In his homeland Iran, he taught and worked in the Industrial Management Institute, and during the Iranian revolution of 1979 was a cadre in the Left and Workers/Employees' Council movement. His works include, *Organization Structure; A Systemic Approach*, 1992, *Diaspora by Design* (with Haideh Moghissi and Mark Goodman), 2009, *Rebirth of Social Democracy in Iran* (Farsi), 1996 *Marx's Method; Foundation of Marxian political* Economy (Farsi) 2012.

Catherine Samary Was involved in international activities of the Fourth International (FI) in Eastern Europe in the 1970th, while being member of the former Revolutionary Communist League/LCR) and of its Central Committee. She is still member of the FI's International Committee and involved in the radical Left, feminist and anti-racist associations in France. She was a co-Founder of the Institute Espace Marx, and is a member of the scientific council of ATTAC-France and of the Editorial board of its

Review "Les Possibles". She was a lecturer and researcher in Economics at the Université Paris-Dauphine and Institute of European Studies. She is a collaborator of the Institute of Research and Education in Amsterdam which has published her lectures, among which (in several languages) *Plan, Market and Democracy – the expérience of so-called socialist countries.* Author of many books among which her doctorate thesis published as *Le marchécontre l'autogestion – l'expérience yougoslave* and many articles for *Le Monde Diplomatique* and other Reviews in different languages.

CHAPTER 1

Introduction: The Question of Transition from Capitalism

From the time of Marx himself, socialists have heralded the "inevitable collapse" of the capitalist system whenever it faced a major crisis, and whenever prosperity has prevailed, proponents of capitalism, even moderate social democrats, have promulgated the eternality of capitalism.

Crisis is inherent to the capitalist system, and its history is replete with periodic and cyclical crises. Capitalism can neither get rid of crises, any more than it can end unemployment or inequality. That said, through state intervention and other mechanisms of control, the capitalist system has always proven to be capable of surviving crises and launch periods of recovery with the intensified concentration and centralization of capital.

Capitalism will neither collapse nor wither away merely as a result of periodic crises or its internal contradictions. Its constant and merciless search for profit and expansion, however, carves an ever-expanding path of destruction of nature and society and prepares the ground for the subjective forces to challenge and confront it. The counter-hegemony created by these forces can, in principle, create a sound political alternative, capable of replacing it with a superior socio-economic system.

For over a century and a half, the socialist left in different parts of the world has confronted capitalism by following one of two broad strategies: reformist/peaceful transition versus revolutionary change. Despite enormous costs and sacrifices, both strategies have, for different reasons, failed and ended up with changing course to a vigorous pursuit of the capitalist path. Obvious examples are the Russian, Chinese, and other revolutions as well as the reformist social democratic movements. Despite setbacks, capitalism over time has only become stronger while the labor movement has grown weaker.

Surely, the failures of both paths have offered many lessons to the socialist left. But socialist forces have yet to find a strategy to curtail the continued onslaught of capital and to offer a viable alternative for it. Great analytical works continue to produce compelling evidence for the atrocities of capitalism, neoliberalism, and imperialism, but the socialist left remains confined to small isolated groups of intellectuals and activists. The recent anti-neoliberal movements, such as the Occupy, Altermondialism, and Social Forums, are no doubt encouraging, but they remained limited. The main issue is how to stand by the ideals and principles and to find doable and effective ways to challenge the ever-advancing march of capitalism. This requires identifying and finding responses to certain serious questions. The old question, going back to the time of Engels, Bernstein, Kautsky, and others, regarding the strategy of revolution versus reform persists, as does the need to figure out which variations of the two have a better chance of success in the context of present day globalization.

Which Revolution and Which Reform?

Marx and Engels, while fascinated with the "revolutionary alchemist" August Blanqui, rejected his notion of a revolution of a minority leading the unprepared masses, and instead, propagated a "self-conscious, independent movement of the immense majority".[1] This is what Marx had earlier called a social revolution, a "radical revolution" which involves "general human emancipation", as opposed to a "political" and "partial" revolution … "which leaves the pillars of the house standing".[2]

As history transpired, however, none of the revolutions that were carried out in their names were revolutions of a conscious majority. They were all political and partial revolutions. Furthermore, none of those revolutions merely erupted as a result of class conflicts, but rather mostly as a result of defeats in wars, international economic crises, or mobilization of national liberation movements against imperialist aggressions. Most Marxist socialist movements initially adhered to revolutionary strategies. But a significant number of them particularly, in Western Europe after the First World War, shifted to reformism. However, both the revolutionary and reformist trends were confronted and had to deal with the specific contradictions of their strategies.

Political revolutions followed a somewhat similar route. Revolutionaries, who were united in the downfall of the previous regime, got into conflict with each other after taking power and invariably radicals and moderates separated. Where the radical revolutionaries gained the upper hand, they resorted to forceful takeover of institutions and massive nationalizations, and there were attempts at wealth redistribution in order to fulfill their promises to the working class and peasantry. However, once confronted with the stark realities, anarchic conditions and major disruptions of production processes, and the intrigues of internal and external counter-revolutionary forces, they realized that they could not resolve the innumerable pent-up demands. Consequently, they were forced to downplay expectations, revise their policies accordingly, and above all, suppress dissent. Ruling alone and rejecting any cross-class compromise and collaboration meant establishing a new dictatorship, not of the proletariat, but of the party, and eventually a single leader.

The Russian Revolution was the classical example. The 1917 February Revolution, with participation by all anti-Tsar forces, led to the emergence of the "dual power" between the Soviets and the Provisional Government. Inaction of the moderate and right wing-dominated Provisional Government on major imminent issues, particularly the War and land questions, led to the radical Bolsheviks' forceful seizure of power through the October Revolution. After gaining only 24 percent of the votes in the election of the Constituent Assembly, the Bolsheviks ordered the Red Guards to disband the Assembly. Their slogan, "all power to the Soviets" gradually turned into all power to the Bolsheviks. Factory Committees (workers' councils), which were one of the most important pillars of the revolution, gradually faded away. In 1917, they were organs of control and administration of factories, and in 1918, they were transformed into state-run trade unions. Later, they became a part of the factory triad (*Troika*), consisting of the plant manager, the Communist Party cell secretary, and the head of the local Union. They were eliminated under Stalin, when the factory triad system was disbanded and the control of factories was handed over to plant managers. Devastating civil war and intrigues of foreign powers had created serious problems. The New Economic Policy (NEP) tried to rationalize some of the earlier radical policies. And with Stalin coming to power, collectivization was forced and rapid industrialization followed, and in the context of the devastating war against Nazi Germany, all the power was shifted to him.

If the Russian and Chinese Revolutions did not have the combined objective and subjective conditions to qualify as a Marxian revolution per se, to certain degrees the German Revolution of 1918 did. This revolution occurred in a country that had produced great political minds, from Marx himself to Bebel, Liebknecht (father and son), Bernstein, Kautsky, Zetkin, Hilferding, Luxemburg, and others, many of whom were alive at the time of the revolution to lead it. The Social Democratic Party (SPD) had more than one million active members before the First World War. Germany had become one of the most advanced industrial countries in the world, with a massive industrial working class, many of whom had created workers' councils (*Rate*). With the collapse of the Empire, socialists gained control of state power, but internal divisions, among other factors, led to the failure of the revolution. The left Spartacists/Communists blamed the right wing and moderate social democrats for siding with the army and reactionary forces, and the right Social Democrats blamed the left wing for prematurely declaring a Socialist Republic and calling for uprising. Tragically, there were elements of truth in both claims. The left was then brutally eliminated, and the center and the right continued with the new Weimar Republic, before their elimination by the Nazis. After the Second World War, the SPD, which had survived in exile during the war, became a strong popular party in the Bundestag. Converting to a totally reformist party, in 1959, it completely de-linked itself with Marxism and got engaged in reforming capitalism.

Some political revolutions in a third-world setting with strong involvement of the left and Marxist socialists produced yet another set of contradictions. The 1979 Iranian Revolution is a case in point, in which while socialists played a most momentous role in the downfall of the Shah, they were defeated with the dreadful consequences of the rising Islamist fundamentalist forces. Amidst political and theoretical confusions, and strong anti-imperialist and anti-capitalist sentiments, the Iranian left followed conflicting and contradictory strategies. Some moderate socialists, guided by the Soviet Union's strategy and infatuated with the assumed anti-American stance of the new regime, supported it, and in some cases, collaborated with it, while the radical left, fantasizing about an impending socialist revolution with the help of the working class, confronted the regime. Both trends were brutally eliminated, and workers' councils (*Showras*) which were mostly created and run by the left, were replaced with the yellow Islamic councils. A democratic and anti-imperialist revolution turned into a reactionary religious revolution, which not only drastically pushed back the Iranian society, but also became a harbinger of other reactionary religious and Jihadist movements that are ravaging the Middle East and elsewhere. The Iranian left, along with the other progressive forces that initiated the first mass-based revolution in a Muslim-majority society, paid a terribly heavy price. We learned the hard way that as long as progressive forces are not in a position to provide a real political alternative, revolutionary upheavals in religious-soaked societies could be too costly for social progress.

All political revolutions of the past failed as a result of both their internal contradictions and their intrigues of the capitalist/imperialist forces. And this was an era when socialism in one country might have actually had a better chance of survival. Now, in the era of neoliberal globalization and the brutal dominance of capital, socialist revolutions face much greater problems and obstacles. Talking of failures of socialist revolutions should not undermine their achievements and direct and indirect contributions to national liberation movements against colonialism and imperialism. Their mere presence also forced capital in many advanced capitalist societies to give concessions to workers' demands and improve the status of working people.

The question here is not whether or not political revolutions are plausible; a combination of factors—objective and subjective, as well as internal and external—can in a specific junctures lead to a political revolution in a particular country. Rather, the question is whether a progressive revolution that does not have the backing of the conscious majority can have any chance of success in attaining its ultimate goals. Of all the categories of revolutions, only a social revolution that is based on the independent movement of a conscious majority believing in the socialist alternative is capable of moving toward the final goal of transcending social relations. But obviously this type of a revolution passes through a very long process, and it takes a type of Gramscian "passive revolution" to create a new cultural and political hegemony through gradual change, or even needs aspects of Otto Bauer's "slow Revolution" for progressive socialization.

Reformist strategies also faced and had to deal with different types of contradictions and failed in moving toward socialism. All the major social democratic parties that came to play a significant role in different European countries ended up distancing themselves from socialist policies. Faced with the onslaught of capitalism and the weakening of labor movements, they limited themselves to reforming capitalism. As right wing parties became more and more powerful, social democrats moved closer and closer to the center and in some cases even to the right of the center.

Reformist social democrats had to work within capitalist institutions, and in order to gain votes, had to follow policies that were appealing to all social classes. Moreover, they had to enter into coalitions with other parties and constantly come up with cross-class compromises. In this process, they gradually distanced themselves from the ultimate goal of socialism, and reforms became an end in and of themselves. Instead of incrementally moving toward socialist policies and goals, they followed the strategy of reforming and trying to curtail the excesses of capitalism.[3]

The best example of this transformation was the German SPD, mentioned earlier. Another good example is the Swedish Social Democratic Workers Party (SAP). In the 1920s, the party advocated "socialization" of natural resources, banks, transportation, and communications. As early as the 1930s, the party began to modify its policies, emphasizing gradualism, more equitable distribution of wealth, progressive taxation, and at the same time, stressed private property rights, and reduction of budget deficits. By the 1980s, with the further dominance of neoliberalism, this party, along with many other European social democratic parties, changed its policies to "liberal socialism", and at times liberalism. The shifts in social democratic parties led to the more radical elements splitting off and forming new left parties like Die Linke in Germany, which along with other left organizations, like the Left Party in Sweden, Syriza in Greece, Podemos in Spain, and the Left coalition in Portugal, tried to push for more radical reforms.

Despite all the shifts to the right, and the continuous assault of neoliberalism, it is important not to ignore many of the achievements of these reformist parties, backed by labor activism. Despite cutbacks, public social spending in these societies is still among the highest in the world. The OECD Social Expenditure Database (SOCX), shows that the EU countries' public social expenditure in diverse areas of social policy, ranging from old age, health and family to unemployment, housing and others, was about 10 percent of their GDP in 1960s and had reached over 25 percent in 2009, with only slight declines by 2012.[4] As another example, all the countries with some social democratic background are at the very top of the Human Development Index (HDI) rankings.[5] The Gini index for these countries also shows they have the lowest income inequalities.

Social democrat's emphasis on democracy is also hugely significant. One of the biggest shortcomings of the socialist revolutionary strategies was the lack of attention to democracy. As Ellen Meiksins Wood has brilliantly argued, "[t]he greatest challenge to capitalism would be an extension of democracy beyond its narrowly circumscribed limits. It is at this point that 'democracy' arguably becomes synonymous with socialism".[6] She reasoned while capitalism has been capable of functioning without democracy, socialism cannot. Democracy is particularly significant at present, when not just the working class, but also the middle classes and even some capitalists are suffering under neoliberal capitalism. Many social movements, including women, national, ethnic, racial and religious minorities, and environmentalists, are severely affected by the atrocities of now globalized neoliberal capitalism. Capitalism itself, as Wolfgang Streeck shows, can no longer lay claim to democracy.[7]

Needless to say, these achievements have now been threatened by the growing onslaught of neoliberalism, as well as the further retreat of social democrats, who have increasingly become nearly indistinguishable from neoliberals.

In other parts of the world, with the expansion of universal suffrage worldwide, some major attempts at political and economic transformations have occurred through the electoral process, and some of them dubbed as revolutions. The cases in point are Guatemala under Arbenz, Chile under Allende (both defeated through US intervention), Venezuela under Chavez and Maduro, and Bolivia under Morales (both surviving to date, despite US interventions).[8] In all these cases, particularly the "Bolivarian Revolution", the newly elected government introduced certain important revolutionary changes in favor of the working classes and peasants, from land reforms and nationalization of major institutions, to expanding social safety nets, increased educational opportunities, affordable housing, and worker-management.[9] Operating in the neoliberal global capitalism, these progressive governments, despite having the massive support of the majority of people, were faced with severe internal and external intrigues and faced enormous setbacks. A case in point is the recent parliamentary defeat of the United Socialist Party of Venezuela (PSUV).

The same electoral opportunities, however, have unfortunately also given rise to reactionary political movements or revolutions. In a growing number of Muslim-majority societies, the Shi'a and Sunni Islamists, similar to earlier Fascist movements, take advantage of the genuine grievances and discontent of the deprived majority and their religious beliefs, and ride the revolutionary tides in hopes of gaining majority votes for establishing a Sharia-based Islamist states. The misguided foreign policies of the USA and its allies in the Middle East have led to the devastations in Afghanistan, the destruction of Iraq and Libya, and civil wars in Syria and

Yemen, creating more opportunities for the violent insurgent strategies utilized by groups like Islamic State of Iraq and Syria (ISIS), surpassing the atrocities committed by the Taliban and Al-Qaeda. The rapid defeat of the so-called Arab Spring had, among other factors, something to do with the growing influence of the Islamists. These developments are particularly threatening the left and progressive forces, who in these countries see decades of their struggles and sacrifices for change stolen by reactionary forces, themselves staunch capitalists.

All in all, the history of socialist movements shows that rapid social transformations arising from swift change of political power, following either a revolution or the election of a radical regime, present strategic dilemmas for the new leadership in power. If the new regime does not rapidly move toward radical political, economic, and social reforms, the structures and agents of the former regime directly and indirectly prevent major reforms and block the fulfillment of promises made. Worse yet, people become demoralized, the movement loses steam, and the previous regime perpetuates, albeit with new faces and players. This also applies to the cases where socialists must enter coalitions with other parties to form a government. If they constantly abandon the pursuit of more radical policies, they will lose the support of the working people and end up being no different than the other parties they have coalesced with.

If, on the other hand, the new regime moves quickly to introduce radical fundamental changes, it faces challenges in fulfilling all the promises and demands, often when the necessary means and resources are not immediately available. The regime therefore moves to modify its policies, attempts to lower expectations, and subdue or suppress popular demands. Confrontations with internal and external enemies and adversaries make the new regime's survival a top priority, forcing it to channel much of the resources needed for implementing social justice policies into securing and consolidating power. Predictably, it ends up losing popular support and encounters new waves of opposition, invariably turning into a new undemocratic and suppressive system.

The level of radicalism needs to be optimized based on the actual and specific subjective and objective conditions; failure is inevitable when radical advances are not carefully calculated and executed. As it is known, social movements either progress or regress. History and the experiences of past revolutionary and reformist movements show that when they are not radical enough they invariably lose to reactionary forces. On the other hand, radicalism above the optimum level leads to adventurism which in a different way impedes progress toward the goals of social transformation. The socialist revolutions and reformisms of the past universally failed to envision, or at least achieve, this optimum.

MARX AND PEACEFUL TRANSITION

Marx's revolutionary positions and his enthusiasms about the 1848 revolutions in France and elsewhere in Europe, and then the Paris Commune of 1871 are well known. In *Class Struggle in France*, which was written one year after the 1848–1849 revolution, or in *Civil War in France* that was written after the Paris Commune, the emphasis is placed on the revolutionary path. Even more emphatically the revolutionary path, and the need for "smashing" the machinery of the state, as suggested in *The Eighteenth Brumaire of Louis Bonaparte*, and his numerous letters to Kugelman and Liebknekht (Wilhelm), are stressed. The 1872 Preface to the second German edition of the Communist Manifesto also has the same emphasis. But he and Engels, particularly in the latter part of their lives, postulated also the possibility of a peaceful transition from capitalism. Elements of a non-revolutionary strategy can even be traced back to their earlier writings.

In 1872, in his *La Liberte Speech* after the Hague Congress of the First International, when Marx succeeded in getting the Anarchist Bakunin expelled from the International, he said "...we do not deny that there are countries – such as America, England ... perhaps ... Holland ... where the workers can attain their goal by peaceful means". But as for most countries of Europe, he stressed that "the lever of our revolution must be force...".[10]

In 1878, in an outline of a draft commentary on the Parliamentary debate on the Anti-Socialist Law, Marx wrote, "[i]f in England, for instance, or the United States, the working class were to gain a majority in the Parliament or Congress, they could by lawful means, rid themselves of such laws and institutions as impeded their development, though they could only do insofar as society had reached a sufficiently mature development".[11]

In 1880, in a letter to Henry Hyndman, the founder of the first Socialist Party of England, Marx stated, "... an English revolution [is] not *necessary*, but according to historic precedents –[it is] *possible*. If the unavoidable evolution turn[s] into a revolution, it would not only be the fault of the ruling classes, but also of the working class. Every pacific concession of the former has been wrung from them by 'pressure from without'. Their action kept pace with that pressure and if the latter has more and more weakened, it is only because the English working class know not how to wield their power and use their liberties, both of which they possess legally".[12]

Another interesting example relates to Marx's reaction in 1880 to the Marxist leaders of the Parti-Ouvrier of France. Marx disagreed with Jules Guesde and Paul Lafargue for their rejection of the Minimum section of the program. Marx favored this section as a practical means "achievable within the framework of capitalism", while Guesde considered the demands as "... bait with which to lure the workers from radicalism". Marx accused them of "revolutionary phrase-mongering". In the preamble of the program that Marx had dictated, we read that the goals "... must be pursued by all means that [the] proletariat has at its disposal including universal suffrage which will thus be transformed from the instrument of deception that it has been until now into an instrument of emancipation".[13]

A most interesting and a lesser-known example is a letter that Marx wrote in 1881 to Domela Nieuwenhuis, a Dutch socialist and later anarchist leader: "...a socialist government will not come to the helm in a country unless things have reached a stage at which it can, before all else, take such measures as will so intimidate the mass of the bourgeoisie as to achieve the first desideratum – time for effective action". He adds, "You may, perhaps, refer me to the Paris Commune but, aside from the fact that this was merely an uprising of one city in exceptional circumstances, the majority of the Commune was in no sense socialist, nor could it have been. With a modicum of COMMON SENSE, it could, however, have obtained the utmost that was then obtainable—a compromise with Versailles beneficial to the people as a whole...".[14] This is a most significant departure from Marx's earlier views on the Paris Commune.

Apart from these examples of Marx's views in the most mature period of his life, one can also see traces of a non-revolutionary path in his early writings. In *The Communist Manifesto*, despite rejecting the reformism of the "conservative, or bourgeois socialism" and those of the "improvers of the condition of the working class", the rights of the workers to pursue their demands legally are recognized. So is the attempt by the proletariat "to win the battle of democracy". The sentence that this phrase is taken from can be interpreted in different ways, as the reference is also made to the proletarian revolution. We read "... the first step in the revolution by the working class is to raise the proletariat to the position of ruling class to win the battle of democracy".[15] Years later, in his 1895 introduction to *Class Struggle in France*, Engels, the co-author of the Manifesto, writes "... [The] Manifesto had already proclaimed the winning of universal suffrage, of democracy, as one of the first and most important tasks of the militant proletariat...". Referring to Bismarck's Germany, Engels adds, "... workers ... have used the franchise in a way which has paid them a thousand fold and has served as a model to the workers of all countries". We further read that "... the bourgeoisie and the government came to be much more afraid of the legal than of the illegal action of the workers' party, of the results of elections than of those of rebellion".[16] Furthermore, it can be argued that much of the ten "measures" in the Manifesto are in a sense reformist.

This brief overview of some of Marx's views shows that unlike the dominant discourse attributed to him following the Bolshevik Revolution, Marx postulated both revolutionary and reformist paths. It is clear that he differentiated between countries that had achieved an electoral system at his time, from those that lacked suffrage. He envisaged for the working people in the former the possibility to achieve their goals through "peaceful" means.

Thus, any country that has universal suffrage—and now the vast majority of countries have this at least on paper—potentially has the precondition for a reformist path for transitioning from capitalism. The main issue is how the socialists and progressive forces can attract the votes of majority working people and "transform" the electoral process "from an instrument of deception to an instrument of emancipation". No doubt, as Marx pointed, "they could only do insofar as society ha(s) reached a sufficiently mature development",[17] and the issue is how these societies can become sufficiently mature for achieving this goal.

Marxian peaceful transition to socialism is by no means limited to electoral victories in an already-existing parliament. Transforming the electoral process into an "instrument of emancipation" needs constant radical struggles and advances. The "maturing" process involves extra-parliamentary activities, raising socialist consciousness, and mobilization of a growing number of working people to articulate higher aspirations. The experiences of reformist social democratic parties and their failures discussed earlier, point to the need for constant incremental struggles toward the ultimate goal of socialism. In the meantime, there should be no illusions about the dominant capitalist class's commitment to their interests; they will not give up easily and will use their ideological and repressive apparatuses to prevent the progressive advances of socialists, resorting to violence when necessary. Democratic socialists, while condemning any type of violence, may be obliged to use "defensive" force. This was a policy that was put forward by reformist socialists as early as mid-1920s, when Otto Bauer of the Austrian Social Democratic Party coined the term "defensive violence", which among others, included strikes, general strikes, even insurrection as a measure of last resort, in response to the violence of the capitalist class.

WHICH SOCIALISM?

The language of socialists is ambiguous even in relation to the main goals of the struggle, socialism itself. It would be futile, no doubt, to try to draw a very clear picture of the ideal post-capitalist society. However, in sharp contrast to Eduard Bernstein's famous dictum that "the goal is nothing and the movement is everything", some theorists argue that defining the goal is the most important task. Instead of going with either of these two extreme views, it is important to have an understanding of the major economic and political characteristics of the desired socialist society, and the necessary mechanisms for moving toward achieving it. Alec Nove, in his important book on the subject, rightly argued that "while the goal is not and cannot be 'nothing', bitter experience teaches us that means affect ends....We may have some idea of the direction in which we wish to go, but the final destination is bound to be affected by the nature of the journey. Indeed whatever the goal, there cannot in social life be a literally final destination".[18]

Marx himself did not attempt to clearly define the post-capitalist society. In his brief depiction in the *Critique of the Gotha Program* he says, "[b]etween capitalist and communist society lies a period of the revolutionary transformation of the one into another". Since the communist society emerges from capitalist society and carries its "birthmarks", Marx envisaged two "phases" for this society. In the "first phase of communism", among other things, individual producer receives back from the society what she/he gives to it by "quantum of labour". In the "higher phase" all distinctions and inequalities are removed and society moves from "each according to his ability, to each according to his needs". For Marx even this so-called first phase is a very radical departure from capitalism in which wage labor, among other things is abolished. May be since this was too idealistic and unachievable immediately in the post-capitalist society, later German and Russian social democrats, and in particular, Lenin in his

State and Revolution, modified these phases, and distinguished between socialism as the lower "phase" and communism as the higher phase.

Here, I do not see the need to discuss the "higher phase" when people are expected to be free of any competition in a classless and stateless society, enjoy the "abundance" of goods and services based on their "needs" and not their "abilities", and "the enslaving subordination of the individual to the division of labour, and therewith also the antithesis between mental and physical labour" is supposedly "vanished".[19] Whether the "higher phase" is achievable or remains a utopian ideal and goal to constantly strive for, is beside the point. This ideal is so far from the present realities that it cannot be put on any serious agenda of any credible left organization. The focus then will be on the "lower phase" of Lenin which became the blueprint for revolutionary socialists around the world.

For the Leninist "first" or "lower phase", we have had the experiences of the "actually existing socialism". In these societies, the most immediate socialist task was "socialization" of the means of production, which took different forms, predominantly through state ownership. Other forms of socialization, particularly in the agricultural sector, were collectivization. In certain cases, also some forms of workers control and self-management were introduced, though short-lived. These regimes not only did not "smash" the "bureaucratic military machine" that was "transferred" to them, but they only [supposedly] "perfected" it. State ownership included a total central planning system, producing a huge bureaucratic structure, and even proved to be technically impossible in a large economy that involved correlation of tens of millions of items in a gigantic input/output model. As for collectivization, the process was introduced by force and led to the disastrous decline of agricultural and food productions. The whole process, amidst civil wars and the right wing's assaults supported by imperial powers, involved suppression of any dissent, and the emergence of an outright authoritarian and suppressive political system.

The important point here is that most of the proponents of the immediate transition to socialism are critical of former existing socialism, but they remain vague about the type of socialism they have in mind. Some reject the experience altogether, claiming that it had nothing to do with socialism. Aside from the main issue of how and with whose support this revolutionary transition would be achieved, the specific features of the desired socialist system also beg a response. Which forms of socialization and to what extent would be followed? Would they want to "smash" the state machinery, as emphasized by Marx, or would they have no choice but to begin to work within the framework of the state "transferred" to them, and modify the relation of power and representation, and expand it? What exactly does "smashing" the state mean? Does it include closing down its institutions and firing the existing employees, or does it mean smashing the relations of power and changing of policies? Would socialization and shifts in land ownership be implemented with force and if so what would be the means to overcome the possible resistances? How different would the wage or compensation structures be? Would competition be abolished, allowed, or encouraged and compensated? What would be the political structure of the society? ... and many other questions. Most importantly, even if the establishment of socialism in one country would be imagined as a possibility, could it survive and compete in the globalized capitalist world?

Many revolutionary socialists, along some anarchists, critical of state ownership and control emphasize "self-management", "worker control", and "direct democracy". Still no clear explanation is provided as to what exactly worker control mean? During the 1979 Iranian Revolution, when we established workers/employees councils (*Showras*) in the large- and medium-sized state-owned and newly nationalized industries, we were exerting full control for a while before soon realizing that this is only temporary and reliant on a complex set of economic and political factors, at different levels of decision-making. Years later in exile, I had a chance to look critically at our experiences and ponder over the root causes of failure of the council movement in Iran. I then posed a set of question to supporters of workers' control. They included: under what conditions, other than periods of crisis, could worker control become a reality? Is worker control a kind of cooperative, and does it involve collective ownership, and if so by whom? Would it be by workers of each plant? Who, other than the workers, can be involved in the process of worker control—engineers, office workers, and others? Can worker control become a universal trend through which workers would run all the firms in a national economy, including large strategic industries? Would worker control be confined to the micro- (firm) and meso- (industry) levels or will it expand to cover the macro- (national economy) levels as well? How does worker control work in industries clustered and linked together through vertical integration and trade linkages, and how this control will be coordinated? What would be the role of different stakeholders in the integrated industries and institutions? And finally, what would be the role of the state? Under what political system is universal worker control even possible?[20]

Work councils, with their functions of worker control in the strict sense of control of production, management, and distribution processes by workers alone, have never existed anywhere. Even in the Soviet Union, as mentioned earlier, the factory committees were eventually phased out.[21] The fate of Yugoslav councils, despite their complexities and achievements was no different. Very small units with few workers may have worker control and ownership, but this is not possible for large, particularly national institutions. Instead, different forms and degrees of industrial democracy or worker participation have been achieved in countries where a relatively strong labor movement and a social democratic tradition have existed. But the concept of industrial democracy and various forms of worker participation have been rejected and defamed by the traditional left for being corporatist, reformist, and a means for class compromise. No doubt these institutions, operating under capitalist relations, have been a means of compromise, but engagement of workers in industrial democracy can be a great educational and organizational opportunity for them to be actually trained for participation in management decision-making and wherever possible in different forms and degrees of self-management.

Surely, industrial democracy is a relative concept and different degrees of its attainment, which ranges from "information sharing" by management to "consultation" with workers, and "co-determination" at different organizational levels—from the shop floor to the firm—are directly related to the strength of organized labor. Considering the conflicting nature of labor–capital relations, the more powerful, better organized and more advanced the workers in a given society, the higher the degree or level of industrial democracy that can be achieved, and vice versa.

As for "direct democracy", it is possible to introduce this system to decide on some specific issues in small towns or districts, or use referenda on some national issues. But surely all decisions cannot be made through these mechanisms, as most organizational decisions need typical professional and hierarchical structures, including different levels of government. Anti-state sentiments, whether openly propagated by anarchists, or shyly by some Marxists, or by the so-called autonomists, are not different from the arguments put forth in the First International. Marx's brilliant notes on Bakunin's *Statism and Anarchy* are as valid today as they were then.[22]

Which Social Class(es)?

Another major category that has remained vague in the discourse of the proponents of revolutionary socialism is with the active engagement of which social class(es) and with whose support do they plan to immediately establish socialism in their respective country? The focus no doubt is on the "working class". But what is not clear is what constitutes the working class today? Is it limited to the blue-collar manual wageworkers, or does it also include the so-called white-collar salaried employees? To be sure, no longer the former constitute the majority of the working population; the vast majority of working people in most countries are engaged in the processing of information rather than materials. If the salaried or the new middle class is also included in the category, then the working class would be significantly heterogeneous in terms of income, social status, and demands. We would have a new set of questions and problems if we follow a different configuration, for example, those based on Erik Olin Wright's model of adding the lower strata of the new middle classes to the rank of working class and removing the upper echelons of skilled workers from that of the working class.

In any of these configurations, it is not clear what is expected of the working class. Is it expected to perform its "historical mission" of establishing the "dictatorship of proletariat"? For some radical revolutionary socialists, particularly in less advanced industrial societies, the answer is on the affirmative without clarifying how and why this "dictatorship" is feasible and plausible at this stage of social development.

The class analysis of some revolutionary socialists, with their focus on working class mobilization, usually accompanies a lack of attention to the new middle class. On the one hand, there is a romanticized and exaggerated delineation of the working class, which confuse the potential and the actual revolutionary capabilities of this class, and on the other hand, a denigration of the new middle class.

The ambiguous and unsolidified status of the new middle class granted, so is the fact that significant sections of this class sides with capital. But at the same time, it constitutes the majority of progressive forces everywhere. Most supporters of anti-capitalist movements, feminist movements, labor movements, Lesbian, Gay, Bisexual, and Transgender (LGBT) movements, youth and student movements, and environmentalists come from different strata of the new middle class. The left has been incapable of recognizing the significance of this extremely significant section of the population in almost all countries of the world. In the middle of the nineteenth century, when this class was almost nonexistent or was very limited in scope, Marx quoting James Mill's *Elements of political Economy*, implicitly recognizes the importance of this class. While Mill referring to section of the capitalist class "which have their time at their command", and through their work "knowledge is cultivated … enlarged …and diffused", and "human capacities … develop", he refers to elements that we now call the new middle class, including "… judges, administrators, teachers, inventors in all the arts, and superintendents in all the more important works, by which the dominion of the human species is extended over the powers of nature".[23] Their scientific, administrative, and artistic contributions aside, in today's world, the new middle classes are extremely significant politically.

While in the final analysis and in relation to capital both wage workers and salaried employees belong to the category of the working class, in practice they are different from each other and categorizing the latter under new middle classes seems justifiable. The most significant and at the same time most difficult task facing socialists is to find out how to mobilize the working class and the new middle class in combination. Without gaining the support of a sizable section of the new middle class, proponents of socialism, almost all of whom belonging to this very same class, will have no chance of pushing their progressive agendas forward in a substantive way. This would entail major revisions in slogans, tactics, and strategies. Furthermore, under the dominance of neoliberal capitalism, suffering is not solely rooted in the class struggle. Racism, sexism, religious intolerance, xenophobia, and wars continue to agonize an ever-growing number of people, as do environmental degradation and ecological disasters. It is not enough to just focus on class, and the social movements fighting for equity, tolerance, secularism, peace, and the environment, are an integral part of the socialist agenda.

While the working class has an enormous role to play in confronting capital, it is no longer the perceived sole agency for social transformation. The new middle class, along with other social "identitarian" movements mentioned earlier, can play a most significant role in the societal transformation. In less-developed societies where there is a sizable peasantry, although capitalist agriculture has turned many of them into agricultural workers, they can be mobilized and play an important role. The combined struggle of the working class and the progressive elements of the new middle class have the great potential of creating a progressive bloc against the dominant class. They constitute the majority of the population in almost all countries. An appropriate strategy, based on specific and achievable goals can mobilize and attract them to the socialist cause. The stronger the social base and public support, the more progressive and radical an agenda can take shape and be put in place.

WHICH ALTERNATIVE? A PREPARATORY PHASE

Socialist left and labor activists are perhaps at their weakest point and have failed to challenge the crisis-ridden globalized capitalist system. This is partly due to the fact that many socialists at times are bogged down in idealistic and impracticable interpretations of the doctrine, riddled with what can be called *ideologytis*. In many cases, this has unfortunately paralyzed rational thinking and praxis, and has helped keep the socialist left in the margins of politics in their respective countries. Practical ways of confronting capitalism and progressively moving toward its alternative are not seriously taken into consideration.

The notion of "phases" in social development and evolution does not mean that there is a distinct end point at one phase from which the clear starting point for the next begins. Social development is an uninterrupted and endless continuum, very much like the spectrum of light, through which many elements of the new formation and structures are germinated and gradually formed within the older ones, as well as elements of the old that perpetuate in the new. This is partly what Marx envisaged for the transition from the post-capitalist "first" phase to the "higher" phase. He wrote, "communist society ... emerges from capitalist society; which is thus in every respect, economically, morally, and intellectually, still stamped with the birth marks of the old society from whose womb it emerges".[24] But what he, and his traditional followers, did not elaborate is the process of transition from capitalism to the "first" phase of post-capitalist society.

Logically, in the same manner that some "economic, moral and intellectual" aspects of the "old society" continue in the new one, some aspects of the new society also have to have at least begun to germinate in the old one. In other words, unless one believes in a jump from one social formation to another, some elements of socialism will also need to start within the capitalist era. Gramsci was among the first Marxist theoreticians to emphasize that the "new order" begins not from the moment of the collapse of the old order but from the process of preparing for the establishment of "counter hegemony" against the old order and at the height of its power.

On this basis, it would be logical to envisage a preparatory phase prior to the post-capitalism phases of socialism. This phase takes place within the capitalist era and its aim is an incessant and steady struggle toward "economic", "moral", "intellectual", and political change in the mentality, condition, and status of wageworkers, salaried employees and other citizens. It also strives toward advancement in gender, sexual, and racial equity, and the overall strengthening of the position of labor vis-à-vis capital and move closer and closer to the "first" phase of post-capitalist society. In the absence of a better name, it can be called *radical social democracy*,[25] to differentiate it from social democracies of today and socialism which is the future of the movement. It cannot be called democratic socialism because it is taking place at a time that capitalism is still the dominant social formation.

Socialist project is no doubt the largest and most complicated project of human history. The lengthy process of transition from capitalism has interrelated socio-cultural, political, economic, and ecological dimensions that go through successive steps and periods. The struggles aim at creating counter-hegemony against the dominant culture and ideology, taking over of the political power, and transforming the economic system. The process involves cultural and political hegemony, transforming the relations of power, reforming institutions of state at the national, regional, and municipal levels, guaranteeing political liberties and freedoms, and includes the introduction of participatory management at all levels from neighborhoods and workshops to the highest levels of decision-making.

The introduction of new economic and social policies, economic and ecological reforms, and changes combine aspects of socialist planning and capitalist market economy with the gradual dominance of the former over the latter. Radical reforms include socialization of finance and banking system, increasing government regulations of industry, business, foreign trade, price control, progressive taxation systems, along with universal education, healthcare and pensions, affordable housing, environmental regulations, and many other reforms. A most important and most complicated reform relates to the issue of work compensation. Unlike what Marx depicted for the first phase, wage labor cannot possibly disappear immediately. It is indeed too idealistic to imagine that abstract labor could be terminated except in a long process. Even it would be hard to imagine that in the early periods of the first phase, the system can get rid of wage differentiation.

While these efforts are made at the national level in different countries, no single country by itself is capable of establishing full-fledged socialism. More importantly, as Istvan Meszaros rightly points out, the "successful social revolution cannot be local or national – only political revolutions can confine themselves to a limited setting, in keeping with their own partiality – it must be global/universal…".[26] This point is part of Meszaros' masterful summary of the main tenets of Marx's political theory, in which he puts forward seven interrelated points, among them: the state must be transcended "through a radical transformation of the whole of society"; "the revolution cannot be simply a political one [and] must be a social one"; and "the absence of objective conditions for implementing socialist measures, ironically, can only result in carrying out the adversary's policies in the event of a premature conquest of power". Meszaros points to Marx's "warnings against voluntarism and adventurism", rejects "limited restructuring of the economy" and emphasizes on "fundamental restructuring of society as a whole without which any transition to socialism is inconceivable".[27]

Corporate power and global dominance of capital is sustained through the power of capitalist states in major economies. These same states also dominate international economic and financial institutions like the IMF, World Bank, and WTO that regulate and maintain the global dominance of capital. No transnational or multinational capital can operate or survive without the full support of its home and host capitalist states. The reason why global corporations and international financial institutions have become so powerful is because of the neoliberal policies that powerful capitalist states have put in place in their respective countries and, through their representatives, in global economic and financial institutions. The establishment of socialism at the global level is dependent on socialist transformations in these powerful capitalist states and international institutions. The introduction and implementation of radical reforms at the national and international levels obviously rely on progressive states coming to power in a growing number of countries, particularly in advanced industrial societies that have strong influences in the global economic institutions. This depends on progressive voters who can elect such states, which in turn depends on the success of left and progressive forces to mobilize public support in favor of progressive candidates.

The aim is to capture the state power, but not with the aim of "smashing" it, but as far as possible in a "peaceful" way, with the aim of changing its "relations" and policies. By gaining the majority in parliaments, progressive forces "could by lawful means, rid themselves of such laws and institutions as impeded their development …".[28] By pursuing "practical means … achievable within the framework of capitalism", socialists can use "…universal suffrage which will thus be transformed from the instrument of deception … into an instrument of emancipation".[29] Obviously, the capitalist states defend the interests of capital, and would do whatever they can to prevent progressive forces from advancing. But the strategy of radical social democracy, while peaceful, is also radical and militant and needs powerful organizational means and confrontational tactics to mobilize the civil society and force capitalists to withdraw from the positions they have gained and maintained. In gradualism, of course, there is always the danger of succumbing to the problems and return to the previous order, that is why, unlike the experience of European social democracy, optimized radicalism discussed earlier should be an integral part of the process.

The success of this strategy depends upon education, progressive independent media, and organization. In countries where unions and civil society organizations are active, making them more democratic and more radical will be the priority, and in undemocratic countries that unions and other civil society organizations do not exist or are severely suppressed, the first aim is to create and strengthen them. New left political parties, non-Leninist and democratic, with clearly spelled-out agendas for attracting a growing number of the new middle class and working people would be essential in mobilizing the civil society. Efforts to establish councils would be an important mechanism for increased public participation. Work councils can act as participatory arms of the unions, and neighborhood councils can involve citizens in their local and regional decisions. New forms of organization—learning from latest developments in organization theory and design, albeit advanced by capitalist and corporate theorists—such as flexible/adaptable agile organizations, holacracy,[30] virtual organization, and others, can be created to mobilize neighborhoods and workplace institutions.

There is no doubt that this is a protracted and very difficult process. However, while this may seem utopian, it has far better chances of success compared with the imagined alternative of toppling capitalist system(s) through political revolution(s) of avant-garde minorities. It needs daring theoretical revisions and practical thinking.

As mentioned at the outset, in the same manner that we have lessons from failed revolutions, we also have the failed experiences of reformisms and social democracy. As it is widely known, social movements either progress or regress, and without optimum radicalism will lose to the forces of reaction. We have learned and should not forget that reforms are reversible. What is needed is learning from failures and achievements of both strategies, and rethink new strategies and tactics. Radical social democracy seeks to meld aspects of militancy of the revolutionary approach with the pragmatism of incremental reform, toward the ultimate goal of establishing democratic socialism.

* * *

In what follows, these themes will be discussed with prominent socialist theorists. Chapter 2 deals with the past experiences, and the failures and achievements of revolutionary and reformist socialist movements. Chapter 3 discusses different notions and concepts of revolution, contrasting the

Marxian social revolution of the self-conscious, independent movement of the immense majority, with the Blanqui-inspired political revolution led by minority vanguards. Some other themes such as the reactionary religious movements, autonomous movements, and anarchism are also discussed. Chapter 4 focuses on the ideas, possibilities, and obstacles of non-revolutionary path and peaceful transition to post-capitalist society. Problems of social democracy and the failures of the reformist strategies, along with the problems of today's parliamentary democracies are discussed. Chapter 5 examines the impact of globalization and the increasing power of capital and the additional limits they impose on efforts toward building socialism in one country. The new opportunities arising from globalization and the significance of globalization of communication and information are also discussed. Chapter 6's focus is the concept of socialism itself and distinguishing it from the experiences of the "actually-existing socialism". Issues related to different forms of socializations and organization of production including self-management, workers' control and different forms of work participations are discussed. Chapter 7 considers social classes, the concept of the working class, new middle classes, and identitarian movements, and their roles as agents of social development. Chapter 8 explores the practical steps for moving toward the ultimate goal of socialism.

Notes

1. Karl Marx and Friedrich Engels, "Communist Manifesto," in *Socialist Register 1998: The Communist manifesto Now*, ed. Leo Panitch, Colin Leys (London: Merlin Press, 1998), 250.
2. Karl Marx, "Contribution to the Critique of Hegel's Philosophy of Law," in *Karl Marx, Frederick Engels: Collected Works, vol. 3, Marx and Engels: 1843–1844*. Translated by Jack Cohen, et.al. (New York: International Publishers, 2005), 184.
3. For a comprehensive overview of Social Democratic parties and their transformations and decline, see, Ashley Lavelle, *The Death of Social Democracy: Political Consequences in the 21st Century* (New York: International Publishers, 2008).
4. http://www.oecd.org/social/expenditure.htm.
5. http://hdr.undp.org/en/composite/HDI.
6. Ellen Meiksins Wood, *Democracy Against Capitalism: Renewing Historical Materialism* (Cambridge: Cambridge University Press, 1995), 15.

7. Wolfgang Streeck, *Buying Time: The Delayed Crisis of Democratic Capitalism* (New York: Verso, 2014).
8. For a comprehensive overview of these "revolutions" see, James Defronzo, *Revolutions and Revolutionary Movements*, Fourth Edition (Colorado: Westview Press, 2011), 429–459.
9. For a most comprehensive discussion of the Bolivarian Revolution, see Marta Harnecker, *A world to Build: New Paths toward Twenty-First Century Socialism*, (New York: Monthly Review Press, 2015). Also, Michael Lebowitz, *The Socialist Imperative: From Gotha to Now*, (New York: Monthly Review press, 2015).
10. Karl Marx, "On the Hague Congress: A Correspondent's Report of a Speech made at a Meeting in Amsterdam on September 8–1872," in *Karl Marx, Frederick Engels: Collected Works, vol. 23, Marx and Engels: 1871–1874*. Translated by David Forgacs, et al. (New York: International Publishers, 1988), 255.
11. Karl Marx, "Parliamentary Debate on the Anti-Socialist Law," in *Karl Marx, Frederick Engels: Collected Works, vol. 24, Marx and Engels: 1874–1873*. Translated by David Forgacs, et al. (New York: International Publishers, 1989b), 248, quoted in Samuel Hollander, *Friedrich Engels and Marxian Political Economy* (Cambridge: Cambridge University press, 2011), 203. This book has excellent discussions on what he calls "revisionism" in Marx and Engels.
12. Karl Marx, "Marx to Henry Mayers Hyndman," in *Karl Marx, Frederick Engels: Collected Works, vol. 46, Marx and Engels: 1880–1883*. Translated by Rodney Livingstone et. al. (New York: International Publishers, 1992a), 49.
13. "The Programme of the Parti Ouvrier," *Marxists Internet Archive*, http://www.marxists.org/archive/marx/works/1880/05/parti-ouvrier.htm.
14. Karl Marx, "Marx to Ferdinand Domela Nieuwenhuis," in *Karl Marx, Frederick Engels: Collected Works, vol. 46, Marx and Engels: 1880–1883*.Translated by Rodney Livingstone et.al . (New York: International Publishers, 1992b), 66.
15. Karl Marx and Friedrich Engels, "Manifesto of the Communist Party", … .257.
16. Friedrich Engels, "Introduction to Karl Marx's the Class Struggles in France 1848 to 1850," in *Karl Marx, Frederick Engels: Collected Works, vol. 27, Engels: 1890–1895*. Translated by John Peet et.al. (New York: International Publishers, 1990), 515–516.

17. See endnote 11.
18. Alec Nove, *The Economics of Feasible Socialism*, (London: Routledge 2010), 154.
19. Karl Marx, "Critique of the Gotha Programme," in *Karl Marx, Frederick Engels: Collected Works, vol. 24, Marx and Engels: 1874–1873*.Translated by David Forgacs et. al. (New York: International Publishers, 1989a), 87.
20. Saeed Rahnema, "Work Councils in Iran: The Illusion of Worker Control," *Economic and Industrial Democracy: International Journal* 13, no. 1 (February 1992): 88.
21. ibid., p. 87.
22. Karl Marx, "Conspectus of Bakunin's Statism and Anarchy," *Marxist Internet Archive*, http://www.marxists.org/archive/marx/works/1874/04/bakunin-notes.htm
23. Karl Marx and Friedrich Engels, *Collected Works, Volume 32*, (Moscow: Progress Publishers, 1989), 287.
24. Karl Marx, "Critique of the Gotha Programme," 85.
25. The term radical social democracy has been in use in different languages by different writers, and there are political organizations like Chile's Partido Radical Socialdemocrata. My usage of the term, however, denotes a socialist-oriented movement during capitalist era, and a preparatory phase for transition to post-capitalist society, combining aspects of militancy of the revolutionary approach with pragmatism of incremental reforms.
26. Istvan Meszaros, *Beyond Capital*, (New York: Monthly Review Press, 1995), 465.
27. Ibid., 938–939.
28. K. Marx, see endnote 11.
29. Karl Marx, see endnote 13.
30. Holacracy is an organizational system based on self-organizing, autonomous, and self-reliant teams, called "holon" (whole), but acting as part of a larger whole.

Bibliography

1. Defronzo, James. 2011. *Revolutions and revolutionary movements*, 4th edn. Colorado: Westview Press.
2. Engels, Friedrich. 1990. Introduction to Karl Marx's the class struggles in France 1848 to 1850. In *Karl Marx, Frederick Engels: Collected works, vol. 27*,

Engels: 1890–1895 (trans: Peet, John, et al.), 506–524. New York: International Publishers.
3. Harnecker, Marta. 2015. *A world to build: New paths toward twenty-first century socialism.* New York: Monthly Review Press.
4. Hollander, Samuel. 2011. *Friedrich Engels and Marxian political economy.* Cambridge: Cambridge University press.
5. "Human Development Reports." *United Nations Development Programme.* http://hdr.undp.org/en/composite/HDI.
6. Lavelle, Ashley. 2008. *The death of social democracy: Political consequences in the 21st century.* New York: International Publishers.
7. Marx, Karl, and Friedrich Engels. 1998. The Communist Manifesto. In *Socialist register 1998: The Communist Manifesto now,* ed. Colin Leys, and Leo Panitch, 240–268. London: Merlin Press.
8. Marx, Karl H. Conspectus of Bakunin's Statism and Anarchy. *Marxist Internet Archive.* http://www.marxists.org/archive/marx/works/1874/04/bakunin-notes.htm.
9. Marx, Karl H. 2005. Contribution to the critique of Hegel's philosophy of law. In *Karl Marx, Frederick Engels: Collected works, vol. 3, Marx and Engels: 1843–1844* (trans: Cohen, Jack, et al.), 175–187. New York: International Publishers.
10. ———. 1989. Critique of the Gotha Programme. In *Karl Marx, Frederick Engels: Collected works, vol. 24, Marx and Engels: 1874–1873* (trans: Forgacs, David, et al.), 75–99. New York: International Publishers.
11. ———. 1992. Marx to Henry Mayers Hyndman. In *Karl Marx, Frederick Engels: Collected works, vol. 46, Marx and Engels: 1880–1883* (trans: Livingstone, Rodney, et al.), 49–50. New York: International Publishers.
12. ———. 1992. Marx to Ferdinand Domela Nieuwenhuis. In *Karl Marx, Frederick Engels: Collected works, vol. 46, Marx and Engels: 1880–1883* (trans: Livingstone, Rodney, et al.), 65–67. New York: International Publishers.
13. ———. 1988. On the Hague Congress: A correspondent's report of a speech made at a meeting in Amsterdam on September 8 – 1872. In *Karl Marx, Frederick Engels: Collected works, vol. 23, Marx and Engels: 1871–1874* (trans: Forgacs, David, et al.), 254–256. New Yok: International Publishers.
14. ———. 1989. Parliamentary debate on the anti-socialist law. In *Karl Marx, Frederick Engels: Collected works, vol. 24, Marx and Engels: 1874–1873* (tran: Forgacs, David, et al.), 240–250. New York: International Publishers.
15. Marx, Karl and Friedrich Engels. 1989. *Collected works,* vol. 32, 287. Moscow: Progress Publishers.
16. Meszaros, Istvan. 1995. *Beyond capital.* New York: Monthly Review Press.
17. Nove, Alec. 2010. *The economics of feasible socialism.* London: Routledge.
18. Rahnema, Saeed. 1992. Work councils in Iran: The illusion of worker control. *Economic and Industrial Democracy: International Journal* 13(1): 69–94.

19. "Social Expenditure Database (SOCX)." *The Organisation for Economic Co-operation and Development (OECD)*. http://www.oecd.org/social/expenditure.htm
20. Streeck, Wolfgang. 2014. *Buying time: The delayed crisis of democratic capitalism*. New York: Verso.
21. "The Programme of the Parti Ouvrier."*Marxists Internet Archive*. http://www.marxists.org/archive/marx/works/1880/05/parti-ouvrier.htm.
22. Wood, Ellen M. 1995. *Democracy against capitalism: Renewing historical materialism*. Cambridge: Cambridge University Press.

CHAPTER 2

Failures and Achievements of the Past

Despite enormous costs and sacrifices, both revolutionary and reformist strategies followed by socialists worldwide failed and ended up with changing course to a vigorous pursuit of capitalist path. To what extent, if at all, socialists themselves are responsible for these failures, and what lessons have we learned from these experiences?

Gilbert Achcar

GA: The only experiences that are referred to as socialist experiences with some historical continuity were those that came as a result of the Russian Revolution, including revolutions that were quite remotely inspired by it, with many differences. To call any of these "socialist" is already a problem, especially when one is speaking of China or Vietnam where you had nationalist, peasant-based military forces that managed to take over their countries and liberate them from foreign occupation, setting up regimes which were from the outset military-bureaucratic centralized regimes. The label socialist does not make much sense in these cases.

SR: What about the Russian Revolution itself or the German Revolution for that matter?

GA: The Russian Revolution is a different case because of the kind of process that took place initially, with the formation of workers' councils, and the fact that the party that led the process was member of a working-class international movement, the Second International. That is the only significant experience that may legitimately be called "socialist" from a Marxist standpoint. The German Revolution, the Paris Commune, etc. were short-lived.

Yet, the Russian experience was affected from the start by a conception of the seizure of power that was implemented in the October 1917 Revolution, a conception that had more in common with the Blanquist conception of government by a revolutionary enlightened minority that takes on itself to educate the backward majority, than it had with Marx's and Engels's understanding of socialist transformation.

The Russian experience was predicated, however, on the idea that it signalled the beginning of the world revolution. Lenin's view of imperialism was that the world had entered into the phase of agony of world capitalism, the era of world socialist revolution, and that therefore "We, Russians, will seize and hold power in Russia, even though we are a minority in our country, until the forthcoming success of the world revolution creates conditions that will enable us to move forward." From such a perspective, the seizure of power was a goal in itself, whereas the conditions for the socialist transformation were to be created later.

This logic was also connected with another core idea of Leninism, that there is only one party that truly represents the working class in each country, disqualifying all other currents as petty bourgeois. This logic paved the way for dictatorship: party dictatorship, not a "Dictatorship of the Proletariat," along with the ban of all other political organizations.

In the field of economy, the Bolsheviks had no clear perspective either and resorted to sweeping nationalization imposed on them by the logic of the events into what was called "war communism." As soon as the war ended, they shifted back into allowing some space for private economy, with a famous speech in which Lenin says, "We were asses" when it comes to running an economy. "We ended up nationalizing everything because that was imposed on us, although we did not have the capacity to manage the economy."

Taking into consideration all the conditions created by war and civil war, it is hard to consider the Russian experience as a model of socialist revolution, as did the Communist movement, and as many Leninist groups of various denominations still do today when they refer to the first years of the Russian Revolution as a positive model for socialism. Basically, the experience of truly building socialism is still to be invented. There is no model whatsoever other than negative: We know from what happened what should not be done. There are thus several negative models, but no significant positive one.

The Paris Commune provided an interesting model of government, but it was alas short-lived, and it is still to be proven that it is sustainable in the long run. The fact that we have negative models is useful nonetheless, at least in indicating the pitfalls that should be avoided if one is not to produce new tragedies.

Aijaz Ahmad

AA: I do not understand any longer what constitutes failure or success. My sense is that the socialist revolution is not an event, is not even a series of events, or stages that we can identify. Rather, it is a continuing process. There will be moments of great victories and there are likely to be defeats. What is likely to happen, very unevenly around the world, is that revolutions will be made and get defeated for reasons external and internal, and when a new beginning is made it will be at a much higher level of culture, ideology, politics, and material basis for creating a socialist society. And then it will be defeated again, and this process will go on until we reach the point that you can reasonably call a society socialist. I do not believe that any revolution so far has actually failed in an absolute sense.

Are the socialists responsible for these so-called failures, the answer is yes and no; in the sense that Marx always insisted that a society could only achieve changes that are possible and potential within the dynamics of that society. History, he said, does not undertake tasks it cannot accomplish. The historic fact is that none of the industrially advanced countries ever arrived at a point where they could even begin experimenting with what a socialist society would be like. The only breakthroughs that were ever made were largely in agrarian societies. Even Russia, which had a fairly advanced capitalist base in some regions, was largely agricultural, barely about 50 or 60 years away from serfdom—roughly, about half a century between the abolition of serfdom in the 1860s and the socialist revolution in 1917. Under such circumstances, the building of socialism was something of a utopian wish. Historically, of course, it had spectacular success in what it did. It transformed an extremely backward agricultural country into one of the most industrialized countries of the world. In certain areas of science and technology, the Soviet Union was even more advanced than any country other than the USA. It created a highly sophisticated educated intelligentsia. It also defended and preserved the classical culture. I once asked my friend Aziz al-Azmeh—who was then based in Budapest—what was the most fundamental change that he had witnessed after the fall of communism in that country? Without pausing to think, he said the death of classical culture.

One also has to think how the Bolshevik Revolution changed the world beyond Russia. Dissolution of the colonial empires was the central event of the twentieth century. Most anti-colonial movements were greatly inspired by the Bolshevik Revolution, and the national liberation movements of the socialist type could not have succeeded without direct support and aid from the Soviet Union. Also, much independent industrial construction was possible in countries like India or Egypt only owing to Soviet aid. I also think that workers in Western Europe possibly got more of Soviet Socialism than perhaps the Soviet working class. The fear of communism spreading from the East to the West compelled the social democrats and even mainstream liberals in northwestern Europe to raise the social rights and living standards of the classes dramatically. Neoliberalism did not take hold of the advanced capitalist countries until after economic stagnation became endemic across the Economic bloc of former Communist countries (COMECON) countries, and the Soviet political system became totally discredited in the West. So, achievements are enormous and the evidence of it all is what happened when the Soviet Union collapsed. What kind of world do we have? You know Luxemburg's famous dictum that the real choice is between socialism and barbarism. What we have now is the outbreak of barbarism at the global scale. So what I am saying is that while all the horrors of the Stalin period and thereafter must be acknowledged, there is also this history of achievements. So, when there is the next attempt to build socialism, it will be done at a much higher level of historical development, in all areas. The same thing is true for China and elsewhere.

SR: There is no doubt the Russian Revolution had an enormous impact on labour movements and national liberation movements around the world, and Russia itself went through rapid industrialization, but of course with enormous costs that we do not need to discuss it here. But, I would like to ask you whether this inevitability of socialism that you stressed would be the result of the so-called objective conditions or the subjective factors that in the long run would put an end to capitalism?

AA: It is not a choice. It is a historical imperative. Humanity cannot survive under capitalism. So in that sense, in your terminology, it is the objective conditions. As for lessons learned from the past, part of the problem is that while the past gives you lessons, history keeps moving on and future becomes very different, and very few lessons of the past are actually useful.

Rob Albriton

RA: Socialist revolutions took off in relatively undeveloped countries that faced very severe difficulties, and despite huge sacrifices and efforts of really well-meaning people, for the most part their struggles in the end failed. This was largely because these revolutions occurred in a world still dominated by capitalist countries. This is a very difficult process. Look at Cuba, which perhaps is still more socialist than most other places in the world. A very poor country, which was very much dependent on the support of the Soviet Union. Cuba is still carrying out valuable programmes of one sort or another, despite all the difficulties, despite basically being an underdeveloped country. But being next to the USA, and operating in a world dominated by capital, it has faced enormous difficulties implementing socialist policies and yet it still has had important successes.

Overall, socialism has had a huge impact historically, even though it is not in power in places that hoped to have socialism. To imagine a world without socialism, you can go back to Bismarck and the origin of the welfare state. The welfare state would not have happened without the threat of socialism. I believe the world is a better place because of efforts of socialism and socialist experiments. Scandinavian countries have taken some steps towards socialism that we can learn from, but they operate in a predominantly capitalist world, a capitalist world that is unfortunately dominated by the USA, which is not only the most advanced capitalist country but also the least socialist. When you have that kind of hegemony in the world, any country trying to move towards socialism is going to meet resistance.

I think there are certainly lessons to be learned from socialist failures. One of those lessons is that to achieve any degree of socialism it is going to take a long time, and it is probably better to move slowly and to struggle for reforms that advance the movement furthest in terms of politicizing people. If you can start with relatively small steps, but steps that open up the possibilities to larger steps, then socialism can go somewhere. It is also necessary to be prepared for unexpected openings that may present opportunities for larger steps forward. Despite the past failures of struggles for socialism, I think we have learned a lot, and I think socialism has had a positive impact on capitalism itself. We do not need to completely discourage ourselves about the possibilities of the future. I think the possibilities are still there and I think there are millions of people in the world that are, to some degree, and in some way socialist. It is important to have vigorous and widespread debates about the best paths forward at this stage of history.

SR: There is no question about the positive impact of the ideals of socialism on capitalism or on human development in general. You mentioned that countries that moved towards socialist revolutions were not among the most advanced societies. This is true, but we have the experience of the German revolution where the social democrats were so powerful, and most prominent Marxists and Socialists were leading the movement. The country was among the most advanced industrial societies, etc. But even there, the socialist revolution failed. I think it somehow relates to what you mentioned about the question of revolution and reform.

RA: We need to learn from past failures, but one can overdo the search of the past for some kind of simple solution, like, for example, if only we had followed Trotsky or Mao, or whoever it is—as if there is one straight path to socialism that somebody embodied, almost like a god, and should be followed. This is a kind of religious thinking, and no kind of religious fundamentalism is conducive to advancing socialism. Sectarian views and infighting among left groups can be very stultifying when it comes to growing the energy of the left. People start calling each other all kinds of names and stop having principled debates about the best avenues of change. What I want to say is that learning from the past is one thing, but turning too much inward and being hyper critical and then trying to find simple solutions is very dangerous to the left.

Kevin Anderson

KA: We have had ups and downs. Right now capital is very strong versus labour and the social movements, though not in as strong a relative position as it was in the 1990s. But there have been periods like in the 1920s when capitalism was in question, which was true even to a certain extent after the Second World War. The Left also had its ups and downs, and not everything was a failure. Where it failed spectacularly, as in the Soviet Union, I would look at these events as transformations into opposite, to borrow a formulation from Lenin's Hegel Notebooks. There have been revolutions but soon they have been transformed into something very different than intended by their participants. No doubt there have been tremendous failures on the part of the left, going back to the authoritarian socialists of Marx's own time, some of whom leaned towards the Bonapartist dictatorship in France. Some left leaders, usually not consciously, wanted just to replace existing ruling group and substitute themselves. The Russian Revolution was our biggest hope and our biggest failure, in terms of the international Left. We have to say two things to qualify that statement, however. One is that all the revolutionaries in Russia were up against very strong forces of opposition, which helps explain (but does not justify) their recourse to terror. Two, we also have to say that the liberal democratic revolutions were not smooth either. The French Revolution of 1789 ended up during the great terror with a very authoritarian regime, and eventually with a moderate kind of authoritarian state under the first Napoleon that continued some of the aspects of the original revolution but not its most far-reaching aims like abolition of slavery.

Revolution or radical social change of any kind is always full of contradictions and that is part of human experience. As the Germans like to say, where there is light there is also shadow, and where there is shadow there is also light. However, it is a very big mistake when many, including much of the anti-Stalinist left, put the blame on the way the Russian Revolution turned out on imperialist blockade, encirclement, and invasion. The liberal Jacobins also used the same reasons to justify their terror. However, such arguments are insufficient, as is the one about Russian economic backwardness. The critique also needs to be a merciless self-critique on the part of the Marxist left, as to why we ended up with a Stalin, or a Mao, etc.

Barbara Epstein

BE: There are two questions here: why socialism failed in the Soviet Union, and in China and elsewhere in the Third World, and why there has been no successful socialist revolution in the USA or in Western Europe. On the first question, I think it is safe to say that a version of socialism based on a highly centralized economy, governed by an authoritarian state, has been shown to have severe limits. In an increasingly globalized economy, such a system was unable to compete effectively with Western capitalism. It also seems likely that at least in the case of the Soviet Union, the increasingly global reach of the media led young people especially to compare their situations, economic, political, and cultural, with the images of Western capitalist societies that they absorbed, and to find their own situations wanting. Members of the elite, much less committed to egalitarianism than preceding generations, may also have been attracted to capitalism as a more profitable system. Due to the economic backwardness of both Tsarist Russia and pre-revolutionary China, forced industrialization was necessary for these societies to even begin to compete with the West. But forced industrialization also caused enormous suffering and relied upon an authoritarian state that squelched democracy. It is hard to say to what extent the revolutionaries, in these societies, were responsible for these failures: without industrialization the economic contrast between the socialist East and the capitalist West would have been even starker, and military conquest would have been possible. But socialism in this form lost both internal support and the capacity to inspire oppositional movements in the capitalist world.

On the second issue—the absence of successful socialist revolutions in the West—I can speak most easily of the USA. I do not think that there has ever been a time, in the USA, when socialist revolution was possible. The moment when this was closest would have been the years immediately after the crash of 1929, when a third of the labour force was unemployed and the economy seemed to be spiralling downward. But the New Deal and the economic and political innovations that accompanied it, while by no means solving the economic crisis, broke the downward spiral, opened up space for a labour/left coalition on behalf of the empowerment of the working class and the common people generally, within the limits of capitalism, leading to a widespread sense that economic recovery and a more egalitarian society were possible. For those on the left socialism remained the ultimate objective, but for the time being the focus was on organizing the unorganized, opposing racism, and breaking the hold of the upper classes over the political arena.

In the late 1960s, in the context of the Vietnam War, massive opposition to it, and the radicalization of large numbers of young people, many on the left thought that revolution was possible if not imminent. But with the end of the war the anti-war movement evaporated rather than moving on to other issues, and it became clear that the radicalism of the previous years had been based on widespread and vehement opposition to the war, not on widespread opposition to capitalism or desire for socialism. By the end of the 1970s, neoliberalism began to appear as a strategy, on the part of the corporate elite, for increasing profits by driving wages down, diverting state funds from social programmes to the needs of capital, and taking advantage of the opportunities opened up by the onset of globalization. The left, at the time, had little understanding of neoliberalism or its potential impact. During the 1960s and early 1970s the view had taken hold, on the left, that due to technological advances poverty had become obsolete, that the elite had learned that keeping the capitalist system functioning smoothly required a well-oiled welfare system and set of social programmes, and that therefore conservatism was a problem of the past. The obstacles to revolutionary change, it was believed, were liberal reform and consumerism. From this perspective, neoliberalism was incomprehensible. In the years after the war, the women's movement and movements of people of colour continued their efforts and the environmental and lesbian/gay movements took off, but these movements had little to do with each other. A better understanding of neoliberalism—which would soon affect all of the constituencies and issues that the left cared about—might have given the left the sense of common purpose that had been lost with the end of the war.

Finally, what lessons have been learned? In regard to the failure of Soviet and Chinese socialism, I think a central lesson is that a socialist system that is authoritarian and lacks, or gradually loses, strong popular support is very vulnerable to outside pressure and to the lure of foreign examples, examples of systems that are seen as more successful. The failure of the main socialist countries to provide a positive example has also undermined the appeal, or credibility, of socialism in Western countries. This is not to say that socialist revolutions would have taken place if Soviet or Chinese versions of socialism had been more attractive. I think that the continued vitality of capitalism, in the West, has imposed limits on the ability of the left to bring about a transition to socialism. But the left could be stronger even in the context of a resurgent capitalism. I think that the main weaknesses of the US left have to do with its failure to build organizations and institutions, and a penchant for an ultra-leftism that makes it seem irrelevant to practical politics and unnecessarily marginalizes it.

Aron Etzler

AE: I would not fully agree with the notion that the efforts of the socialists have been all failures. Many positive and progressive aspects of today's society have been the direct or indirect result of what revolutionaries and reformists of the past had achieved. This is particularly true of countries like Sweden or other Scandinavian and some other societies. In these societies, successful working-class movements have changed the countries for the better, and some of their achievements are hard to be reversed. Many people now see the contemporary form of capitalism as a natural phenomenon, but this is not the case—it is rather a result of the political hegemony of the right. In this view, our current neoliberal epoch is the final station, while I think it is more of a parenthesis. The setbacks that we have seen since the late 1970s cannot go on forever and I believe it is a temporary setback and in a longer term we will have movements that actually point towards socialism. If we should be afraid of anything, that would be the processes that seem to be spinning out of control, such as ecological devastations with their enormous economic and social consequences, or the geopolitical problems and confrontations that we now face in light of the rising new cold war. If we survive these catastrophes, I believe the chance of moving towards socialism is higher than the possibility of continuing with capitalism forever. The pendulum seems to swing a lot slower than politically active people expect, simply because changing institutions and ways of thinking takes actually a lot of time. For instance, in our country, Sweden, to attain universal suffrage took decades. That is the same thing as public ownership in institutions, something that in many cases are pretty far away from the market-oriented capitalism we have been taught to see as the only way of organizing production. It has taken a lot of time to build, and also a lot of time to change the expectations from people, but in a country like Sweden, it has had an enormous impact on the way people see society—it is why even people who vote for bourgeois parties tend to hold elements of a socialist worldview. And that is what real success looks like.

SR: I totally agree that it has not been all failures and there have been major achievements, but I think it is important that we look at the failures in order to learn from them. I would like, in particular, to ask you to discuss this question in relation to the experience of the Swedish Social Democracy, with its enormous historical significance. When we look at its history we see that it begins with a more radical perspective and higher demands and then gradually moves towards right and liberal democracy, even in some instances close to neoliberal policies.

AE: The idea that Swedish social democracy has constantly been getting less and less radical overtime is not true. Social democrats had periods of adaptation and conflict with capital, with some periods of backlash. For example, in the 1920s there was a setback as a result of very conservative economic policies, but in the 1930s, 1940s, and 1950s they bounced back. When they were established after the Second World War in the 1950s and 1960s, they began working on the project of social welfare. In the 1960s they were challenged in relation to a foreign policy issue, the war in Vietnam. Later, they vigorously criticized the class society of Sweden, and in the 1970s we see a most intense reform period and huge expansion of the welfare system. So I argue for instance that the 1970s were more radical than the earlier period. Now in Europe we are witnessing that some social democratic parties are moving to the left, for instance we see in Britain with the election of Corbyn, or rise of left parties like Podemos and Syriza. This points to the fact that moving to the right is not at all a "natural" development for social democracy—it is just a political conjuncture.

SR: Was not it the case that in the 1920s the Social Democratic Party, SAP, advocated for the "socialization" of natural resources, banks, transportation, and communication, but in the 1930s modified the programme, stressing private property rights and reducing deficit, etc.? In any case I do not deny that there have been ups and downs and fluctuations for European social democracies, but as we come to the present time, we witness a shift towards the right. Why is it that a section of these parties had separated themselves from the main party and had created left parties, like your own party, the Left, or Die Linke in Germany?

AE: Sure, the Social Democrats moved from classical Marxist ideology to the idea of a peoples state in the 1920s, but that was in my view an intelligent remake that opened the way for a much larger success in the 1930s. Now, what happened in the early 1980s was something else: That was a retreat.

In the late 1970s, the right wing came back, not only in Sweden but also throughout Europe, and brought proposals that they could not have dared to put forward for almost 50 years. It was the end of the Bretton Woods era, an era of big change in the American policies. Many people today think this was a natural development, but I see it as a political development that the right wing used the crisis of the 1970s, the heightening of the oil crisis, and the stagflation of the period. It appears that social democracy did not have the answers to all of these questions, but this does not mean that they could not have gotten the answers. I am not determinist, but believe that lack of prospect for the future led to a very defensive attitude for the Swedish Social Democrats. The Social Democrats did not really know what to do. The Swedish welfare state was built and Social Democrats really did not know how to get themselves a project for the future. There is a famous sentence by the Swedish prime minister Olof Palme addressed to Ingvar Carlsson, whom he had assigned to write the programme for the future, that says "I don't know it is the programme or it is me that each time I read it, I fall asleep!" Palme himself in the mid-1970s was figuring if they should go further along socialist path. He was very reluctant to touch the interests of the richest oligarchs in Sweden. He was reluctant to move beyond what they called functional socialism, which is a current of social democratic thinking that believes society should be functioning along socialism without touching the big companies and ownership. Of course that cannot be done. This is one of the lessons that we should learn. I think Social Democrats in Sweden are well positioned and they have changed society very radically in one way, but if you do not touch ownership in the end, it will bite you. They were not prepared to do that (and still they are not). But not be willing to move beyond the limits of capitalism also put an end to the Social Democrats ideas to develop Sweden. In that particular political situation, it meant that they gave away the initiative to the right, which emboldened by international currents, managed to do a tremendous comeback in Sweden.

Sam Gindin

SG: The socialist project is a remarkably difficult, long-term project and it is not clear yet whether we have failed or "not won yet." We do, of course, have to take some responsibility for particular problems in our analysis and organizing. Methodologically, there was a tendency to treat Marxism as a science that gave us laws that definitively determined the path of capitalist development. Though Marxism can be very useful heuristically in pointing us in certain directions, looking for unchangeable laws is a mistake.

This particular error led to underestimating what we are really up against. It led socialists to expect that the system would more or less collapse because of inherent laws and socialists would then be in a position to take advantage of this breakdown. At the same time, we overestimated the extent to which the contradictions of capitalism would automatically lead to workers becoming revolutionary. And this meant we misjudged what it would take to build the working class into the kind of social force that could transform itself as part of transforming society. Such "optimism" neglected what capitalism did to distort working-class capacities, narrow their vision, and push them to focus on the short term because of pressures to survive—leaving little time for political participation and longer term strategizing. All this distorted the nature of the organizational question, the importance of radical education and how much it would take to move people. It is necessary to think of organization not just in terms of taking over the state but of a myriad of complex tasks given that we are virtually "starting over"—

fundamental questions like how to just get and keep socialism on the agenda and how to win the people over to this extremely challenging and contradictory process. If, for example, workers magically took over the world today, would they know how to run it differently? The answer is very likely "no" since there is little that has prepared them for this in their experiences under capitalism and much that has undermined the needed capacities.

On the question of organization, Lukacs rightly emphasized that it was something especially undertheorized by Marxists. Many Marxists thought the Bolshevik experience provided an answer and all that was needed was to adapt it to modern times. But we need to rethink, in spite of the continuities in capitalism, a great deal about the current world. This is particularly the case in the West where the working class has made significant gains and has—so far—been ready to make concessions in order to hang on the bulk of these gains. In the context of globalization and the failure of communism and social democracy, a crucial barrier to change is pervasive despair about possibilities. What makes the question of organization so fundamental is that it involves creating structures through which people can act and a sense that they are building something—the confidence that struggle *matters*.

Peter Hudis

PH: I think that the main barrier to an anti-capitalist perspective in the last century has come actually from socialists and the left, and I think they are largely responsible for these failures most of all because of the legacy of Stalinism, which discredited the idea of socialism in the eyes of tens of millions of workers around the world, and of course it created authoritarian and totalitarian repressive regimes that in no way, shape, or form could possibly have represented socialism. Stalinism is not just a historical issue, but it is something that the left must continue to grapple with today. But, of course, that begs the question of what led to Stalinism and what can we learn from that. Obviously there were objective factors such as the material backwardness of the Soviet Union or China during the time of the revolution, or pressures of imperialism, hostile forces from outside trying to suppress these revolutions, and many others. But these are hardly the only ones; there were internal factors that led to Stalinism as well.

I think that there are four basic problems that the revolutionary left, including the anti-Stalinist left, is responsible for in terms of the crisis of socialism. One is the relation of socialism and democracy. The failure to understand that you cannot have socialism without democracy and cannot have democracy without socialism, has taken a terrible toll of the movement. That is why I do a lot of work to reinvigorate discussions of Rosa Luxemburg; she was one of the foremost Marxists who understood, way back in the beginning of the twentieth century, that any effort to repress democracy would necessarily prevent a movement towards a socialist society coming into existence, no matter how revolutionary the regime happens to be. She was criticizing people that she was very closely associated with, in the Bolshevik party, Lenin's party; and she issues that critique not just in 1918, but as early as 1908. She had a very sharp criticism of what she saw coming. In contrast, Trotsky argued in 1918 that democracy was a cumbersome mechanism that the revolutionaries could simply discard.

The second thing that damaged the cause of socialism is unilinear evolutionary determinism. This is a notion inherited from nineteenth-century socialism and radicalism which was itself derived from bourgeois utilitarianism and Social Darwinism. The idea that society has to go through strict pre-determined stages and you cannot reach a socialist society, especially in the developing world, unless you first go through a bourgeois stage of development headed by the national bourgeoisie, has proved very counterproductive. This perspective had a certain degree of validity in the nineteenth century, and even in the first years of the twentieth century, but in most of the twentieth century this notion of two-stage revolution became a great hindrance.

SR: Before discussing the other two points, I would like to ask when you refer to the legacy of Stalinism, you mentioned we should of course see what led to Stalinism. To what extent, could what you said about Stalinism also apply to Bolsheviks' policies and Lenin himself?

PH: This is a complicated question of course. First of all, Lenin was not an original thinker on the level of Marx, except in three areas: One, his theory of imperialism, which was excellent; two, his greatest contribution was his return to Hegel in 1914–15, during the collapse of the Second International; and three, his notion in *State and Revolution* that the state had to be not just taken over but smashed. But in terms of organizational theory, which he is most famous for, I do not think he was original. As Raya Dunayevskaya wrote in 1958 in her book *Marxism and Freedom*, Lenin saw his role very modestly as applying the traditions of German Social Democracy based on the Erfurt Program of 1891 to Russian conditions. Lenin certainly understood the role of a democratic stage on the way to a socialist revolution. However, like others of his time, he viewed this democratic stage as not itself socialist, but as a bourgeois democratic phase that an underdeveloped country must go through before it would be able to implement socialist content in the revolutionary process—what he called the democratic dictatorship of the workers and peasant. My problem with Lenin is what he does after the 1918, after the seizure of power. I support the Bolshevik Revolution, and, as Rosa Luxemburg said, the Bolsheviks alone dared and took the initiative at the moment of crisis and it was a magnificent revolution, both the February and the October Revolutions. But my biggest criticisms of Lenin is, (1) his shutting down the Soviets as independent organs of workers' power; (2) his imposition of single-party control and making illegal other left wing revolutionary parties in addition to bourgeois ones; and (3) under the pressure of imperialist invasion and the problems Russia was facing, he basically treated democracy and direct workers' participation in the revolution as something that could wait till later. These problems planted many seeds that Stalin was able to take advantage of. I do not think there is a straight line between Lenin and Stalin. Lenin did not see this coming and did not prepare his followers for the dangers of a counter-revolution from within, except perhaps towards the very end of his life—and by that time it was too late. So some of his policies are responsible for Stalin's rise to prominence.

The one thing I emphasize in Lenin's favour is that towards the end of life he did not have a stagified or unilinear understanding of historical stages, as most orthodox Marxists did. If you look at the second congress of Third International, especially his speeches in 1919 and his discussions with people like Soltanzadeh, Galiev, and others, he discusses the possibility of an underdeveloped country transitioning directly to communism, not just socialism, without going through the capitalist stage of development. This is a remarkable shift from the earlier period of his life, when Lenin shared the Plekhanov's deterministic view that Russia must experience a lengthy period of capitalism before it could be ready for socialism. So at the end of his life and seeing the experience of the revolution, he began to modify many of his views. I think this is part of the impact of his study of Hegel in 1914–15. But, unfortunately, what he never did was to rethink his elitist view of the need for a centralized vanguard-party form of organization in light of his investigation of Hegelian dialectics. And I think to this day this is one of the major problems inflicting radical movements.

SR: I wish we had more time to go through the historical analysis and discuss further some of the points you mentioned, particularly Lenin's notion of the two-stage revolution. I also have a problem with some aspects of the theory of the two-stage revolutions, but I believe, much to Lenin's credit, he realized that the then relatively backward Russia would not have been able to directly move to socialism. Also, I would strongly differentiate between the February and the October Revolutions. I appreciate your critique of Bolsheviks' abolition of the Soviets, but I would also question the abolition of the Constituent Assembly. Moreover, Lenin's contribution in developing a distinct party of the working class is also extremely significant, but of course, as you rightly pointed out, it was an elitist organization.

Sorry I interrupted your four points you discussed in explaining the reasons for the defeat of socialist experience. Could you please mention the other two remaining points?

PH: The two other factors leading to the failure of socialism are in sense even bigger factors. One is that prior to the 1920s, I do not think any Marxist after Marx, let us say until the 1920s at the earliest, understood that the object of critique of Marxism is not to abolish the unequal distribution of value—the distinction between the amount of value produced by the workers versus what they consume in wages—but rather to abolish value production itself. Any revolution that simply tries to redistribute value more equitably without uprooting the social relations that gives rise to value production is inherently self-defeating.

The other factor was a dogmatic assumption that Marxists and socialists are not supposed to envisage an explicit alternative to capitalism, not talk about a new society, because Marx supposedly did not indulge in utopian blueprints. This did great damage because it left the radical movements unprepared to figure out what to do when they did seize power.

Ursula Huws

UH: No doubt Leninist parties made many mistakes, but until we know what right looks like, it is not really fair to blame people for being wrong. You can only do what the circumstances allow you to do, and what people are willing to do. Just focusing on the mistakes made by the leadership may miss the point. It is what the actual working class and the people are prepared to do or to risk that decides whether you finally win or not. Problems with the leadership were mainly lack of attentive listening, failure of intellectual understanding, a failure of democratic accountability. Intelligent analysis of what the actual situation of working-class people is at that particular juncture is very important. I am not saying that revolutions are just made by people autonomously rising up. Of course there is a need for leadership and organization, but I want to stress that without understanding where the class is and what is prepared to do, we cannot achieve any change at all.

SR: You are absolutely right in emphasizing the factor of the preparedness of the people and the working class for radical change. But I would like to know whether you see any problem on the part of socialists themselves, the way they led the revolutions, their strategies, and their understanding of Marx, etc.?

UH: We cannot talk about socialism in an abstract way. Socialism contains many strands. The vanguard Leninist party jumped ahead of itself, failed to understand the contradictions within the working class and between the working class and other class positions—such as distinctions along lines of gender and ethnicity, the complicated petty-bourgeois positions—that lots of people still occupy, etc. They absolutely failed to understand the contradictory nature of the forces at play. They had an oversimplified idea that everyone had common interests. If you read Marx on Paris, there is a very detailed analysis of the different class positions. It is necessary to do empirical work like this on each specific situation.

Also, many socialists did not and do not understand the nature of capitalism and capitalism's enormous capabilities to adapt to new circumstances.

SR: In your writings you have very clearly elaborated capitalism's extraordinary ability to survive, by generating new commodities, generating new forms of production of new goods and services and create new markets.

UH: There has always been a simplistic notion that capitalism will implode from within as a result of its inherent contradictions. Capitalism is much more creative than that, because it harnesses the capabilities of human labour. I think some Marxist intellectuals, some of whom I would characterize as, what Henry Bernstein once called Marxologists rather than Marxists, have a disrespect for what is going on empirically in the world, and this has led them into some real errors, major errors. Some among the current generation—I hate to caricature them—but there are some that I think of as new Marxist theory boys, who seem to see capitalism as a homogenous single entity, a single undifferentiated thing which absorbs your labour and sells you goods, and do not see that capitalism consists of many competing capitalists, aggressively competing with each other. This failure to understand how capitalism works is very evident in the debates about surplus value and how it is produced. It leads them to the error that value creation and value realization are the same thing. They do not seem to see that there is an enormous gap between value creation and value realization. This is particularly true under the conditions of globalization.

Michael Lebowitz

ML: Revolutionary and reformist experiences failed for different reasons. If by reformist we mean the experiences of social democratic governments, we cannot parallel them to the experience of the revolutionary movements. The reason is that characteristic of social democracy has been the acceptance of the necessity and logic of capital. It attempts to incrementally make inroads on that logic, but ultimately succumbs to the logic itself. Social democracy is subject to what Marx explained as the tendency of the working class to look upon the requirements of capital as self-evident natural laws. They may be able to make some inroads, but when crises emerge, between the choices of giving in or moving in, social democrats tend to give in precisely because they have not broken with the logic of capital. Therefore, you end up with the tendency for the enforcement of capitalism with a human face. Much like Syriza.

This is quite different from the revolutionary perspective. Your implicit reference is to violent overthrows of existing regimes, be it the Soviet Union, China, or Cuba. However, we have to distinguish between the beginning of the process and what follows later. The process may begin by a forcible overthrow, or by winning an election, but what is important is what you do after that.

As for the question of the extent to which socialists have been at fault, whether they came to power through violent overthrow or through electoral process, they neglected what I call the second product, a neglect of understanding the central point that Marx poses when he talks about revolutionary practice, the simultaneous changing of circumstances and human activity, or self-change. By changing circumstances we change ourselves. Socialists in the twentieth century neglected the question of self-change, the question of what kind of people are formed in a society in which the decisions are made top-down. If we forget about the second product, we will forget about the way people's capacities are built. The question is what happens when a new regime comes into power with the perspective of a vanguard that believes we must advance very rapidly and accordingly we cannot allow the working class to make mistakes.

SR: Your reference to the experiences of social democratic parties that came to power in Europe is absolutely right. My reference to reformism is a perspective that has the aim of socialism, and although operates during capitalist era—as it cannot end capitalism abruptly—it does not accept the logic and necessity of capitalism. Part of this incremental approach is somewhat related to the faults of socialists that you mentioned, that is "human development." I believe it is a long process and obviously should happen both before and after the establishment of socialist system. Also, I would like to ask you to elaborate on a very important point you raise in your book *Build It Now*, where you say the twentieth-century socialism focused on the development of productive forces, means of production, with no attention for relevance of social relations in which people live.

ML: On the first point, I worry about your stress upon a long process and a great amount of preparation in advance. The process can begin with a forcible revolution and overturning of the existing order. Even if this process begins and advances led by a minority, it does not require a long period of preparation. Once you have gained access to the levers of power within a country, you use that power and decide what needs to be done at that point. In the Soviet Union after the October Revolution, workers gained lots of power in the workplaces. What happened was that this power was taken away from them. It was taken away by the fear that workers would become self-oriented. They removed workers' control and prevented workers from developing their capacity. What would have happened if the workers instead of the bureaucrats could have developed their capacities? What would have happened if they had built upon the social relationships of worker-management in enterprises? This was a question that Alexandra Kollontai posed in 1920, that instead of self-development of the masses, we had self-development of bureaucracy. So I think it is wrong to focus on the long process of preparation. Revolutionaries must always attempt not only to capture the old state, but also at the same time to build people's capacities to the extent that is possible by local struggles so that they can make decisions, and gain some sense of strength and dignity.

SR: The big question here is how? How the working class or people can come to power? All the revolutions that you mentioned occurred during wars and national liberation movements, and from the start had to fight against internal and external enemies, without being much prepared, and ending in establishing another rule by force.

ML: Firstly, I do not want to make a distinction saying what was and was not a revolution, or that revolutions should be defined solely in terms of forcible taking of power. As you know, I always talk of the Bolivarian Revolution; that power was gained through an electoral process. A revolution is not defined by how it comes to power but by the positions that it takes to change things. We recognize there will be enemies and they will try to crush anything. But the question is: What you do when you have the ability to make decisions. For example, Iran during the revolution introduced worker-management, the Councils movement. What happened to it, and why did it disappear? This is a question I am asking you. Building on such mechanisms in workplace and community levels strengthens people to prevent the loss of the project.

SR: It is a long story that I have written about it, but here very briefly can say that while no doubt the *Showra* (council) movement in Iran was a most amazing feature of the 1979 Revolution, it was doomed to failure. The workplace councils were formed and run predominantly by the left, while the new regime was controlled by the Islamist populists, who were against the councils because they were not under their control. In the large strategic industries, the site of the most important workers/employee councils, the left activists belonged to different left organizations and parties with conflicting policies towards the regime. There were theoretical confusions about the concepts of workers' control and councils. The leadership positions of the councils were predominantly occupied by the revolutionary new middle class—the workers alone were by no means in a position to run these large industries and without the help of progressive engineers and managers. The industries were heavily reliant on state subsidies, on the one hand, and imported technology and components from multinational corporations, on the other. With the hostage taking in the American Embassy in Tehran, and later the beginning of the Iran–Iraq War, the Islamist regime consolidated its power, wiped out the real workers/employee councils, and replaced them with the yellow "Islamic Councils."

ML: Yes, this is an unfortunate experience. As I have said with respect to similar problems in Venezuela, the matter is ultimately resolved by class struggle. Nothing is doomed to failure: In class struggle, there are no guarantees, no inevitability. Of course, workers are never able immediately to make key operational decisions in large industries. That is a given. The question is then what you do to prepare them to do so once you have power? How do you introduce ways in which they build their capacities? This is something that was not done in the Yugoslav experience despite the many years in which workers councils had juridical power in socially owned enterprises.

SR: Now if you would elaborate on your point regarding the difference between focusing on the development of productive forces as opposed to the relations of production.

ML: This deals with the issue of human development and the necessity of focusing on the second product, the human product. When you focus on human activity, then you cannot avoid the question of social relations. But what is the link between human development and productive forces? The argument, based on the misinterpretation of so many Marxists following Lenin, was that we need to have enormous development of productive forces and then suddenly we reach a point, a new stage in which we can provide all the things we had promised. This perspective completely ignores human beings, and the development of human capacity that I mentioned earlier.

Leo Panitch

LP: Where does one begin? Let us start with those capitalist countries where the working class was able to form its own parties and its own trade unions and on that basis to make a broad appeal to the population in an open way, in a legal way, as representing the working men and women including new immigrants. This is different from those countries where representation and the advancement of the workers cause was pushed underground, was made illegal. In those countries where liberal democracy prevailed—which the workers movement had a good deal to do with bringing about—there was an assumption that once reforms were won they would be won forever. This was famously captured in T.H. Marshal's "citizenship and social class" with its notion of successive stages of reform for working people, with civil rights (allowing for trade union association) being followed by political rights (the right for workers and women to vote) being followed finally by social rights (the welfare state). This was presented as happening in an almost inevitable teleological way. We see now in the twenty-first century that many of the social reforms that were won have been lost under neoliberalism in the context of increased capitalist competition, and the loss of working-class identity, which has partly occurred through the bureaucratization of trade unions and the de-radicalization of socialist parties. I think the biggest mistake proponents of this notion of gradualist cumulative reform within capitalism made was to assume what was being achieved at each stage could be consolidated primarily within the state rather than through the continuing mobilization and education, led by the active membership of the working-class parties and unions that won these reforms so as to expand class identity and solidarity, and develop collective capacities among working men and women, including those who can enrich the working class as recent immigrants. This orientation was abandoned. The unions increasingly became collective bargaining machines, processing grievances against employers like lawyers, representing workers like insurance companies. The parties became election campaigns machines, replacing political education with television advertising.

SR: It is good that you differentiated the situation in liberal democratic countries and those countries lacking democracy, and where socialists could not operate legally and had to resort to underground and resurrection, inspired by the Russian revolution and then the Chinese and others. Many mistakes were made on their part, leading to their disastrous defeats.

LP: There is no question there were many mistakes, but I want to say first that it is wrong to think that if people had not followed the Bolshevik Revolution with all of it mistakes, false steps and even crimes, Russia could have ended up with something like the Swedish Social Democracy. You are absolutely right that it was different conditions that produced different strategies. Political groups do have choices, but the conditions under which those choices are made can be so very different. So unlike in the countries where it was possible for workers to openly organize unions and to freely engage in elections for representative and accountable governments, the Bolshevik Revolution took place in a country where this turned out to be no real option. For this very reason, I was never in agreement with those Trotskyists of my generation who—after recognizing clearly that social democratic parties had made their peace with capitalism, but were nevertheless very critical of Stalinism and the Soviet Union—hoped to revive what they saw as the pre-Stalinist revolutionary spirit and purpose and form of the Bolshevik party that was led by Lenin. But what they did not understand was that the conditions were no longer there for that type of Bolshevik party or strategy. The very language of Bolshevism, which maybe was relevant in the conditions of 1917, not only in the East but also, to some extent, even in the West with all the general strikes, etc. after the First World War—was no longer relevant by the 1970s. The sectarianism, the marginalization, and the arcane disputations among these groups were not there because their members were in some sense born to be sectarians. They became sectarian because they were employing a Bolshevik language and dreaming of Bolshevik strategies in conditions that were no longer there, and this was bound to marginalize them.

SR: The question is that even in the countries that, as a result of political and economic conditions, the only path is seemingly revolutionary and insurrectionist, the socialists' engagement in insurrection without being prepared to provide an alternative, can be disastrous.

A good example is the Iranian revolution of 1979, which, as you know, the left engaged itself in a revolutionary process without knowing what will replace the old regime and what are the consequences of a premature insurrection.

LP: Well, this is an old story in revolutions. We need to remember that the French Revolution gave rise to Napoleon and eventually to the reassertion of the monarchy. We need to remember that the 1848 revolution ultimately failed, and a generation of revolutionaries, very much like you and your comrades, spent the rest of their lives in exile and could never go back. But would you say the 1789 or the 1848 revolutionaries should have just stayed home and tended their fires? These were social explosions, and even if it is true there were leaders, these were still leaders amidst social explosions who were not just acting out of sheer revolutionary voluntarism. And, of course, unintended political consequences can result from such social explosions. Look at Egypt today. One can only hope that future generations in Egypt will be able to look back and see a figure like Sisi, who even as a military secularist lacks any trace of a Nasserite third worldist anti-imperialism, for the counterrevolutionary he is, given the reactionary role he has played in attempting to stifle the revolutionary spirit that was the undoing the old Mubarak regime. Now I cannot say for the Iranian case whether there was a way of dislodging the shah, given the role he played in the US-led drive for a global capitalism, that would not have entailed the type of insurrectionary moment that occurred in 1979. The situation in each country is obviously different. If you look at the Cuban revolution I think you can say Castro was probably right to opt for armed revolution against the advice of the Cuban Communist Party leaders, and they ended up of course being part of the new regime.

SR: The question is not whether revolutions should or should not happen, as a combination of factors—objective and subjective, as well as internal and external—can in a specific juncture lead to a political revolution in a particular country. The question is rather whether a revolution that does not have the backing of the conscious majority (Marxian notion as opposed to Blanquist-type revolution of a minority) can have any chance of success in attaining its goals. Most of the revolutionary left have followed the latter with inevitable consequences.

Catherine Samary

CS: There is of course the question of what you mean by socialist, as claims of being a socialist are very different, each having a different understanding of the question you raise. There are objective and subjective reasons for failures of different revolutionary and reformist experiences. The isolation of the Russian revolution and the failure of the revolutions in the core capitalist countries pointed to the difficulties confronted in the semi periphery of the capitalist system, where revolutions occurred. But then, of course, there is the very deep and big problem of lack of experience. Socialists were confronted with the real organic contradiction of the capitalist system, the very unjust systems and inequalities. The Marxists, the socialists, and those who wanted to change the system, were forced to invent ways of confronting the system. They were faced with the realities of class divisions. There was, for example, the important question of the role of peasants, which I do believe was an issue that was underestimated by Marxists, particularly in countries where peasants formed the majority of the population.

There were also non-class issues, the question of bureaucratization within the revolutionary process and organizations, which contributed to the failures. As well, one can point to the revolutionary transformation of the party, and in the context of isolation, the problem of concentration of power in a single party, and the fact that they resorted to suppression of democracy with the hope of defending the revolution. The question of bureaucratization and the absence of pluralism were key issues. Rosa Luxemburg, while defending the revolutionary process and even the Soviet form of organization, raised these issues and, as you know, criticized the suppression of the parliament, the Duma, and the eradication of pluralism as something very dangerous for the revolution. Here you have an element of the responsibility of subjective forces.

CHAPTER 3

Which Revolution?

The Marxian social revolution based on a "self-conscious, independent movement of the immense majority", in contrast to Blanquist revolution of a minority leading unprepared masses, is a long process. In your view, how can this be achieved and what is involved in the process?

Gilbert Achcar

GA: I should start by saying that the phrase "Dictatorship of the Proletariat", which Marx borrowed from Blanqui but used very little indeed, is a very bad formula, even if one takes into account the theoretical elaboration that Marx gave in his critique of the Gotha Program; or, for that matter, even if, like Engels, one refers to the Paris Commune as the model of the Dictatorship of the Proletariat. The phrase is bad because "dictatorship" refers originally to an absolutist rule based on force, not on democratic consent.

A formula like the one you mentioned referring to the conscious movement of the immense majority, points to the necessity of social consent, the need of a democratic consensus for socialist transformation. It also points to the fact that no party with a socialist orientation, claiming to represent the interests of the majority and wanting to implement a project of socialist transformation, can envisage the seizure of power without the support of a clear majority of society. There is an obvious contradiction between such a conception, and seizure of power by a minority.

In the case of Russia, the October Revolution looked more like a coup than like a revolution; there were no large masses involved in the assault on the Winter Palace, Petrograd was not even on general strike. Later on, when the Bolsheviks faced problems with the elected Constituent Assembly, they had the option of organizing a new election; instead, they just dissolved the Assembly.

The Sandinistas in Nicaragua were actually the first example of a radical force coming to power by revolutionary means that ceded power after losing an election. They were also the first to preserve democratic freedoms under their rule. The contrast between Sandinistas and Bolsheviks is quite significant in that respect. The Sandinistas in the 1980s got much closer to a democratic conception of socialism.

In addition to political transformation, which should be backed by majority consensus, there is also the issue of economic transformation that is far more complex. There, you need to calculate very carefully the consequences of your acts. In light of previous negative experiences, we know that running an economy is very far from being easy, and that a precipitous sweeping nationalization of the economy is the shortest way to bureaucratization.

SR: In today's globalization, if a regime decides to move toward full socialization and nationalization of the economy, it will be faced with major obstacles, ranging from capital flight, brain drain, to trade sanctions, and so on.

GA: Of course! Kautsky says something in this regard, which is true. I am one of those relatively few who are not afraid of quoting Kautsky, and who disagree with his demonization (or any "demonization" for that matter). He said the socialist transformation is like re-building your house while living in it. You cannot destroy it all at once, you need to re-build it sector after sector, taking the time it needs. If you destroy all walls at the same time, the roof will collapse over your head.

SR: This relates to the questions of revolution versus reform, and what kind of revolution and what kind of reform, and issues related to premature movements toward taking power through abrupt revolutions, and the need for socialist education, and so on. In your view, what exactly should be done to move toward the goal of a revolution in conformity with a Marxian perspective?

GA: I think that the concept of revolutionary transformation remains valid. The Gramscian concepts of "historic bloc", "counter-hegemony" based on "cultural hegemony", and winning the consent of people, are very useful here. These views belong to a democratic socialist perspective. The point, however, is that the transformation of the state is not something that can be achieved gradually. If there is majority consent for its radical transformation, the state should definitely be radically transformed, starting with its repressive apparatuses, because it is a state of an essentially bourgeois nature, molded by capitalism over a very long time. It needs to be thoroughly changed, lest it should turn into a key instrument of counter-revolution.

SR: Don't you think that there is a contradiction here? On the one hand, you say that when we do not have the support of the majority, we cannot take power abruptly, but, on the other hand, you say change cannot come gradually and needs drastic measures in taking over the state.

GA: There is no contradiction here: revolutionary political power should involve support and participation of a vast majority, and it is only once this hegemony is achieved that the government and apparatuses of power, the bureaucracy and the armed forces, are to be radically transformed. These are not neutral institutions, they have a class nature. If the revolutionaries have achieved counter-hegemony, they would have also won over an important section of members of the bureaucracy and the military, who will play a crucial role in helping to bring about the radical change of their institutions.

SR: So it is not the question of "smashing" the state, a popular notion among some socialist left, or is it? Some consider "smashing" of state as an attempt to close down all institutions and fire civil servants and armed forces personnel. I believe that this is a wrong understanding and that what is needed is to replace, or if you will, "smash" the dominant relation of power, and not the institutions themselves, whose continued services the new regime needs.

GA: No, it is definitely not a matter of closing down all institutions and firing civil servants and armed forces personnel! Even the Bolsheviks did not contemplate that, and kept as many people in place as possible. This is actually the kind of caricature that terms like "smash" (like "Dictatorship of the Proletariat" for that matter) easily induce in the minds of those who hear them, and also,

I must say, the minds of many who use them. What is essential for the survival of the revolution and in order to lay the ground for the socialist transformation is to purge the higher ranks of these institutions from the reactionaries and put in their stead supporters of the popular majority. They must also be thoroughly democratized, through implementation of the principle of election of officers. And the pay scale within these institutions must be radically compressed, with a radical reduction of high-ranking salaries. The Paris Commune showed the way in that respect.

SR: If we go back to the previous point regarding the question of gradual or radical change of the state, I would like to add that in a parliamentary system even if you are not a majority, but you are a strong opposition, you can impose policies in favor of labor, improving working conditions, providing educational opportunities, and so on and these become state policy and part of a gradual change. We can probably say that while the ideal is to transform the state in its entirety and move toward the final goal, changes can be introduced gradually.

GA: There is no contradiction here again. The fight for reforms and gains for the people is the main means through which socialists can gain the support of a popular majority. So, of course, there must be many encroachments on the capitalist logic before socialists come to power. In Western countries, there were major progressive reforms implemented after World War Two, but there have been serious setbacks over the last three decades. This shows that it was not capitalism that did become progressive, but that the balance of forces and the strength of the workers movements after World War Two, as well as the competition with the Soviet Union, were such that capitalism had to make a lot of concessions to the working class. As the balance of power changed, with the collapse of the old left, the weakening of workers unions, along with the demise of the Soviet Union, we have witnessed the unfolding of a very vicious offensive which is taking us back to nineteenth century capitalism.

Aijaz Ahmad

AA: We can have an extensive discussion about this distinction between Marx and Blanqui for which there is no time. Let me offer just two remarks. First, Blanqui was in prison but was still the generally recognized leader of the very Paris Commune which transformed

Marx's thinking on the revolutionary process and the nature of the state during the transition to socialism. My second submission is that although there is a world of difference between Blanqui and Lenin, there is also something they share. Both believe that you need a dedicated, experienced, and tightly organized minority to lead the revolutionary offensive but also that no revolution can succeed unless the great majority of people actively participate in it. This is well encapsulated in Lenin's image of the spark and the prairie fire. We can come to this same question from another side as well, more modestly. A great achievement of the Occupy Wall Street was that it invented the slogan that we are the 99 percent. Movements like that can fizzle out but leave a legacy. These were anarchists and very naïve sort of anarchists. They suddenly appeared on the scene with a dramatic act of disobedience, as any anarchist vanguard would, believing that they represented the 99 percent who would then be inspired by their action. It is only when the masses did not take up the lead of the anarchist vanguard that the Occupy movement fizzled out. But one can argue that they were following Blanqui. I also think that Marxism should go back to that one line in the Communist Manifesto, where the young Marx [and Engels] wrote that communists form no political party, they organize the proletariat as a whole. I would amend that to suggest that Marxists ought to organize not just the proletariat as a whole but also the great majority of the people as a whole. Capitalism has by now turned the great majority of humanity into an immiserated mass chasing wage work.

SR: There is no question about the working majority, my point is that revolutions of the past were mainly Blanquist and where not the revolution of conscious majority.

AA: In August 1917, Lenin writes that there is no reason why the functions of the state cannot be distributed among two million people. That was the intention. The revolution was led by a minority but was actually made by millions of people, the army, peasantry, workers, and others, and the civil war was fought by immense number of people. Nor do I understand how the Chinese or Vietnamese revolutions could be called Blanquist.

SR: Of course, in all revolutions a majority somehow gets involved, the question is about the consciousness and independence of this majority.

AA: I think the question of majority and minority is no more applicable. The Bolshevik style frontal seizure of Winter Palace is not in the cards anymore. It is not possible. The historical development of the productive forces has made it impossible to make that kind of seizure of power. This was clear to Antonio Gramsci already in the 1930s. He recognized that state power in the advanced capitalist countries was not concentrated at the very top, as in Czarist monarchy, but dispersed throughout the territory. Means of surveillance and information are much more advanced, as are the electronic media of ideological control. The security apparatus—army, police, and so on—have a far deeper reach into even the urban slums and the countryside. Middle classes are more numerous and more prosperous. Systems of electoral representation have created a very widespread liberal, bourgeois subjectivity. There is now very little consent for clandestine vanguardism. Popular enthusiasm for a socialist overthrow of capitalism has to be obtained *before* taking power. Lenin used to say that the backwardness of Russia made it easier to make the revolution but much more difficult to build socialism. I think Lenin was more right than he knew. I think that the problem may have now reversed itself. The advanced level of capitalism makes it more difficult to make a revolution. But if a revolution is made in an advanced country, transition to something resembling socialism would be easier. Meanwhile, on the ground today, we have this working majority, and what unites them is labor.

SR: Exactly. The main issue is how this laboring majority would be mobilized, particularly at a time that as a result the mobility and growing strength of capital and weakening of labor organizations, we have less labor movements.

AA: We need to look at the structure of capital today. Unlike the finance capital that Lenin theorized, or even the finance capital that existed 30 or 40 years ago, we have no more national capitals, or national monopolies. There is such integration in a vast majority of places; the capital that is actively engaged in a given country tends to be a peculiar amalgam of national and international components that interpenetrate. This imperialism of transnational finance capital is completely different from the imperialism of the colonial period that Lenin and his colleagues had conceptualized. We have to figure out how to struggle this. Inventing modes of struggle appropriate to this imperialism of our time is a very different theoretical question.

SR: Particularly that today's financial capital is no more predominantly related to the industrial and commercial capital and is almost totally independent of it, and is mostly trading in money, bonds, and other things.

AA: Yes, what we have is speculative capital and distinguished from industrial capital. On the other hand, the collapse of communism in Soviet Union, China, and elsewhere gave to the world capitalist system roughly a billion more workers, and this has been fatal for the wage rate. Also despite the so-called large rising economies like China, India, and Brazil, and for all the spectacular industrial and manufacturing growth in China, the industrial proletariat is in all such countries a very small proportion of the population. Manufacturing capital can no longer employ any considerable proportion of the labor that is coming out to the market. So you have not only an army of the unemployed, you have in fact a situation that a great majority will always remain unemployed. Then, we have ecological problems and so on. What we need is a theory explaining all that. My sense is that, as Gramsci says, it was only with the rise of the Paris Commune in the 1870s that the logic set in by the French revolution of the late eighteenth century reached a point that some new alternative form of revolution became faintly visible, and then it took another roughly half a century for a truly different logic—the logic of the Bolsheviks—to explode on the world scene. After the French Revolution was contained by the end of the nineteenth century, it took 150 years for a truly different revolutionary form to arise. The Bolshevik form is now clearly exhausted, just as the earlier French revolutionary form had been exhausted by the time of the Paris Commune. We don't know what the new revolutionary form will be or how long it will take to emerge. We only hope that this interval shall be much shorter. History has been speeded up. Immense numbers of people are on the move. But we are in a transitional period. I believe that this immense proliferation of social movements, ecological movements, the Latin American contests over state power, and so on are struggling to find a new revolutionary form. These are transitional phenomena, because we don't know how to unite these great forces in a shared project for socialism. Hundreds of groups are in search of a revolutionary model. Some theoretical breakthrough will come. But one thing we do know is that the extraordinary achievements of the Marxist proletarian revolution and ideology has been that it has led to the rise of a very large number of revolutionary subjects. Whereas in the mid-nineteenth century Marx quite correctly identified the proletariat as the leading force for revolution, we now have a huge number of revolutionary subjects who want to have their own revolutions. Women want their revolution, indigenous people want their revolutions, and oppressed castes want their revolution. These are revolutionary times but very different from what we had anticipated.

SR: True, but at the same time, unfortunately, we have immense number of reactionary religious elements who want to have their regressive revolution, and for reasons that we know, have become most active with most disastrous consequences.

AA: The defeat of the socialist revolutionary project was bound to produce an immense reactionary backlash to take back all the gains the revolutionary projects had made over a century or more. Race and religion have played a key role in this transition back from socially progressive Reason to atavistic, primordialist, identitarian, even millenarian Un-Reason. For one thing, a retreat from the politics of Equality has necessarily led to savageries in the politics of identity. A millenarian attachment to religious identity and even religious violence is also the other side of the politics of Despair. That is why so many of the wretched of the earth get recruited into those sorts of crusades. Even so, the least we need to remember is that these religious movements are not mere ideological phenomena, or matters of pure Belief. Each of such movements is diligently set into motion by identifiable forces, in pursuit of quite specific objectives, which also means that each of them has a specific history that needs to be understood in its own context. Cumulatively, they are all part of the overall reactionary character of the current historical moment. But they must not all be seen as just so many expressions of a unitary essence called "Religion". Each has a historical materiality of its own. The USA does not sponsor Jihadists for reasons of Belief. Both the Lebanese Hezbollah and Saudi Wahhabism obviously use "Islam" as a legitimating rhetorical device, and indeed at some level, matters of Belief are also involved, but the two can hardly be reduced to being merely different expressions of an Islamic Essence. What is interesting about each of them is not what they believe about what is truly "Islamic" but the radically different profane projects they pursue in the real world.

Rob Albriton

RA: On the question of revolution, imagine a Blanquist revolution in a country like USA, which is obviously hard to imagine. Modern industrial states have huge standing armies, have huge stockpiles of weapons, a very powerful capitalist class and a right wing media. You cannot take on these states through a quick revolution or a coup d'état. This might work in a relatively weak third world country, although as we see, it cannot even be successful in a country like Syria, with so much misery for its people and so little real headway toward social progress. In industrial societies of today, a peaceful road is to be preferred if at all possible, a road that does not necessarily mean that you don't have aggressive demonstrations, strikes, and political struggles. One might even run in an election depending on the circumstances. To build counter-hegemony, you need to use every possible public forum to put forward your ideas. The ideological struggle becomes extremely important, at least for a very long time. Today, if you refer to yourself as communist in the USA, 99 percent of the people would think you are an evil terrorist. You have to start with reforms that are practical and people can understand.

A lot of people are hurt by capitalism and there are lots of movements on the ground in response to this. But the movements do not necessarily understand the extent to which capitalism is actually blocking their success. So you have to work with movements, support the more progressive and more radical movements and try to get them seeing not only how capitalism is hurting them, but also the need to unite with other movements that are in the same predicament, and ultimately join a broad anti-capitalist struggle. So you are right, it is a long process that involves ideological struggle, hegemonic kinds of political struggles, and education. In a country like the USA, it probably will take at least a couple of generations, if not more, depending on the unfolding of historical circumstances. So you have to start where people are hurting the most and where there is possibility of some success in short term, and at the same time, where there is also the possibility of mobilizing a fairly large number of people toward more radical and political ways of thinking. You keep making steps, and steps can get more ambitious with time. We are in a very difficult position now. We see in the USA and many of countries the disturbing phenomenon that far-right wing populists are mobilizing the people. It is unfortunate to see how issues like immigration combined with reactionary nationalism are being utilized to popularize racist and fascist ideas among the masses in many parts of the world.

SR: It is not just the USA, but European parliamentary elections in France, Germany, and Britain, also point to the same problem.

Kevin Anderson

KA: I think we have to nuance a little bit this idea of putting the Marxist notion of revolution on one side and the Blanquist one on the other. As you know, of all the French revolutionaries, Marx had always the most positive things to say about Blanqui and had a tremendous admiration for him. The term Blanquist came to the Marxian lexicon at a later time, and as you mentioned, it differentiated between a vanguard taking action on its own and a conscious movement of the immense majority. Marxian notion of revolution was also different from that of Lassalle who did believe in mass movements but focused only on the working class and excluded the peasantry as completely backward and reactionary, a view that was followed by German Social Democrats like Kautsky.

Let me also note here that it is a myth that Marx dismissed the peasantry as a non-revolutionary force. He said it was conservative in the context of the Bonapartist coup of 1851, but this has been misinterpreted as his general view of the peasantry in the modern capitalist epoch. In fact, he viewed the peasantry as an important revolutionary subject, as seen in the attack on Lassalle's dismissal of the peasantry in *Critique of the Gotha Program* (1875), or in his enthusiastic support of Engels's *Peasant Wars in Germany* (1852), a book that Marx thought had contemporary relevance.

The "immense majority" is not a very precise term either, whether in terms of social consciousness or levels of revolutionary potential. Moreover, for Marx even the working class is multi-layered. Thus, I don't think the notion of the 99 percent versus the 1 percent would make much sense in this regard.

SR: I intentionally differentiate between these two types of revolutions because I believe all revolutions that were carried out under Marx's name were the type of vanguardist and Blanquist, and were political rather than social revolutions. Besides, when you don't have the involvement of a conscious majority, whether working class or non-working class elements, then you end up with situations like what we have witnessed so far. In other cases, like our own revolution in Iran, the unprepared masses can be taken over by reactionary forces, with the disastrous consequences, of which you are aware. I think we need to prepare for a social revolution involving the conscious majority rather than having a minority leading the unprepared masses, and a seizure of power prematurely.

KA: I mainly agree, but I think "majority" is a very general term and that we also have to talk of specific social classes, or social groups. No doubt that it is a long process, not only in a sense that it takes a long time for a mass movement to mature and develop, but also because there will be many ups and downs over the decades. We are in a very different situation today because until the 1980s, there were many mass movements in many parts of the world that held to at least a supposition that there was a real possibility of a positive overcoming of capitalism. But since 1980 and especially since 1989 that has changed. Look at the recent slogan "Another world is possible". It not very affirmative, but it reflects the empirical reality of where we are. On the one hand, like the protagonist in a traditional French novel, we are now in our 30s and we lost our illusions. That was the positive, cleansing effect of the collapse in 1989–91 of most forms of statist communism. But along with these illusions, the Left also lost the confidence that a new world is possible, both because of the strength of capitalism and probably even more so our lack of confidence in our own capacities. That is why the results of the Russian Revolution or Chinese Revolution, let alone the Iranian Revolution, should give us pause. I had contact with the Iranian left as early as 1978, and I can say that it certainly was not free of authoritarian tendencies. Had they come to power in Iran, I am not sure how well that would have turned out. Because of so many of these things, I think we lack confidence in both the possibility of overthrowing capital and even more importantly, in our capacity to transcend it in a positive manner.

Capital seems so impregnable today, similar to the way it appeared in 1900. But what is even more difficult than in 1900 is that we did not then have the sometimes-negative experience of having taken power in the name of socialism, which we have now. The other big disillusionment concerns social democracy in places like Sweden or Germany where they could not achieve what they wanted, even with their more limited goals compared to the revolutionary left.

SR: Exactly, and that is why in my first question I referred to the failures of both revolutionary and reformist strategies. Now, these social democratic parties have moved to the right and some of them follow a neoliberal policy. But the main question remains, what factors led to these failures. No doubt one factor has been the power of capital but at the same time, there have also been the factor of our own weaknesses, both theoretical and practical.

KA: Since the Russian Revolution, or at the very least since Stalinism, there is what we can call a democratic deficit of the left. Marx and most socialists of his day had a critique of liberal democracy but understood the difference between liberal democracy and conservative authoritarianism. That distinction has been lost to many among the Marxist left. In part of the Marxist left, one can find fans of characters like Ahmadinejad, Putin, Assad, and many others, even the gangsterish breakaway zones in Eastern Ukraine. This problem goes back to Bonapartism in the mid-nineteenth century, where there were people on the left supporting it. But today, it is a much larger problem. Marx regarded himself as the left wing of the democratic movement. You mentioned social revolution, but Marx was also interested in political revolution. Even today, authoritarian regimes are common, most of all in the Middle East and North Africa, and we need to support democratic revolutions there, as Marx would have. Marx was living in a world where there were no democracies as such. In that period, the USA was the closest to a democratic system of any large country, but was marred by slavery as a major part of its economy and society; and everywhere, women lacked the vote. Even England, which had many liberal freedoms, had a huge property qualification that excluded the working class from voting, and other major countries were monarchies and authoritarian dictatorships. When Marx advocates revolution, he sometimes does not distinguish which type of revolution he is talking about, because he sees revolution as a multi-faceted process that has to have a social dimension if it is going to be successful. Of course, he sees the difference between the 1848 revolution and the Commune of 1871. Even the Commune was against an authoritarian regime and democratization was part of its agenda.

SR: No doubt that all of those revolutions were political revolutions and it was expected that the state and bureaucrats would bring social revolutions.

Barbara Epstein

BE: In the late 60s and early 70s, when the radical movement was at its height in the USA, most of those who talked about revolution took the revolutionary movements of the Third World, especially the Chinese revolution, as their model; the Bolshevik Revolution and Lenin's conception of the vanguard as conspiratorial and as consisting of professional revolutionaries also contributed, though the Soviet Union was not seen as a positive example of revolution. Here, I am talking about the USA; Maoism also took hold in France and elsewhere in Continental Europe, much less so in Britain. This model revolved around a vanguard party which, with the presumed support of the working class and/or peasantry, would seize power, depose the existing ruling class, destroy capitalism, and rule in the name of the people.

There were two problems with this model. First, while it was understandable or even necessary that revolution take this form in dictatorial societies such as Tsarist Russia or pre-revolutionary China, it was not appropriate for the USA or other western societies. In modern societies in which governments are elected, and in which freedom of speech and freedom of association are at least ostensibly protected, a seizure of power on the part of a small group would not be accepted by the majority, except under exceptional conditions, such as in response to a coup. The conspiratorial methods that were necessary in Tsarist Russia would be likely to discredit an organization in the USA. In a society that is even formally democratic (i.e., with voting rights but lacking equality in other respects), a revolution is not seen as legitimate.

Second, revolutions that rest on the seizure of power by force are very likely to rule by force. Violence is an element of social life that will probably never be entirely eradicated; it is bound to be an element of revolutionary change. But if it is the main vehicle of revolutionary change, it will likely remain the basis for the new social order. In the absence of widespread support for the new social order, the need for violence to keep it in place is likely to increase. The record of twentieth century revolutions that have been accomplished largely by force is not good.

A democratic revolution must have the active support of a considerable sector of the population, and at least the passive support of a solid majority. The question is how to bring this about—speaking now not in the abstract, but about what might be possible in the present day USA. I think that what we need is a coalition of organizations, groups, projects, and individuals committed to building a society dramatically more egalitarian than the one that exists, a society based on the common good rather than on private profit, and on cooperation rather than competition. Opposition to racism and discrimination of all kinds, to militarism and war, and the pursuit of a harmonious relationship with the environment and with other living creatures would be fundamental principles. Socialism would not be a fundamental principle; though there would be many socialists and socialist organizations in the coalition, socialists would not regard themselves as necessarily the leading sector, but as holding one perspective among others. There would have to be an acceptance of diversity that would include deep differences in perspective, based on the understanding that even after a revolution everyone who is here now would still be here, including religious people, people whose cultural tastes vary widely, and so on. Different organizations within the coalition would focus on different tactics: some would engage in public education, some in civil disobedience and direct action, some would focus on electoral work. While there certainly could be discussion of what tactics are appropriate under particular circumstances, there would have to be an acceptance of a range of tactics.

SR: The emphasis on organization is indeed significant. In one of your writings, you take issue with anarchism and argue that the young radicals who consider or call themselves anarchists are not necessarily followers of Bakunin—in the same manner that Marxists follow Marx—and are anti-authority and favor decentralized structures based on affinity groups and consensus. This is an important issue that I would like you to elaborate.

BE: Traditionally, anarchism has meant a rejection of the state, and that remains an element of the outlook of contemporary young anarchists. But I think that for many of them what is central is a commitment to egalitarianism: anti-racism, anti-sexism, anti-homophobia, and, for many, also anti-capitalism. I agree with them on egalitarianism; I differ with them in that I think we need a state of some sort, though quite different from the state we now have. Many young anarchists are against organizational structures on grounds that they easily become bureaucratic. But others point out that traditionally anarchists have had organizations; the Spanish anarchists, who are regarded as a kind of model by many, had extensive organizations. It is only recently that anarchism has come to be associated with a rejection of organizations. I understand that in the wake of Occupy, many young anarchists are re-examining the question of organization, having seen how quickly a movement based on spontaneity and without organizational structures can evaporate. I am also told that the question of the state is open for discussion in anarchist circles. The questions that are not open for discussion are those concerning equality.

I think that the strengths of the anarchist perspective lie in their sharp critique of the present—they are right, for instance, that the state and the political arena are far removed from ordinary people, an especially young people—and their vision of a future egalitarian, decentralized society, based on cooperation. The weaknesses of anarchism, I think, lie in the absence of any conception of how to get from here to there, a penchant for purism and a tendency to focus on principles to the exclusion of practical reality. An example: while I agree that more decentralization would enable more people to participate in politics, I don't think decentralization should be regarded as an absolute principle. We need organization for society to function, and that includes large, formal organizations, such as a national state, as well as small, voluntary organizations. Local communities cannot deal with environmental disasters on their own; they require large organizations with large resources. I would not want to count on local voluntary committees to keep schools or hospitals running, or to keep the roads in good condition. We need a national state to fund and administer public education, a good national health service, Social Security, Medicare, and so on. I have never heard a persuasive argument against any of this.

What disturbs me most about contemporary youth anarchism is the attraction toward a confrontational and often provocative stance for its own sake. The black bloc, a tactic that involves large numbers of people wearing all black, including black masks, running together and sometimes committing minor acts of property destruction, has come to be surrounded with a romantic aura. Another confrontational tactic is the "fuck the police" march, which involves collective taunting of the police. In some demonstrations, broken windows are an invitation to looting. I see no political purpose in any of this. The aim is to provoke the police to violence, leading to a riot. The theory behind it is that fighting with the police will appeal to all those who feel oppressed by the police and other authorities, and will ignite a mass revolt. This is "propaganda by the deed", the outlook of the insurrectionist wing of the anarchist movement, The most famous instance was the assassination of Tsar Alexander II, in 1881, by the Russian anarchist organization, Narodnaya Volya. The assassination led to a wave of repression that destroyed the Russian revolutionary movement for some 20 years, and to the rule of his much more repressive, and reactionary, son, Alexander III. The wing of the anarchist movement that aims to build mass movements has traditionally avoided such tactics because they restrict the movement to the few who are willing to engage in them, and because the usual result is increased repression.

One lesson to be drawn from this is that like the movements of the 60s, in which many of us called ourselves Marxists, but we meant very different things by it, anarchism is the dominant influence among contemporary young radicals, but it too has many interpretations. On the question of violence, anarchists range from pacifists to the Insurrectionists described above.

Aron Etzler

AE: I must say that only using the term Blanquist makes me happy, ha ha! I have not heard it in at least 15 years. It is an unusual term, as the fact is that no major change can be achieved by the Left through "Blanquist" means. Actually, this has been the strategy of the right, as shown by Naomi Klein. It has been the Right that has had the means to resort to extreme measures and implement extremely un-popular policies. Their "shock doctrine" is to grab any chances they get. But for the Left, the logic is much more democratic: we need to convince people to be able to get their support. There is an interesting phenomenon that we see not only in Sweden but also in many other countries, that when people get to choose what kind of policies should be implemented, they tend to prefer solutions from the left. They don't like privatizations, or they don't like inequalities, and they simply prefer policies from the left. But, they doubt that these policies can be implemented. They doubt the feasibility of these policies. So, the most important task for the left is to show people that it is possible to have progressive policies. In other words, to say it in an old-fashion way, we need to educate people about the possibilities, about economy, politics, or the significance of public ownership, as a most significant means of providing services, such as hospitals, schools, transportations, and so on. Then, there is the question of winning the elections. Many people on the left think that change of society will take place some 50 years from now, or, even worse, they are waiting this to happen in another country. Maybe because they are afraid of the responsibility that comes with power. There is a paradox that a section of the left says that it wants to break the power of capital and wants the working class to take power, but at the same time is highly critical of gaining power—it corrupts everyone, we are told. This belief often results in just avoiding power, resorting to complaining, instead. I think it is rather sad. We should discuss how to avoid the pitfalls of power, but never decline the possibility to change our community for the better.

I think a socialist strategy needs working class parties to come to power, and believes that we should use the power, expand on it, make reforms, and for each reform accomplished, we would move to a higher one; thus, continually expanding people's power through elections and practical examples. This is actually close to what Marx envisaged, and very far away from what Blanqui advocated.

Sam Gindin

SG: Revolutionary change does need leadership since people develop unevenly, and logically, you have to start somewhere so you start with a core of people who are already committed and ready to organize toward radical change. But the key is to develop a base and critical to this is developing the working class—broadly defined—as a social force. As for social democrats, the difference is not just that socialists have more radical polices. It is that while social democracy is concerned with entering the state to introduce good policies, the socialist project is primarily about developing popular *capacities*. Unless we can develop the ability of working people to analyze, think, strategize, and debate democratically, and unless we can create spaces and structures through which to do so, and at the same time lead campaigns and struggles, we won't be able to achieve our goals.

Many workers don't disagree that capitalism is a bad system; what limits their activism is the question of "what can you really do about it?" They simply don't see any institutions through which they can participate in that might change this. Their unions are limited; they can certainly affect some things but not the larger structures that dominate their lives and shape their options. And social democratic parties have in fact become a barrier to change, part of the problem. So workers turn to their personal lives, make adjustments, and try to survive. That is why the fundamental role of socialist organizations must be education to clarify the context of their problems, but linking this education to struggles, and this crucially includes creating structures that people can struggle through. By this, I don't just mean electoral and political organizations, but all sorts of organizations—feminist organizations, organizations fighting against racism, organizations working in the community, and so on. In emphasizing the importance of education and its link to struggles, my experience in the trade union movement confirmed that though there are workers who are curious and interested in intellectual activity, workers in general see education in the abstract as a luxury or as irrelevant to their lives; it must matter to their lives and so only becomes relevant when it becomes part of their struggles.

SR: I would like to follow up on this last point, particularly that you apart from your scholarly backgrounds, have had major involvements in labor movement in one of the most important and one of the largest workers' unions in North America. It would be good if you elaborate on this question of capacity building and organization.

SG: Let me give you one experience that highlights the link between structures and struggle, in this case structures involving education. Toward the end of 1970s, the Canadian Autoworkers negotiated a paid educational leave for a portion of the workforce that allowed them to have four weeks away from work, attending courses in our educational center, with wages paid. This was intended to create a new generation of leadership. These were not technical courses, but courses on philosophy, economy, and history with a strong dose of Marxist ideas. By coincidence, the start of these programs coincided with the coming of a new generation of workers to workplace, and the neoliberal attack on workers was also emerging. Much of the content was oriented to fighting neoliberalism.

SR: This is very interesting. You put together theses course and these major motor companies were paying?

SG: Yes. We negotiated money from the companies that they had no input into. (Their first response to the proposal was why would we pay you to teach them Marxism?). In order to carry out these courses, we developed a cadre of 200 workers to act as facilitators/teachers and to some degree were also developing as left organizers. We expected that over a ten-year period, we could put 10,000 workers through theses courses and through shorter (one-week) courses such as on black leadership, women leadership, the environment, and so on. And we came fairly close to that target. As long as the union was engaged in fighting the corporations, the program was successful. After taking the courses, the student-workers would return to the workplace and plug into on-going struggles; the days of action, the fight against free trade, demonstrations against cutbacks in unemployment insurance or health care, and so on.

But then the situation changed, both nationally and internationally and the union culture of struggle was eroded. So when the union began making concessions, the dynamics of the education also changed. If, for example, participants argued that we should fight concessions, this now embarrassed and contradicted the leadership. The union increased control over what could and could not be discussed and the instructors, vulnerable to keeping their union-appointed positions (and not wanting to be returned to the line) internalized the fact that there are things they cannot talk about. Moreover, since they were away from work for a long time, they had a limited workplace base in terms of running for local positions. They justified their own compromises by arguing (to themselves as well as others) that even if they no longer raised the larger issues confronting the unions, they could focus on smaller, but still important "safer" issues, such as childcare, affirmative action, and pay equity. So, the unions ended up with a situation in which the cadres that the union trained to teach the originally radical courses were neutered both in what they taught and in becoming political activists in the union.

There are two important lessons here. The first relates to the relation between struggle and structure. The structure was great but it had to be linked to struggle. When the struggle wasn't there, the same structure actually played a negative role. The second relates to dealing with what those who have finished the courses would do when they returned to work. The education we provided was impressive but what we failed to do was to develop them as *organizers*. The result was that a lot of the students felt, after taking the course that they were superior to (even somewhat contemptuous of) the workers in the plant; they themselves were now socialists and "got it" while the workers in the plant did not. The difficulty in winning fellow workers over was difficult and the necessary skills to do so hadn't been developed, so they felt more comfortable taking their newly formed radical ideas into the community, where they could find people who were already on the left—working, for example, on Cuba and Nicaragua. Rather than becoming working class leaders inside the workplace, they ended up separating themselves from their workmates.

SR: So they became a new worker elite? This is in a sense part of the reality of the impact of social mobility and shift in social status, and an important factor to consider in labor organizing.

SG: In some ways, they did see themselves this way, but still as "progressives". They mostly operated outside the union and if at that time we had real socialist parties in Ontario, many of these workers would have been picked up by these parties and would have learned how to organize and do things that unions could not do. So, the absence of left parties also left them in limbo—which is another lesson: in the absence of left parties, even a powerful union's progressive workers may have a very limited impact.

SR: This is most interesting particularly that it relates to linkages between labor unions, progressive political parties, and political process. Also relates to the linkage of national and international levels. As you mentioned when things change at international level, it had impacts on the local. I will get back to these points later.

Peter Hudis

PH: Revolution is the transformation of the conditions of everyday life in terms of uprooting fundamental conditions of alienation. Revolution that does not address the problem of alienation has not addressed the fundamental problem of the existence of capitalist social formations. I think that Marx was completely correct in his critique of Blanqui who he respected as a revolutionary activist. Nevertheless, Marx's understanding was that you couldn't make a successful revolution that uproots the law of value unless it involves a huge number of people, the majority of working population as active participants, and not as passive spectators. This is why he argued against any putschism or revolution from above, or any kind of approach that goes behind the backs of the working class.

However, I don't think that Marxism is solely a theory of class struggle, although class struggle is a very central aspect of Marxism. I think Marxism is a philosophy of liberation that looks at whatever social relations exists in which human being are dehumanized and alienated and tries to elicit opposition against those conditions and give them theoretical articulation and clarity. Marx of course lived in an era when the industrial working class was that primary force and therefore he emphasized its centrality. But it has been very evident throughout most of the twentieth century, certainly in the last 50–60 years, that the working class is not the only subject of revolution. Now, we also have women's struggles, struggles of youth, struggles of national minorities, struggles against racism and imperial domination, peasants' struggles in certain historical contexts. So the basic concept that Marx had against Blanqui is as valid today as it was 150 years ago, even though the alignment of social forces that we would conceive of as part of the majority revolution has radically changed. But again, I want to stress that Marxism is not a set of conclusions that one simply applies to different situations. It is not an applied science. It is not a formal method; rather Marxism is a methodology of elucidating from changing realities the possibilities for social transformation.

As an example of this, Franz Fanon, who I just finished a book about, was not coming from the orthodox Marxist tradition, and was not looking at the industrial proletariat as a revolutionary force in Africa; he was looking at the peasantry, the lumpen proletariat, the youth, and to a lesser degree women. He looked at them because they were the majority of the population fighting colonial domination, and the industrial proletariat was just 3 or 4 percent of population in the countries he was dealing with in Africa. In my argument, this did not make Fanon a lesser Marxist, it made him more of a Marxist. If he had come and simply said that the labor movement in Nigeria or Algeria has to be the vanguard of the revolution, he would have sounded as if he was repeating Marxist conclusions, but repeating Marxist conclusions when you are dealing with a different reality is not consistent with Marxist methodology. Marxist methodology should say let me reconstitute or recreate the dialectic from a series of realities I am confronted with. Fanon remained true to the basic Marx critique of Blanqui that you cannot make a successful revolution that does not involve the bulk of the exploited masses.

SR: Your emphasis on Marxist methodology somehow reminds me of Lukacs' point that methodology is the only thing that distinguishes Marxism, even if its substantive propositions are questioned. You rightly talked about other subjects of revolution, women, youth, national minorities, and so on, but this brings up two questions to my mind; one, how can we bring about these transformations, and bring together and mobilize all these very diverse forces to become active participants in a revolution, particularly the type of revolution you have in mind, which aims at eliminating the relations of value production and alienation? In terms of Fanon and Africa, you may agree that the case was easier because, like in other national liberation movements, leaders could mobilize the people around one single and achievable goal of kicking colonialists out of their country. My second point is this: in talking about all these new subjects of revolution, when it comes to value production, wouldn't it again go back to the labor element?

PH: Actually, I do not agree with Lukacs that the methodology is the only thing that distinguishes Marxism; Marxism is also defined by a set of normative principles of how a truly free society should be organized. Certainly, Marx's work is rooted in an understanding of the role of labor in society, but one does not have to directly experience industrial capitalist production to experience alienation. In today's capitalism, we have a smaller industrial proletariat than ever, but we have a greater proletarianization of everyday life. A good example of this is that in the USA today we face with the creation of the so-called precariat. Even in academia, about 75 percent of professors are part-time instructors with no possibility of full-time employment, and another 10–15 percent are working on contract. The number of academics with tenure position is drastically shrinking, and it may disappear within 15 or 20 years. The laborer is increasingly detached from the objective conditions of knowledge production. This is one of many examples of the proletarianization of areas of economy that are not themselves proletarian labor.

But the main response to your question is that there is no way to make people revolutionary. There is no way to instill revolutionary consciousness into people's minds. People become radicalized through their experience, and we are living in a historical era in which it is very unclear what the direction of revolution is, especially in the industrially developed West. We don't know the answers to many questions about what revolution truly means in the twenty-first century. What we do know, is that there cannot be any exit from capitalism without some kind of revolution, and there cannot be a successful revolution that repeats the errors of the last 150 years. It has got to target the fundamental social relations of domination, central to which is value production. No doubt, value production is rooted in the labor process, but the value form also mediates other relations of society. Men–women relations themselves take on a value form, as do the relations between the races. The basic challenge for radicals is how to articulate and address people who feel upset about this alienated reality but who may not understand why they are upset about it.

SR: Two points I would like to ask you to expand upon; one, there is no doubt that in a capitalist social formation, everybody and everything is directly or indirectly affected by the relation of value production. However, what is not clear is how all these diverse proletarianized groups that you rightly mentioned would be involved in value production. The second point relates to what you pointed out that one cannot make people revolutionary and people themselves become revolutionary. Would this be something similar to what the so-called Autonomist Marxists and theorists like Antonio Negri argued? I know that you are critical of them.

PH: In terms of the second question, there is some crossover between the Autonomist Marxists and Marxist Humanists, which is the philosophical perspective that, as you know, I am part of. In fact, Negri very early on had credited Dunayevskaya's *Marxism and Freedom* as an inspiration in his work. But I have a criticism of the Autonomists as they tend to idealize the subjective dimension and often impute more to struggles than actually exists in them. Most important of all, they do not grapple with the central question of the emergence of counter-revolution from within revolution. Negri seems to think that the multitude automatically overcomes all barriers to its self-development, but this automaticity, history has shown, cannot be relied upon when movements are left bereft of a vision of the future. But nevertheless, there are some similarities. I do believe in spontaneity, and I do think there also is a very vital role for organization—because I believe in the vital role of critical theory. If people are involved in day-to-day struggles and are deeply dissatisfied with their alienated conditions of life and labor, does it mean that they understand why they are dissatisfied? Do they know that socialism represents an alternative to their dissatisfaction? As you well know, in many parts of the world, including here in the USA, many people who experience alienation vote against their self-interests and ally themselves with reactionary forces, because they have so little theoretical understanding of what is really at the root of their distress. So, exactly because of the diversity of potential revolutionary forces, now more than ever, there is a need for a solidly rooted theoretical project that addresses different manifestations of oppression and alienation, and communicates to common people what is the nature of their distress—and its alternative. I don't think it is automatic that people who suffer oppression become revolutionary. As a matter of fact, history shows the opposite, that people often become dehumanized, internalize it, and they take it out on their fellow citizens. That is why I say revolution is very much an open question. But I think the biggest problem that we are facing today is that there is no vision of an alternative to capitalism, not even in places where there are socialist movements like Greece, Spain, or Venezuela. You don't have a clear articulation of what is the alternative to capitalism and so therefore people who are frustrated with the system cannot see an alternative to what exists. I think the role of the left today is very different from what it was in Marx's time, or Lenin's time, even very different from what it was 50 years ago. I see the central cardinal role of the left is to fill this void in articulating the concept of what is a genuine viable alternative to capitalism. If people do not know about this, how can we expect they would rise to the challenge of overthrowing the existing system?

SR: I am glad you are emphasizing this very important point. This is exactly why I started this project, because we always talk of socialism and crisis of capitalism, but we don't have a clear idea of post-capitalist society. But it is not just the question of WHAT we are aiming for, but HOW we can move toward it, and I believe the latter is far more complicated than the former, and because of their interrelations, the higher the aims of the former, the more difficult would be the means of achieving them. How to educate, how to organize, and how to mobilize forces, are part of my other questions.

Ursula Huws

UH: The Marxian social revolution is a long process. Consciousness should change for a large number of people. At the individual level, it has a starting point. It can start from experiencing some sort of shock. There is a specific moment like the sound of "kerching!" in an old cash register. A moment that a worker who has put her soul into doing a good piece of work, suddenly realizes that this work has been appropriated by someone else who does not give a damn about her. For me, I witnessed this moment when I was working as a trade union organizer in the 1970s among workers in the publishing industry. The workers, despite not being paid well, were very proud of the job they had. Then suddenly a shock came; for instance, if they asked the employer for a very modest concession and the employer just refused outright, or if they were sacked. And then you could see the most conservative workers would become very radical on the picket line. That individual change in consciousness can very quickly be connected with a more general consciousness and connected with other workers and then you have a collective consciousness that has to be multiplied across social divides. People have to understand they have something in common, and experience this quite concretely. There are also historical moments that suddenly erupt very quickly into something much bigger.

These moments can erupt very unexpectedly. But education and organization are crucial in the process, without which you will have a situation like the Occupy movement, or in Seattle, where people wave rainbow flags, just protesting at abstractions like globalization and neoliberalism. People, working 70 hours a week, taking shit from their employers and not daring to say anything to them, will, in their own time at the weekends, participate in these demonstrations and raise the rainbow flag against globalization. There are some incredible disconnects in the popular consciousness. We can of course blame some of our comrades in the left intelligentsia for encouraging these ideas of the so-called "multitudes" and so on.

But it is interesting to note that we are now witnessing something remarkable happening. We are seeing a sort of crack in the global neoliberal perspective, and we see a sort of resurgence of some of the ideas of the 60s and early 70s on the left. This is symbolized, for example, through the current attraction to three quite different figures: one is the Pope, with his crowd-pleasing anti-capitalist things to say (perhaps cynically) but which resonate with a new generation in a way that was unimaginable years ago. The second one is Jeremy Corbyn, (a British left Labour MP and anti-war activist) who has astonishingly attracted tens of thousands of people who had not voted in the last elections, and now follow him and has gained the majority of support in the Labour Party and has even attracted many others outside the party including the youth and the anti-war movements. The third one is Bernie Sanders, (an independent US Senator and a Presidential Candidate for 2016, advocating social democratic policies) who is not as radical as Corbyn but nevertheless well to the left of other democratic candidates and who is attracting a large following, especially among the young.

These three figures, none of whom are Marxist revolutionaries, have attracted so many people who are disgruntled with the right wing politics of today. This suggests something of a sea-change, in which the hegemonic neoliberal values are being challenged from below in a new way.

Michael Lebowitz

ML: The argument in the Communist Manifesto is about revolutionary change. Aspects of it relates to the question of "winning the battle of democracy", which deals with a process of constantly interfering with the logic of capital and making inroads into it. This does not necessarily mean that you need to a have a self-conscious independent movement of the immense majority in advance. The question is where does this self-consciousness come from? It is the process of struggle that brings this about. Marx emphasized the need for organizing the working class, and that is the main distinction with Blanquists who were oriented toward a conspiratorial take over. The Bolsheviks in pre-October were definitely involved in organizing the working class. The German Social Democratic party was certainly involved in organizing the working class. But having said that, there is no need that they should form the self-conscious immense majority. If you say the only socialist revolution is the one that should involve the self-conscious independent movement of the immense majority, then you should say that October Revolution should not have happened.

SR: It is not the question of should or should not, although I believe after the February Revolution, there could be other paths, which is beside the point. Part of the failure of the Bolsheviks and the eventual establishment of another authoritarian rule had something to do with the lack of these qualifications.

ML: Well, no doubt there were problems, but were these problems because the level of development was too low, or were these problems because they did not empower the people?

Leo Panitch

LP: We are now in the second decade of the twenty-first century. If we are at all historical materialist, we need to take our distance from the types of tactics and even strategic notions that people had—even the most brilliant and committed people—in the middle of the nineteenth century. We also need to notice that anarchist ideas have become very common in the last 20 years; they have inspired in many ways the anti-globalization protests around the world and other kinds of protests. Many of the most impressive young people today either explicitly think of themselves as anarchist or have been influenced by anarchist ideas. This is because of how they have experienced, and very consciously reacted against, not only vanguard parties but also electoral parties. But they will go on protesting forever, and we will go on protesting forever with them, unless there are organized political vehicles interested and capable of going into the state and transforming it. Now how does one know under what conditions you can build a majority, and what is the sufficient number before you can say you have the "conscious majority", to employ the rather vague phrase you quote from Marx against Blanqui. I have never been a Leninist, and I have always expressed very strong criticisms of vanguardism and of the types of party organization based on democratic centralism. That said, one has to begin somewhere, with a cadre that is committed to creating the type of political organization oriented to developing people's capacities to understand, support and take part in transforming the state as a necessary part of fundamentally changing social relations. So can one say that the problem with that the Russian Social Democratic Party was that it represented only a "minority", whereas the German Social Democratic Party represented a "majority"? The German party was massive and its membership was largely supportive of it, not least because it created trade unions that fought for their rights, and because it got them into the state as individual voters. When it came to supporting the Kaiser in World War One, and thus avoided being labeled traitors by the old regime, it wasn't that the party leaders betrayed their members overwhelming commitment to socialism. They were actually afraid of challenging their members' underlying sense of nationalism. They were afraid of challenging their members' adhesion to the unions only because it gave them a higher wage, and whose leaders, as Rosa Luxemburg had put it so well in her Mass Strike pamphlet, did not want revolution even if they still spoke in terms of socialism at party meetings. The Russian party, we have to remember, did have almost a million members, so in that sense, it also was a mass party before it was forced underground. And as Rosa Luxemburg also recognized that as the old Tsarist regime crumbled through the course of World War One, and Kerensky could not quickly consolidate a parliamentary regime as so many local soviets sprang up, power was left lying in the streets and the Bolsheviks were well enough organized to pick it up. But Luxemburg was also right to say to them, after they soon banned opposition parties, you are destroying the conditions whereby workers will be able to continue to develop their capacities. If you ban other parties, and many workers are supporting those parties, how do you know who is a supporter of the reactionary party, by the clothes they are wearing? Some of seeds of the Stalinist dictatorship were planted right then and there, but that there were no Bolsheviks in Egypt during the heady days that brought down Mubarak capable of picking up the power in the streets did not produce such a great result either, did it?

SR: I am glad you mentioned the German experience, as it vividly shows the failures of both reformist and insurrectionist strategies. After the collapse of the empire, the internal divisions between the moderate/right wing and left wing of the Socialist Democratic Party (SPD) played a major role in the failure of the revolution. The right wing sided with the army and reactionary forces, and the left wing prematurely declared a Socialist Republic and calling for the uprising.

LP: But those are very specific judgments.

SR: My point is that not every insurrectionary moment is beneficial for socialists. This is particularly the case in today's world with all reactionary religious fundamentalists on the move. In your *Renewing Socialism*, you have a very interesting quote from Raymond Williams who says when people get to the point seeing that the price of contradictions is yet more intolerable than the price of ending them, then they move to revolution. No doubt, this happens when you have no other choice, and you have a political revolution. But unfortunately, if we look carefully at almost all these political revolutions, the costs of abruptly ending the contradiction have been far higher. We have so many of these examples, but I refer to my own experience in the Iranian revolution. That revolution that the socialist left played an enormous role in it, with all the mistakes of all organizations, whether moderates or ultra-left, ended up being disastrous not only for the left, but also for the working people, women, and the whole country. The degree of social, cultural, political, and economic degradation is unbelievable.

LP: I entirely agree and I think that anybody who is honest needs to be extremely conscious of the costs and dangers of such a revolution and needs to understand that so many people are reluctant to engage in it because they have the instinctive sense of the cost of the enormous disruption that such a massive change would entail. I think we need to be in that sense very sensitive not to reject such cautious people as reactionary. But in the moment when a regime is toppling and there is an array of social forces (including reactionary ones, as in your country) engaged in insurrectionary activities against the old regime, it is very difficult not to get caught up in it. It really depends on the conjuncture, but the primary task needs to be to develop people's capacity to be able to eventually get to the point when there is the possibility of socialist change.

Catherine Samary

CS: This is a very important and difficult question. At the time when Marx was elaborating the idea of revolution, there was no experience of a workers' party. There were mass organizations that entered the First International but there were no "political parties" clearly distinct from social movements. The Paris Commune began to give a place to "strategic" political issues about the articulation between mass social movements and state power; but it is 1905 and October 1917 in Russia which raised the revolutionary stake as a political issue for the "workers' movement", and the need for the role of permanent political parties. This type of organization (bringing to the workers a revolutionary consciousness from "outside") could be interpreted by some critics as a form of Blanquism, because of the role played by a vanguard group leading the masses. But firstly, Lenin's orientations were articulated with real revolutionary upsurges and not minority actions. He fought against "infantile leftism" and was in favor of militant involvement in Parliament where they existed, and supported mass revolutionary initiatives in Russia (even very violent ones, because of violence of the tsarist oppression.) As you know, the soviets were already invented by the masses in the 1905 revolution. The whole Russian process was far from a kind of "Blanquist" minority putsch. Secondly, the Leninist distinction between political organizations or parties and mass movements is useful. Of course, in practice, there is always a danger of the "leading role of the party" which would mean the substitution of the "Vanguard" with the mass movement (the "Vanguard" speaking and acting on behalf of the masses without their control). But the need for a permanent political party is to be linked with the need for the continuity of the struggle, for education, learning lessons from the failures, and other functions that political parties need to perform, functions that the mass movement (with its ups and downs among other difficulties) cannot do it by itself. No doubt, respecting the mass movement's democracy and choices is a key issue for self-emancipation. And the capacity to convince a majority is a stronger and efficient proof that the party's choices are the right ones.

So let us break with false answers to a real question: how to invent a democratic and efficient form of political activity for an emancipatory project? Of course, answers are to be found in different contexts. But we can be sure that any kind of "organization" can become bureaucratic and oppressive. But putting aside the notion of organizations (and parties) is not the solution. One of the functions of a political party fighting for an emancipatory project should be to integrate a conscious fight for democratic procedures within its own ranks, in its relations with mass movements, and within those movements themselves. That should be part of the education of its members to criticize the idea that "politics belongs to parties", and exclude any monopoly of decision making on social and political choices. So political parties can be pluralist and useful in a democratic society and in relation to the mass movements. No doubt, we can criticize bureaucratic and authoritarian trends within the Bolshevik party, even before the Stalinization of the party. There was less and less pluralism and counter power against what became the dominant single party. The context of civil war facilitated also the trend toward the suppression both of its internal (very rich) debates and of a pluralist political system. This trend, criticized by Rosa Luxemburg, is not fatalistic or unavoidable.

But the real question is, what are the institutions and mechanisms needed for conflicting and complex process of decision making in a mass movement and in a society where emancipatory goals are put forward as the main ends? How can "politics" be transformed, and not be monopolized by parties acting for their own power?

SR: No doubt. I am not questioning the need for leadership and political parties, and leadership can come in different forms and at different levels. My emphasis is on the mass movement and the extent in which the political consciousness and preparedness are needed for a major social change and socialism. What lessons do you think we can learn from the experiences and mistakes of Bolsheviks or other revolutionaries?

CS: In talking about the need for leadership, we have to differentiate between a self-proclaimed leadership, and the genuine leadership chosen by the mass movement. Also, there is the question of the capability of the mass movement to criticize and change the leadership. Lenin had tried to introduce some measures against bureaucratization. The issues of limiting privileges of those who have responsibility, and rotation of leadership, or even the possibility of dismissing some leaders, should be remembered. The second aspect is the Gramscian approach of the kind of organic intellectuals that mass movement is able to produce. That is the leaders who come out of the movement itself, with specific knowledge linked to experience, along with appropriation of all past knowledge and the support and trust of the masses. Also, there is the need to fight against the separation of the roles and functions of the party and the mass movement, with regard to decision-making responsibility. I do believe that politics must belong to the whole population and to broad movements and they must find the way to express it. New forms of socio-political movements can be a combination of associations and political organizations, avoiding the kind of hierarchy that differentiates between parties (or leaders) and the masses.

SR: On the question of revolution, in one of your writings, "East Europe: Revisiting 1989s Ambiguous Revolutions", you set two criteria for a revolution, one a mass mobilization and the other a radical change. But there is also the question of the direction of change. We can have mass mobilization and movement, but it can also be taken over by reactionary elements and this would be regression rather than progress. We experienced this during the Iranian revolution, and more recently, we are witnessing it in much of the Middle East and the so-called Arab Spring.

CS: Of course, and as far as 1989 is concerned, I stressed the counter revolutionary dimension and also more explicitly have discussed it in a recent article. But I also underlined that self-organization of the masses was very limited in that period, which facilitated manipulation and opaque transformation from "above". But coming back, more generally, to anti-capitalist revolutionary processes, first, we have the question of preparing for radical change in order to increase the chances of going toward the desired progressive direction. Here, we are faced with a tension or contradictions that can be summarized by reference to Marx's criticism of the so-called utopian socialists, against any kind of abstract and preconceived "model" elaborated by a minority outside of mass movements. This is both true and false. Of course, the first difficulty (as far as "preparation" is concerned) is due to the limits of what you can implement within the capitalist system. I think the revolutionary currents are confronted with two dilemmas and risks, in a sense two suicide: One is the idea that within capitalist society, we can experience socialist alternatives, self-managed organs, and so on almost without limits. The risk, however, is that—as the experiences of many cooperatives and self-managing institutions show us—the pressures of capitalist environment is such that these institutions can very quickly be channeled to the system, be transformed and submit to capitalist logic, thus losing their subversive potentials. They even fail their reformism without having the capacity to resist and fight the system. This is one aspect that can be related to the question of the direction of change that you raised. But the other risk is to wait, without preparation, for the final moment of general strike that may never come (or that may come but without the conditions of resisting negative trends, like rapid bureaucratization, or "vanguard's" substitution of which we spoke earlier). I do believe that in any case, we have to get prepared (putting all efforts in the democratic self-organization of masses and their controls on decision making) but with consciousness about the dangers of adaptation to the existing system. We also have to look carefully what the mass movement is inventing (without preparation) and take into account the lessons of the past failures. And no doubt, we have to be aware of the dangers you pointed out about the possibility of reactionary forces taking over and manipulating the mass movement. There is no guarantee, unless there is pluralism, self-organization, radical democracy, constant education, and trying to maintain the resistance's potentials, and refraining from participating and joining the institutions of power where we have no possibility of implementing the programs we are fighting for.

CHAPTER 4

Peaceful Transition

While for Marx "the lever of … of revolution must be force", he excluded countries with "universal suffrage", where "workers can attain their goal by peaceful means". Now that the vast majority of countries have universal suffrage, to what extent and under which circumstances can a peaceful transition to socialism would be possible.

Gilbert Achcar

GA: This has been possible for a long time in some countries, at least in theory. We are speaking of bourgeois liberal countries, with limited state power under civilian control, and where the armed forces do not interfere in politics. It is not only a matter of universal suffrage, but also one of established democratic institutions. The less these conditions are available, the less it is possible to achieve a peaceful transition, and the more risk there is of removal by force of an elected progressive government.

So you need to achieve a strong democratic consensus in society, you need to win over the hearts and minds of a major part of the armed personnel, in order to avoid a situation like that of Chili, where Allende came to power with majority support, but was toppled by the army backed by the CIA. Of course, there is another strategy influenced by the Paris Commune and Bolshevism that advocates the creation of workers militias to defend the revolution. The choice of strategy must, however, depend on the concrete conditions of each case. There is no universal strategy for revolution.

Aijaz Ahmad

AA: These remarks are about historical possibilities, where Marx was wondering if the combination of the great majority of the population getting proletarianized in one way or another, and the vast majority of people are achieving universal suffrage, could be used for transition from capitalism. Marx does not follow these conjectures theoretically, but what he tried to theorize very seriously was the possibility of bypassing the capitalist system and go directly to a postcapitalist system. These questions remained inconclusive. These are speculative questions and belong to a much older historical phase. History itself has also bypassed these phases. Already by the time of Gramsci we have very serious theoretical consideration of the fact that once the bourgeois subjectivity has been created among the masses of people, does the Bolshevik model of revolution making still apply. This is the real question. Unlike some people who try to turn Gramsci into an academic sort of cultural theorist, he was a Leninist. He was trying to rethink Lenin in the condition that was developing in Western Europe. Today, most countries are at a higher level of industrialization than early Soviet Union was, and many countries have gone through parliamentary democracy and universal suffrage. In this situation, the question of the relation between socialism and the parliamentary form cannot be evaded easily.

SR: The question is, can this vast majority of people who, as you rightly say, are suffering economically, politically, culturally, ideologically and ecologically, be mobilized and organized, and through an electoral process form a progressive government that could represent them? Of course there is no illusion that the capitalist class with its powerful repressive and ideological apparatuses of state would not easily give up, and the majority could also use elements of force to confront them.

AA: I have two brief responses. Firstly, the use of force and violence is not a theoretical question and is a strategic question, and strategic questions can only be posed in concrete circumstances. They cannot be posed in the abstract. The other thing I want to say is that the revolutionaries have never chosen violence. Violence is the weapon of choice of the rulers and oppressors.

SR: It is true that oppressors have always used violence, but I am not sure if we can say that the oppressed or the revolutionaries have never used violence.

AA: I did not say that revolutionaries have never used violence. They often have. My point was that there is no revolutionary history based on having some commitment to violence per se. All revolutionary violence has been counter-violence. And where it should or should not be used is a practical and strategic question.

Rob Albriton

RA: I think that, at least, a relatively peaceful transition is almost necessary, because a violent uprising will just be crushed and or lead to a very lengthy civil war that is likely to result in the defeat of the revolution. Of course it's not that easy to get elected even if you have spent some time trying to build up a counter hegemony, as long as there is a really powerful capitalist class that essentially pays off the politicians, as is happening in the US and to a lesser degree in many other places. One area of reform would be to push for removing the complete domination of big money from the political arena. But ironically, it has been going the other way, particularly in the US, where laws that were constraining the buying off of politicians with millions of dollars, have been removed. One could have a campaign arguing that these changes in the US are a radical loss of democracy in America, a country that has always presented itself to the world as a leading democratic power, and now it can no longer do that. What I mean is that while winning state power through the ballot box would not be easy, in so far as you have an elected government, you have to go that way, even if the elections are not quite fair because of the role of money in them. So I don't want to have a black and white line between peaceful and violent because you can be peaceful but quite aggressive.

SR: Of course, street demonstrations, strikes, a general strike, and many other confrontational approaches may be utilized.

RA: Yes, strikes, particularly general strikes, while they don't necessarily lead to revolution, they're a statement about where people are at, and a widely supported general strike could be a significant event.

SR: What you rightly said has become even more complicated in today's globalization, and even if progressive forces come to power and take control of the state, they will be faced with very serious problems that can discuss in my next question.

Kevin Anderson

KA: If we look at France in 1968 there was, to a great extent, a non-violent movement. Almost all the major institutions, except the military and police, were occupied by mass movements with a revolutionary character. I don't think one shot was fired. Here the role of the communist party in demobilizing the workers and getting them to accept new elections and a big pay raise was crucial in the movement's defeat.

Marx talks about electoral changes, as you have quoted in your article about the possibility of workers attaining their goals through peaceful means. But when Marx talks about the possibility of peaceful transition, he adds the qualifier that the peaceful movement might need to be transformed into a forceful one by resistance on the part of those interested in returning to the former state of affairs. The example he gives is the American Civil War, where the rebels were suppressed by constitutional and lawful force. And recall that he regards the changes that resulted in the American Civil War—especially the freeing of the slaves without compensation to the master class, which destroyed it—as revolutionary. But all that came about not because Lincoln intended such a thing. His program was actually very conservative, as he wanted to free the slaves gradually and with compensation. But the force of circumstance, especially the revolutionary subjectivity of African-Americans and the intransigence of the slaveholders, forced confrontation and eventually brought about revolutionary change.

At a general level, I think peaceful transition to socialism is possible, as Marx points out, in countries with a long history of constitutional government rule and democratic processes. But there is a second aspect that we have to mention as a qualifier as a result of the twentieth century. In the nineteenth century countries like United States did not have standing armies or large-scale police forces, let alone a national security apparatus (FBI, CIA, NSA, etc.). Today we have a national security state as an aspect of modern capitalism, which those in my Marxist-Humanist tradition term state capitalism. This power is not going away easily; surely it is going to resist and has a lot of levers of power that it can use. Even if as in France in 1968 the revolutionary movement could take over factories, transport, mass media, schools, etc., repressive institutions like the military and the police -- unless they themselves were also internally splintered by the movement—would likely be able to suppress such an uprising.

We can say there is a two-fold process since Marx wrote; on the one hand, as a result of 40–50 years of grassroots social movements, we have greater democratization of society, wider freedom of speech and many other rights throughout much of the world. On the other hand, we have the rise of the power of surveillance, policing, the use of highly sophisticated technology. For example, the Los Angeles police possess the StingRay, a semi-secret device that can get all the cell phone numbers and information of not only the demonstrators but also the by-standers within the immediate area when deployed near a demonstration.

Barbara Epstein

BE: I believe that any movement for socialism should be nonviolent for three reasons. First, now more than any time in the past, the military power of the state is overwhelming. It is foolish to imagine that we could win an armed contest with the state. Talk of a violent overthrow of the state has no relation to reality. The second point is that in a formally democratic society, the public will regard an armed challenge to the state as nothing more than an attempted coup and a threat to democracy. Thirdly there is the question of ethics, or of what is sometimes called prefigurative politics. A movement for a different kind of society should as far as possible exhibit, in its internal relations and in its external behavior, the values that it would like to see embodied in a better society. Those values should include nonviolence. This is not to say that violence can always be entirely avoided; there is, for instance, the right to self-defense, or defense of the vulnerable. But far too often it seems that those on the left who talk about the need for violence are looking forward to it with anticipation. For the vast majority of people, violence is a serious problem. Enthusiastic talk about violence makes the left appear as part of the problem—or maybe as adolescent.

SR: While no doubt non-violence should be the basis of a majoritarian movement, there are cases or moments, particularly towards the mature stages of a movement, when balance of power between the repressive state and progressive forces are shifting, in which some use of force might be necessary. These could take different forms, from general strikes, closure or takeover of buildings or infrastructure, or even openly confronting police and the military establishment. I would like to ask you to elaborate on the point you raised in one of your books on nonviolent direct action during the civil rights movement in the US. Although the book, *Political Protest and Cultural Revolution*, is very clear, it would be good if you would discuss it here.

BE: Absolutely. I think it is a mistake to rule anything out. I don't believe that violent confrontations can be ruled out—and in fact they will take place whether we rule them out or not. The usual example is World War Two. Nonviolent direct action would not have had any effect on the Nazis, or on similar regimes. But I also think that to the extent that it is possible, it is important for a socialist or democratic/egalitarian movement to maintain the ethical upper hand and exhibit its values in its behavior. Violence should be resorted to only when absolutely necessary, and not just as revolutionary bravado.

SR: That is very true. In terms of the electoral process, some argue that since the electoral system in most countries is controlled by big capital and power, therefore it cannot be a means for achieving real social change.

BE: Certainly participation in the electoral system is a problem for the left, especially in the US, with the two-party system. It is very difficult for the left to be heard in this context. But one of the functions of the left is to put pressure on this system from the outside—and having allies within the electoral system make that a lot easier than without them. I would never argue that the left should drop everything else and do nothing but run candidates for office. But the more characteristic mistake of the left is to have nothing to do with elections. In the late 60s and early 70s the electoral system came to be seen by many on the left as nothing more than a trap, and the idea circulated that anyone who was involved in electoral activity was selling out. But for most Americans, politics meant elections. From that perspective, the left was abandoning politics. I think that the question of whether to participate in electoral politics and if so at what level and in what way is a practical question: it depends on the circumstances. When there is room for left participation I think it is a mistake to refuse. The right, by the way, has for decades engaged in both electoral politics and community organizing, and has regarded these activities as complementary, not contradictory. I think we could learn something from this.

Aron Etzler

AE: It is hard to answer this, as we have not achieved socialism. We cannot know until we get there. But I believe prospects are better now. We just have to seek winning elections, at the same time expanding people's public actions, seeing both as one whole process. A recent example we can find in Latin America, where you have this process of continuous education of the people, expanding public action, and winning elections. No doubt this process has its own limitations, partly because losing election often means losing important changes. Note that compared to a revolutionary Blanquist tradition the losses are limited. In those traditions like in the dismantling of Soviet Union the backlash has been much worse. In Russia they have sold most of the public properties, have had horrible results in social policies and have generally lower democratic consciousness. This strengthens the idea that you have to consolidate every move forward democratically. You don't need to bother about this, if you are a small group of people sitting in a cellar talking about revolution, because then you are dealing with fantasy. But if you are serious about changing society, you have to be very serious about democracy, about bringing people along, building democratic culture, and going forward with serious changes. You cannot change society for the better of people plotting behind their back.

Sam Gindin

SG: When we talk of revolutionary change, we have to theorize the state much more carefully. Social democracy tended to assume that once you form the government, you have taken over the state. On the other hand, Leo (Panitch) and I have argued that it is also wrong to reduce the state to an instrument of the bourgeoisie. States have, over time and through their role in managing the contradictions of capitalism, developed unique sets of capacities. States are constrained by depending on capital accumulation to provide jobs, generate taxes, and sustain their legitimacy but they have a degree of autonomy in doing so and this raises very complicated questions about how to actually begin transforming such states. You cannot just 'smash the state' since every society needs states in the sense at least of collective administrative institutions but can you view this as a process and take over pieces of it? And what would the role of public sector unions in particular be in any such transformations?

Consider in this regard the position of the Ontario Council of Hospital Unions, which represents many long-term care health workers. It is illegal for them to strike but more important, their members are opposed to striking—they don't want to leave old and disabled people without the service. Moreover, a strike would isolate them publically and most likely weaken their cause. So what do you do? The leader of this section of CUPE posed the possibility of a work-in instead of a strike. The idea is to select a particular site and then, instead of striking, bring in *extra* workers from other shifts or other hospitals to *increase* rather than remove the service. This puts management on the spot—would they block these workers from coming in and be blamed for removing a vital service or would they step aside—and essentially allow the union and workers to organize the service? And if that happens what you're indirectly starting to do is to raise the question of a different kind of state, with workers playing a different role and operating on different principles.

The bigger question you're raising is that of a frontal assault on states. Given state power and the international context, this would only be possible if we had the most massive, deep and united base. The point is that as soon as you enter a revolutionary situation, divisions will crop up and be exploited by the enemy, and we can't succeed against the power of the state if we're in a minority. We cannot write off existing democratic practices as 'bourgeois democracy' both because they are in fact more than that and because it carries with it popular legitimacy. We must win this battle through expanding democracy and bring people along with us. Of course, as was evident in Venezuela, you also have to have a base within the army and the police to neutralize them as much as possible. With the broadest base in civil society and divisions in the army and police, their use of force would more likely be constrained. The depth of what we build in civil society is the only protection we ultimately have.

And this gets us back to the intimidatingly difficult question of what happens when you actually come to power. If this involves not just winning elected government but also 'transforming the state', what might that concretely mean? Among other things, we need to prepare by moving towards forming councils of workers and clients across various sectors (such as the hospital or social services sectors) that can address a different kind of state—as opposed to leaving unions and clients to express their separate and often competing interests. On the basis of such structures and people mobilized along class lines, the arrival of a friendly government can then be the occasion for putting all kinds of demands on the state to support progressive initiatives and such new forms of organizing, moving the state towards the long-term changes that truly supports and deepens democracy.

SR: This question becomes far more complex when you deal with societies that are not democratic, there are no independent progressive parties, and workers have no unions and if there are unions they are mostly yellow unions organized by government and others. We have had the experience of revolution and our failures. The discussion of a non-revolutionary path becomes even more difficult in dictatorial systems. Any idea what can be done?

SG: This is the kind of thing we have to learn from you because you have that experience, though there might also be lessons from our own earlier history in the 30s, before unions were legitimated and established. Two points seem especially crucial. First, a lot of the work has to be done in the community outside the workplace; class exists beyond the walls of where the work is done. Where the work is concentrated in one place but the workers themselves are dispersed across large urban spaces, this creates additional problems. Second, where does the confidence come from to overcome present circumstances? Here the 30s are very relevant. In those circumstances, workers on their own tended to see unionization as a crazy, impossible idea. Communists played an absolutely critical role overcoming this. They had an analysis of capitalism, a vision, the international ties, which reinforced a sense of being part of a larger struggle, were part of an organization that helped overcome inclinations to individual demoralization. All this and their commitment to the long-term contributed to their seeing unions as being possible in spite of the 'reality'. Workers did not become communists in any significant numbers, but the readiness of communists to take on the fight gave workers the confidence to join the struggle. Even were anti-communist, when asked (as I once did of one retiree who had been there in the 20s) how workers as far back as 1928 came to attempt to form a union in Ford Motor Company, gave credit to communists as the only ones who were crazy enough to think it was possible.

Another important point was that a lot of the organizing ended up being with the unemployed, which seemed in a sense counter intuitive, because you needed the power of those with jobs. But as it happened, many of the unemployed eventually became leaders and as they got jobs they extended their organizing into the workplace. In South Africa, organizing in the townships was critical in part so that the townships would not become places to recruit scabs to replace unions militants. And so too it was important to organize in schools, where students eventually entered the workforce and their previous struggles affected their workplace organizing. In Brazil, during the dictatorship, the church became a crucial organizing space. The point is that the kind of organization that is needed is one with feet inside the workplace so it is grounded in sites where workers have potential economic power, but also with feet planted outside the workplace so as to avoid the trap of thinking only in terms of particularist union concerns. So organizing can be done in communities, in schools, among the unemployed and not necessarily just in the work place. I think those things were very important.

SR: These are most interesting examples of organizing under different conditions.

Peter Hudis

PH: I think there is a bit of conflation of two issues in this question. There is no question that Marx in different passages in the last decades of his life envisaged the possibility of a socialist government coming to power without violent revolution in England, US or Holland. But I think that is a different question than suggesting that Marx felt that a socialist society could come into existence without violent struggles. I think these are distinct issues. The country Marx in particular thought faced such a possibility, because of having the closest thing to universal male suffrage at that time, was the United States. In relation to the United States he emphasized how the southern aristocracy waged a most violent counterrevolutionary war against Lincoln. Marx felt that the working class could come into power through democratic non-violent means in some instances, but if the slave owners made such a violent counterrevolution, what would the capitalists do when it comes to maintain their property rights over labour power and private property in the means of production? He had no illusions that a counter-revolution would very quickly follow a democratic socialist government coming to power; he said it is likely there would be 10, 20, 30, 40 years of civil war. So I think Marx was very skeptical about a peaceful achievement of socialism. What he wanted—in contrast to the anarchists was for working class movements to be trained in the exercise of political power, so that they could organize the mass of the populace to fight such a counter-revolution. Unfortunately, history has proven him to be right. I am not an advocate of violence, but I think it is hard to conceive that the bourgeoisie would ever kneel down and accept a socialist program, simply because a majority of people are in favour of it. This happened to Allende in Chile, and even is happening in Venezuela, which is not even a truly socialist government (it is more of a social democratic welfare state).

SR: You are absolutely right and there is no doubt that capitalists and their functionaries would not give up easily and will resort to violence. But in a real Marxian revolution, "the mass of the populace" is organized to "fight the counter-revolution", as you clearly elaborated in your reference to Marx's analysis of the American Civil War. The other point relates to the problem of socialism in one country to which we will come back to later. Also I would like to add a point here about Marx's view of socialists coming to power. As I mentioned in my article, Marx in response to a Dutch socialist, Nieuwenhuis, says, "…there is nothing specifically 'socialist' about the predicaments of a government that has suddenly come into being as a result of popular victory". This is in line with what you said earlier. But in the same letter, referring to the Paris Commune, we see a significant departure from Marx's earlier views on the Commune, where he declares it non-socialist and says they should have made compromises. In other words, shifting from criticism of the communards not smashing the state machinery, to criticism of not compromising.

PH: I don't see contradiction in that letter, which I like very much and have referred to several times. I don't think that Marx changed his mind about the Paris Commune. Even when he was very enthusiastic about the Commune in 1871, he realized that it could not be considered a socialist revolution, because you cannot make socialism in one country, let alone in one municipality. He saw the limits of the Paris Commune in that it remained in one locale and did not spread to other areas, and in a sense was doomed to failure one way or another. Marx never expected that the Paris Commune would by itself produce a socialist transition. What he thought the Commune created, was a non-state form of functioning politically, a sort of dictatorship of the proletariat. It is important to note that for Marx, as he explicitly states in the *Critique of the Gotha Program*, the dictatorship of proletariat is not a stage of socialism, it is a political form that comes in between capitalism and the initial phase of socialism or communism. It is a system that still has value production, you still have capitalism but the working class has obtained political power over the state because it has obtained effective power over society. He also did not think of the dictatorship of the proletariat as a phase of socialism, because under socialism there is no proletariat. The proletariat would be abolished with the abolition of classes—which is the essence of socialism.

SR: We will discuss this further in another question dealing with features of socialism.

PH: Marx explicitly refers to a "political" form that comes between existing capitalism and a future socialist/communist society. The dictatorship of the proletariat is not a transitional society. I find no evidence in Marx's work that he ever believed in a transitional society to socialism. He thought the dictatorship of proletariat is a transitional phase that is a political form, not a stage of socialism itself. It does not constitute by itself the creation of alternative economic system. So Marx sees this period of the dictatorship of proletariat in a much more limited sense. Of course the problem is that now this term is not a useful one because of the way it has been abused by post-Marx Marxists; Marx did not mean dictatorship in the way we use the term today, as the despotic control of the state over society. He meant by it the complete opposite—the freely-associated control of society over the state!

Ursula Huws

UH: I would like to believe that it is possible, and in my daily activities I behave on the basis that I believe that it is possible: the Corbyn phenomenon, Die-Linke phenomenon, Podemos, Syriza, and others are all good indications in Europe. But let us look at history: Chile, Iran, and elsewhere. Capitalism is brutal, and does not give up easily. There is also increasingly a kind of complicated slippage between how people are treated in their capacity as citizens, and in their capacity as workers. In the latter case they are treated more brutally in many ways. One of the tricks of globalization is increasingly to disconnect the two. You have an increasing number of immigrant workers with no voting rights, working in the capitalist heartland, alongside the work activities that are exported from the capitalist heartland to countries that do not have universal suffrage or established democracy. All along the value chain, you see that disconnection is happening between citizenship and employment. This also sets people as citizens against those who are not seen as citizens. Denmark is a very clear example of that; they boast to have the best democratic system in Europe but they also have the most racist immigration policy. This is a contradiction of the European social democratic model. The UK is at the other extreme, having very little in terms of social rights, but relatively open borders (although of course still with a savagely racist immigration policy). We see it in the southern United States where Mexicans have very few rights. This relates to a research that I am doing now on 'crowdsourcing' which enables employers to employ people across borders, ignoring any labour protection regulation. There are many examples that show the dismantling of what is left of the social regulations that the workers movements of the twentieth century had managed to negotiate at the national level, through suffrage, through national institutions of democracy, and the social democratic gains in different areas such as pensions, safety regulations, working hours regulations, and health services. So these are the realities of our time, and people who thought that these gains were steps towards a socialist future are disillusioned now.

SR: That is true, and the question remains as to what are the real alternatives and how to move toward them, that I hope you would discuss in other questions.

Michael Lebowitz

ML: We cannot mystify universal suffrage. We have universal suffrage in the US and many other places and we see how they are fooling the people. There is universal suffrage, but at the same time we have capitalist domination of the media, police, the judicial system, etc. Universal suffrage by itself cannot be a solution, and it is only one aspect of the process. Marx argues that while in contrast to the revolutionary path, it might be possible for the working class to come to power electorally in some countries, he was not saying it is the way.

SR: There is no illusion about the democratic systems of today. The reason why I ask this question is that the focus for vast majority of Marxists have been on the revolutionary take over, but Marx also envisaged an electoral possibility, through which the working class can transform the democratic institution of the bourgeoisie from a "means of deception" to a "means of emancipation". I am particularly interested to ask you, as a supporter of the Bolivarian Revolution of Chavez who came to power through universal suffrage and electoral process. Also in *Socialist Imperative* you discuss three perspectives on democracy that would be great if you discuss it.

ML: The argument of the three perspectives on democracy was to first of all reject the perspective that dominates in capitalist society, the perspective of consumer choice, where the concept of democracy is that everyone is free and as an atomistic individual is free to choose. I argued that this is not real democracy and contrasted that to two other perspectives. In one, I used the analogy of the orchestra conductor, which refers to a society run by vanguards at the top who make the decisions and transmit these decisions to below through various transmission belts. In this situation democracy is seen as an opportunity for others to comment on plans and decisions made above. I argued if people are limited to commenting on decisions coming from above, they cannot develop their capacities. You know my focus has been what kind of people are developed under certain relations. I gave some examples from Cuba, where they have enormous participation in discussing the proposals that come from the top, but very little opportunity for the people to come up with proposals from below. And finally I contrasted these two with the third perspective which is my focus and deals with human development, and with creating the instruments and the means and forms in which the people can develop their capacities. This is the characteristic of the concept of democracy that is discussed in Latin America as Socialism for the twenty-first century.

SR: Does the human development process that you rightly emphasize happen during the capitalist period or after that, or both? I am particularly interested in the period prior to the post-capitalist society.

ML: It is a continuous process that happens before and after. In *Socialist Imperative* I discuss the future of socialism and the state and in the concluding chapter I make the argument that we have to make the state from below, and for this we have to build the institutions that develop human capacity. This has to happen before, but if it does not happen before [the end of capitalism], it has to happen after that. For example, take Venezuela where I spent several years. Before Chavez there were many local practices and organizations that developed people's capacities, and it is out of these local institutions, ideas and struggles that Chavez comes. The new Venezuelan constitution emphasized the centrality of participation and protagonism as the only way which you can develop people's capacity, both individual and collective. Once that Constitution was adopted, it acted like a signal that local organizations referred to and stressed human development, and led to some further experiments in local decision-making. These experiments led to the creation of the communal councils subsequently enacted as a law which became an encouragement for the areas that had not developed such institutions. These experiments played a very important role in developing people's capacities. Further, when Chavez emphasized the importance of the communal councils, he said these councils are the cells of the new socialist state. Obviously these neighbourhood councils had to link with others and create something larger, which became the concept of the commune. These became a mechanism for coordination, but from below. Finally, one of the last things that Chavez talked about in one of his last speeches was that he asked why some ministers have not made the communes as the center of their focus. In the televised cabinet meeting, he told Nicolas Maduro, I entrust to you my life and the communes—*Comuna o nada* (without communes, nothing). This statement generated an enormous interest in the communes, and enormous movements from below that we don't hear about it in the media. So developing people's capacities does not need to be fully achieved before the change. Obviously you need the old state; that is why I came up with the idea of "dual state socialism". The old state engages in policies which are fighting capital and deals with national and international issues, until such time that the new state has developed its capacities to take over. What is important in the Venezuelan experience is how the top stimulated the bottom, how it created conditions for building a new state from below. We need to understand this as dialectic between old and new state.

SR: Your notion of dual state as distinct from "dual power" is a novel and very important concept that hopefully should be developed further. I also wanted to make few points regarding what you discussed earlier about the three perspectives on democracy. You rightly criticized the conductor-conducted relations. But at the same time, we cannot deny the need for coordination, particularly in large organizations, both horizontally and vertically, and from below and above. Some of the notions stressed by the so-called autonomists or some anarchists, such as horizontalism or non-hierarchical organizations are too idealistic and out of touch with reality. There is no possibility of having a non-hierarchical large organization., without vertical division of labour.

Leo Panitch

LP: Marxism is not a proven theory of revolution; its greatest contribution is to help us better understand capitalism. Marx as a politicized journalist brilliantly analyzed some revolutionary moments, particularly in France. But I think we need to stop getting ourselves into these situations of discussing these questions and debating these questions only on the basis of this or that quotation from Marx, and that was my point about being historical materialist means understanding different conditions under which we need to be discussing these things. How could Marx foresee, when he listed the Netherlands, Britain and United States, which other countries would end up after 1945 being liberal democracies. Because it wasn't until after 1945 that more than handful countries that even had secured mass suffrage and competitive elections in a stable way.

SR: The point is that if the working people, the majority of people have the capability of really getting their true representatives in the parliament and influence policy, then there might not be a necessity for abrupt political revolution.

LP: But only under conditions that the party organization which makes them representatives is also capable of making them accountable, open to recall, as well as capable of ensuring they remain cadre and organizers rather than professional politicians who are careerist 'parliamentary representatives'. If I have made any contribution

I think it really lies in this. We now can see after over a century of such parliamentary activity that the elected representatives of social democratic parties became enmeshed in the structures of the state and they lost their role as developers of the capacities of the people who put them there. Roberto Michels predicted all of this a hundred years ago in his *Political Parties: The Iron Law of Oligarchy*, a book that far too few socialists whether reformist or revolutionary, have read. We have to believe that we can develop peoples' capacities so that you have a genuine democracy. It is not enough to say what if workers have 'true representatives' in parliament. What kind is true? There have been moves in this direction in the last 30 years. The Green Party in Germany made up of many people who were kicked out of the Social Democratic Party in the 70s; initially strongly made a case for recall, the circulation of parliamentarians, etc. Similarly, the Workers Party in Brazil was based on the notion that when people get into the parliament, get in to the state, their main role has got to be to continue to be organizers.

SR: It is beside the point that even the German Green Party when got larger and more influential, put aside many of their 70s organizational arrangements, but you are absolutely right and there is no illusion about today's representations in liberal democracies. The question is how socialists and progressive people can use democratic mechanisms to push for their agenda, and how to change these institutions. In one of your works you refer to the Marxism's traditional failure to address the necessary institutions for democratic socialism, this is very important.

LP: I often feel uncomfortable when people label me as a classical or orthodox Marxist, just because I have retain my socialist commitment and because I think certain aspects of Marxism, even without deploying much of his value theory, help us understand the dynamics of the capitalist system. I have always been like this. When I was young, one of the first articles I published (in *Capital and Class* in 1978, and subsequently included in my *Working Class Politics in Crisis* book in the mid-80s) was about the limitation of Marxism in relation to delimiting specifically the institutions necessary for a transition to socialism. I argued that Marx and Engels swept all of the difficult questions—well, at least most of the difficult questions—under the carpet with terms like the 'dictatorship of the proletariat', the 'smashing of the state', and so on. I think that it is incumbent upon both our generation as well as the next generation of people who remain committed to a socialist future beyond capitalism and are trying to prepare for it institutionally, to develop a Marxist institutional analysis, so as to understand better both the limitations of the institutions of capitalism, whether corporate organization or state institutions, and also of working class institutions, including the ones who were engaged in and the new ones thrown up by revolutionary struggles.

SR: Because of the influence of Leninism, much of socialist institutional analysis has been based on Leninist type organizations.

LP: Well we need to be open-minded about this. As I said earlier, I have never been a Leninist. But I do recognize that many of the most committed, knowledgeable and impressive cadre, many of the best organizers very often came out of Leninist organizations. I don't think that this can be replicated easily today. Yet, as I also said, often their commitment to the Bolshevik model of revolution made them much less effective—sometimes made them actually very ineffective—than they might have been as working class organizers. My father was a Social Democrat, as well as a workplace activist that at one point was elected president of his local trade union, and who saw first hand that the Communist leaders of the union often made a hash of things by following the 'party line'. But at the same time I saw that my aunt, who was a Communist who had joined the Party out of the sweatshops, had an understanding of exploitation that was deeper than my father ever got from the CCF—Co-operative Commonwealth Federation (which was the social democratic forerunner of the NDP in Canada). No doubt, there were all kinds of defects of both types of parties that we would want to learn to avoid. I think if we are going to try to develop this new institutional strategic thinking, it has to be based on recognition of the advantages and limitations of both types of organization we have known in the past, but not to replicate them, as they have run their historical course. We need to be creative institutionally, understanding that institutions arise also in the context of different historical conditions.

SR: This is very important particularly in relation to the present globalisation. In the past, the Left attempted to create national organizations with the hope of establishing socialism in their respective countries. Now, with globalization more obstacles are created that we will discuss in the question.

Catherine Samary

CS: Unfortunately I don't believe in the possibility of peaceful transition to socialism. Even the experiences such as those of Chili's Allende, or Portuguese revolution of 1973 and similar cases point to the failure of such attempts: the combination of repressive (military) coup and of massive corruption or integration within the system gives a vast range of means for the dominant classes to break democratic revolutionary processes.

But there is an additional difficulty, linked to recent developments. The capitalist system in its last phase is confronted with major structural crises, combined with the crises of the world order. Incapable of resolving the crises through social progress for the masses, it has resorted to the use of the crises to increase social attacks and, for that reason, it needs the suppression of democracy. Even in countries where they have established parliamentary system, we witness that main decisions (on socio-economic issues) are taken outside parliaments and without the intervention of elected members—which themselves are not really controlled by the electors after elections. There is a big crisis of representative and parliamentary democracy (abstention becomes the dominant "vote" and elections mean nominal changes without real changes). I don't mean that the answer is to suppress parliamentary system, but we need to transform democracy and combine it with radical political, social and economic changes dealing with property and human rights. The big questions of daily life of the people, the question of employment, the question of dignity, the question of access to public services and so on, which are the questions of democratic choice, are less and less taken within parliaments. Even we see it in European countries, where we witness more and more what is called Ordoliberalism, which seeks to impose market competition on the constitutions through powerful non-elected institutions. This prevents any democratic debate on economy, or on social issues—without speaking of property. Multinational firms try to protect themselves against new nationalizations, social and political control, while all social protections tend to be removed from constitutions and labor codes. All the past gains are in the process of being destroyed. There is also the transformation of the armies into militias and private armies and the criminalization and repression of resistance. So, more than ever before, I don't believe in the possibility of a peaceful movement for social and democratic rights without major class confrontations with the dominant classes that are in control of all kinds of international and national repressive institutions. The answer is more than ever also, the mass movement, the self-organization of the mass movement and the capacity of the self-defense of the mass movement—and of political, moral de-legitimation of the 1 percent powerful rulers who destroy social rights, human rights and environmental rights. Of course the movement has to consolidate its legitimacy in the democratic process and in new constitutions and the articulations of international rights and institutions—linked to the protection of nature, health, human rights, dignity, etc.

SR: We don't of course have any illusions about problems of the present democratic systems in Europe, North America, or elsewhere, all of which are to different degrees dominated by big capital and rich interest groups. The idea is to struggle for real and deepened democracy with genuine representation of the majority of citizens. If we put aside the parliamentary way of coming to power, we have to resort to political take over, which depends on whether we have strong support and mass base among the majority of people, that we discussed in the question related to what kind of revolution, by whom, and how.

CS: We have a big mass of population, women, youth and workers who are suffering under the capitalist system, and we have to find allies within different parts of the population, and find ways of organizing—around concrete issues concerning daily life, and the alternatives that need to be found. These need to be articulated from the local to the national, continental and global levels. We can take the case of Syriza in Greece and Podemos in Spain. The answers to radical social assaults of capital have been general strikes and mass national movements on very concrete issues, like health, housing, and so on. But strikes and struggles have not been sufficient to stop the assaults. The traditional political parties have been discredited. The dispossessed are suffering from inequalities in all fields and have become "indignatos" (indignant) often rejecting parties. But they need to transform their upsurges into a political force, raising the issue of changing the "power" of making laws and giving people constitutional rights. There have been movements in squares, in streets, even self-organized network of the 99 percent in the US, but these have been insufficient and needed to be transformed into organized political movements—like Syriza in Greece, and Podemos in Spain. Podemos, in particular, coming after the spontaneous movement of the "Indignatos" (reflecting a crisis of political representation through parties), expressed the idea that it is not enough to be *against*, but you also need to be *for* something, and that you need to win the elections. So you can criticize the limits of elections, of parties and of parliamentary democracy that are reduced to elections, but you have also to win the legitimacy to change the laws and to organize an alternative, which can be a Constituent Assembly that would enact new laws for the establishment of a new democratic system. So you need a combination of fighting within the system and against the system.

SR: This is exactly what I was raising earlier about parliamentary change.

CHAPTER 5

Globalization and Socialism in One Country

With increasing globalization and internationalization of all cycles of social capital, what new opportunities and obstacles have emerged for proponents of socialism? In the era of globalization, is socialism in one country possible at all?

Gilbert Achcar

GA: Socialism in one country was never possible at any time, and it is even less so in the time of globalization, to be sure. The predominant view of the transition to socialism in most of the twentieth century was predicated on the idea that the Soviet Union was a socialist state and that relying and depending on it could pave the road to socialism. The Yemenis and the Cubans held such views for some time. The truth, however, is that socialism in the Marxian sense of the term can only be established when global capitalism has been overthrown, at least in its main economic strongholds: the USA, the European Union (EU), and Japan.

Here we come back to the crucial issue of the difference between the political, or political/military seizure of power, and the economic transformation. The first one is qualitative and takes a relatively short time. The second one is a matter of balance of forces at the local and global levels. Because as long as capitalism is dominant in the global economy, it is impossible to eradicate it at the national level in a sustainable way. Workers power will need to coexist with capitalism for some time. From the historical experience, we know that the rapid eradication of capitalism, through sweeping nationalizations, leads to disaster. That is where Kautsky's idea, which I mentioned earlier, becomes important: the socialist transformation of the economy needs to be gradual. It will involve bargains with the capitalists, depending on the balance of forces, until the historical global conditions for the socialist transformation are met.

SA: In one of my arguments, I ironically said that we can have socialism, when the global economic institutions like the IMF, WTO, and World Bank pursue socialist policies put forward by representatives of major member states that have become socialist. Obviously, this is a far cry from where we stand now. But while global capital, through powerful capitalist states, international economic institutions, and multinational corporations and banks, has become more powerful than ever, globalization has also created new opportunities for the proponents of socialism, particularly in relation to the globalization of communication and information.

GA: There can be no doubt that international economic institutions are needed for a globalized economy. The point is how to change their nature and agendas. The IMF and World Bank were originally institutions of Keynesian inspiration, with quite different agendas from their present ones.

Aijaz Ahmad

AA: I answer the second question first. The answer is simple. Socialism in one country has never been possible. The necessity was imposed on Soviet Union by the failure of revolutions in Europe, Germany in particular. At the time the Bolsheviks took power, it was assumed that there will soon be a revolution in Germany and that backward Russia will be pulled into a revolution by advanced Europe. No one had a fantasy that Russia could make a revolution by itself. In this sense, this was not only Trotsky's position and it was Lenin's and Bolshevik position. It was only when they were stuck with a fatality that no other revolution was going to be made, and were invaded by a number of countries and counter-revolutionaries, then they had to defend what they had. They could not abrogate the state they had created and tried to do what they could to make a transition to socialism. They needed a legitimating ideology for it, so a new ideology of "socialism in one country" was created, and Stalin tried to legitimize it.

As for opportunities and obstacles of globalization or that of the present state of capitalism, the opportunity is the extreme proletarianization that is taking place across the globe. The proletariat no longer resides predominantly in the advanced capitalist countries of the Euro-American zones. The vast majority of them live in other parts of the world. Proletarianization is also significant in terms of the proportion of the global population. Communications have made it possible to coordinate revolutionary momentum in a way that has never been possible before. That can take so many different forms that we do not need to choose. We have a variety of peasants' movements that can be coordinated; it can be trade unions or political parties of different kind or it can be the Social Forum type coordination. What was once possible at the national level is now possible at the global level. There is now a much more articulate intelligentsia of the left-wing type across the world. We would be myopic not to see that millions upon millions of the people are on the move around the globe. So what is going to happen is that there will be new structures and flexibilities on the ground and around the world. There is going to be different centers of coordination. No more do these centers need to be in any specific cities as Moscow once served as the center, and the totality of these different forms of politics does not have to be authorized by the Third International type centralization. We don't really know what the future revolutionary forms will be. That will be discovered in practice, by building revolutionary politics. As of now, we only have transitional forms, very fragile and episodic.

SR: It is true, but at the same time we are faced with new obstacles. Now, we have organized capital at the global level, with its international financial organizations, regulating capital's global dominance, along with multinational corporations and credit-rating agencies, and not to mention its military wing, NATO.

AA: No doubt these are obstacles. It is true that nation states, with the exception of USA, are weaker today in respect to capital. Even for the USA, when Barrack Obama went to India, he took 200 top businessmen with him. Heads of states in the OECD countries have simply become salespersons for transnational corporations of their respective countries. However, if we are talking of the revolutionary movements, talking of masses of the people transforming the world, state oligarchies all across the world are nothing but the managing committees for the bourgeoisie of their respective countries. They enforce labor regimes and while these states are weaker in relation to capital, they are much stronger in relation to labor. I am not surprised if IMF would want to curtail prerogatives of Mr. Modi's government in India, or similar governments elsewhere. Such government already serves the interests of international finance capital as assiduously as the IMF itself.

SR: I am not referring to the governments of today that represent the interest of the capitalist class, but refer to obstacles that a progressive left government would face in case of coming to power and wanting to follow a pro-labor policy. Then these institutions of capital that I referred to could easily create serious problem for them, and we have many examples.

AA: Yes, there are contradictory movements. I would rather have nation states that represent the interest of people, but unfortunately there are not. If you do have states of that kind and these institutions that you referred to try to curtail them, then you will have a very different kind of fight. In any case, the fight goes through struggle against one's own state. There is no way of confronting imperialism other than through these national states. The first thing that I mentioned was the imperialism of the finance capital. We have to think of some strategy to have mobilization against that. The idea behind anti-globalization is good, but the problem is that they have not accepted an action plan, and organizations like Social Forum came to a blockage, because it became speech making and debating society, and could not move to the next stage which would have involved the framing of a broad common program of principles and objectives on which all could agree, spelling out what a transition to socialism would look like.

Rob Albriton

RA: I don't think socialism is possible in one country, except ironically in the USA, and we know it would be the last country to move toward such path. Again, it is not the question of socialism everywhere or no socialism at all. It would mean that some countries would become more and some less, and at some point, one or two counties can have a kind of breakthrough and rightly claim that they are henceforth socialist countries. So it has to start somewhere. Unless you have the whole of Europe becoming socialist at once, or the whole of Scandinavia should become socialist, the process is going to be step by step, through which some countries will get further than others. I think that without a very strong international socialist movement, at a time that we have a strong capitalism on a world scale, just one country implementing socialist policies isn't going to survive. It can't.

SR: You rightly say that considering all the subjective and objective obstacles at both national and international levels, there is no other choice but to move gradually and to different degrees push forward to implement policies toward socialism. This is what I call radical social democracy that unlike social democracies of today constantly and aggressively aims at socialism, by constantly educating and mobilizing the working majority. Another point you rightly mentioned earlier is that a peaceful path or resorting to force is not black and white. There will be serious confrontations, and you don't just aim at toppling the old regime. While you use experiences of revolutionaries of the past, you try to foster changes and gradually and increasingly move forwards your goal of moving beyond capitalism.

RA: Yes, you do not follow Mao's famous quote: "power grows out of the barrel of the gun". There are other ways of exerting pressure, and in any case, I think that the international dimension is extremely important, and the Left in every country should make every effort possible to build a strong international movement. Now there are different efforts, like the World Social Forum, peasant movements, aboriginal movements, labor movements, feminist movements, human rights movements, and so on, but more and more work has got to go into establishing, strengthening, and radicalizing trade unions, building a real international movement that can work together globally. I don't know whether it is possible to reform the UN, the World Bank, IMF, or WTO, but either they need to be radically reformed or replaced by altogether different institutions.

SR: No doubt with the international economic institutions of capital such as the WTO, the World Bank, and IMF and the imposition of their neo-liberal policies, no single country will be able to push for its progressive agendas. And since no country can have an autarky and live in isolation these days, it cannot ignore these external constraints. The socialist world will also need these types of international organizations, of course of a different type.

RA: Of all the problems, I would almost say the most serious ones we face are international or global: inequality, poverty, unemployment, ecological problems, and so on. There has been in recent years a lot of emphases on the local, getting people to mobilize on the local level, to fight local issues—and that is something that is not to be ignored—but I would tend to place a lot of emphasis on the international level.

SR: That is true, but of course change at an international level is ultimately based on the local level, and they are closely linked.

RA: Yes, ultimately you have to link up the local struggles with the international. Even now, there are countries that are more progressive. They have powerful trade unions in place, have socialist parties, and although they are not radical social democracies, they have institutions in place that can push for reform at the global level. One area is reforming the UN, which is not an easy thing to do. In the politically dominant Security Council, one great power can stop any policy move, and this state of affairs is absolutely undemocratic and appalling. The whole international financial system should also be reformed, and what we call the economic surplus should turn toward human and environmental flourishing. This obviously requires a different financial system.

SR: Also, there is a need to confront the power of multinational corporations and banks. Now, finance capital, which has become almost independent of industrial and commercial Capital, is dominating the world economy. You are absolutely right about the need for reforms at the international level, which is of course possible only if progressive governments are elected in the powerful capitalist countries.

RA: That it true.

Kevin Anderson

KA: Socialism was never possible in one country. It is certainly not possible in a small or medium size country like Venezuela. It was not possible in Russia either, despite its being a very large country, because it was so economically undeveloped.

One thing that globalization does is to internationalize struggles. For example, we have had a struggle in Mexico about police kidnapping and murdering leftist youth and we had demonstrations over this up in California. Today, what happens in one country can be immediately reflected globally. New forms of solidarity have been created. Look at the Arab revolutions of 2011 and how widely they spread throughout the region. Not since 1848 had such things had happened, even surpassing 1968 in terms of the number of governments overthrown. But at the same time there are more obstacles to radical movements. Capital is so much mobile, and repression is also mobile. These are contradictory developments.

I don't think that the nation state has disappeared and I don't think we have yet a global capital that is not differentiated by the national capitals, for otherwise the USA, China, Europe, or Russia would not have constant rivalries. Also I think—and this puts me in a minority among the left—that progressive forms of nationalism are still worth looking at. The most obvious example is the Palestinian movement, which is a national movement, but one can also mention the Kurds. A part of the international left has a position that condemns all forms of nationalism. But among our modern-day heroes are the Zapatistas of Chiapas, Mexico, who call themselves the Emiliano Zapata *National* Liberation Movement (EZLN), which is a movement based upon oppressed, indigenous peoples of southern Mexico. Palestinians, Kurds, and indigenous Zapatistas have a sort of national or ethnic consciousness that is certainly revolutionary. Of course, we are not in an era like in the 50s and 60s' when there were large numbers of progressive nationalist movements in many parts of the world, but we should not exclude national movements completely by talking of globalization as an accomplished fact, as if there is already a single global capital or capitalist apparatus, and therefore that all movements have to be global and not local or national. Nonetheless, we are in a new era.

SR: Two points here; no doubt that there are some genuine and progressive elements in nationalist movements. But I think the nationalist movements of the 50s and 60s had a linkage with the so-called national bourgeoisie that is now almost missing because of continuous internationalization of capital and the fact that there is no country that is not under the domination, to different degrees, of big capital. We have small or medium size national capital in different countries, but they are economically and politically insignificant in terms of the ability to support a genuine nationalist movement. The second point is that, undoubtedly serious rivalries do exist among big capital of major economies, but at the same time capital has now international financial and trade institutions, through which to impose neo-liberal rules and regulations. These are mechanisms that did not exist at the time of Marx or Russian Revolution. This makes any movement toward socialism in one country very difficult.

KA: No doubt the second point is something that undermined social democracy. As you say, some of the members of these institutions come from countries that are social democratic, and it is hard to differentiate them from the right-wing members. We have seen how the IMF has acted in the past decades, and now the way EU is involved in strangulation of Greece. This points to the fact that the social democratic model was also unsuccessful, just as the Bolshevik type model was unsuccessful. By the 70s, there was economic stagnation. This is before Thatcher and neo-liberalism, and there was Keynesianism in many of these countries, but economically they were running out of steam.

SR: Absolutely right. These social democratic governments moved toward right because of lack of radicalism, and also because of pressures of the global dominance of neo-liberalism.

KA: Yes, that is important. The other way to look at it is what the French call it *les trente glorieuses* [glorious 30 years]. The period 1945–1975, after so much both capital and physical resources were destroyed by war in Western Europe, allowed a relatively low-wage economy to be created that over time and under pressure from labor and the left was turned into modern welfare states.

Barbara Epstein

BE: Globalization opens up the possibility of greater communication, internationally, among movements of the left. What happens in one country has more impact on the thinking of movements of the left elsewhere; movements are more likely to spread from one country to another, as in the case of Occupy. Beyond that, I can't think of any advantages to the left from globalization. Globalization has enhanced the power of capital at the expense of the power of labor, the left, and popular movements generally. In the past, progressive social change has often been facilitated by splits in the ruling class and by the support of some part of that class for elements of a left agenda—as in the 30s, when a sector of the ruling class came to believe that recognition of labor unions and some sort of welfare net were necessary, and in the 60s, when a sector of the class came to oppose the War in Vietnam. This is not happening, at least not on the same scale, today. In the wake of the crash of 2008, I expected that much of the ruling class would conclude that neo-liberalism was a mistake and that there needed to be a significant degree of regulation of capital. This has not happened, I think because the wealthy were not harmed by it. The response of the left to globalization has to be to strengthen our own international ties, and to rebuild organizations of the left, within the USA and other countries and also internationally. Without a stronger and more visible left, it is difficult for people to believe that something other than the current status quo is possible. I think this lack of confidence that something better is possible is an important factor in the consolidation toward the right suggested by recent elections in Britain and elsewhere.

SR: I would also like to have your views about the second part of my earlier question about the possibility of having socialism in one country, and whether globalization has made it more difficult.

BE: I think it is a question of momentum, of whether movements against austerity and toward a more egalitarian society can gain the upper hand in a number of countries simultaneously and thus begin to challenge neo-liberalism internationally. A lot depends, I think, on whether large numbers of people, in a number of countries, become convinced that a more egalitarian society is possible. I doubt that any country can become socialist in an international vacuum. Furthermore, it seems to me that in the USA and Western Europe, a shift toward socialism itself is highly unlikely any time in the foreseeable future. A shift away from neo-liberalism and toward more equality and toward states less grateful to the corporations and more responsive to the people as a whole could take place. Such a shift could be a step toward socialism itself. But I think it's a mistake to pose the issue as if a continuation of neo-liberalism and socialist revolution are the only options.

SR: You are absolutely right.

Aron Etzler

SR: In addition to the question of globalization, I would like to ask you to comment on another point. In response to an earlier question you mentioned how Swedish capital created problem for the social democrats. Aside from the power of capital in Sweden and in other European countries, in the era of globalization, Social Democrats are now confronted with global corporations and international institutions of capital and their aggressive neo-liberal policies. I think one of the best examples that I am sure you know was when in the mid-90s, the Swedish government of, I think, Goran Persson wanted to introduce some important improvements in the pension system, the credit-rating agency of Moody's reduced the AAA rating of Sweden and created serious problem for the Social Democratic government. My argument is that now it is more and more difficult for social democrats to follow socialist policies in their respective countries.

AE: Yes, for sure in the present period, capital has become far more powerful and international institutions like the IMF and others have created bigger obstacles for socialist policies, and EU itself has become more conservative. But the question is that whether this trend is the result of globalization in itself? I am not absolutely sure about this. Globalization has been defined as deregulation—although more accurately it is seen as global regulation for profit. Nevertheless, it is possible to think that globalization can also be a means of socialist regulation.

SR: That is true. The institutions like IMF, the World Bank, or WTO are consisted of representatives of right-wing governments that follow neo-liberal policies, and of course if one day progressive forces replace these governments, then the policies of these institutions would also become progressive. So as you say, it is not globalization itself but the type of globalization and in this sense neo-liberal globalization that is a main obstacle for moving toward socialism. Also in terms of deregulation, as you said, they are very much involved in regulation. They are regulating global economy on the basis of their economic perspective.

AE: True, but this cannot possibly continue like this. We can see the disastrous impact of these policies in different parts of the world and reactions to these policies. Environmental problems are threatening life, and these and many other economic and social problems cannot be resolved through deregulation and less government. Actually, I believe that we move toward a period of state capitalism. Socialism is not around the corner, but some kind of planned state capitalism is a possibility.

As for the possibility of socialism in one country, I don't think it is possible. However, the political processes of taking steps toward socialism start from the country level. Latin America is a good example, as one or two countries start and others follow. In Europe, we may be able to follow the same process. While Greece because of its debt problem and other issues cannot move to socialism alone, any move toward that direction in the region, for example, coming to power of a left government in Spain, can help the left government in Greece. The paradox is that political conquest takes place in national state, and so it has to start in a country, but has to spread.

As for obstacles and opportunities of globalization, I think first we should note that globalization in a sense goes back to the fifteenth century. As Giovannl Arrighi or Immanuel Wallerstein has argued, banks and corporations were also very powerful in the sixteenth century. Capitalism in a sense has always been globalized, and I think what defines globalization in our era is that there are super-national political organizations, and also there is a shift of industrialization from the more advanced industrial societies to the so-called former third world countries. A new economic and geopolitical landscape is created, but I am not really sure that globalization is the best way to describe this. At least you have to add that the power is shifting toward a multipolar world. You have to add that democracy, while being undermined by supra-national treaties, also is in many ways more rooted in values and practices. Attempts to enshrine neo-liberal policies in the supra-national organizations and treaties are no doubt very real. But as mentioned earlier, it may not necessarily remain like that. For instance, the supra-national negotiations about preventing climate change will mean stronger regulations, more government action, and less of the free trade mantra. I believe that neo-liberalism that has been dominant in the past 20 or 30 years cannot be continued in future and will be challenged.

SR: Well, let us hope so, but there should be a major force to challenge this very powerful trend. On the question of history of globalization, no doubt we have had internationalization of capital for a very long time, and indeed international trade is almost as old as human history, but globalization as it is now is indeed new, not only in terms of globalization of production with its industrialization and de-industrialization effects, but also globalization of finance which is no more primarily linked to trade and investment. Also, now we have globalization of communication and so on. All these have indeed created major qualitative changes to the functioning of capital and societies at the global level, and it is better to differentiate between today's globalization and earlier internationalizations.

AE: I think you are right about that. But what I am saying is that this system cannot continue like this, and we see the decline of empires. We see the rise of China and decline of the USA and Europe. I think the solution to the present crisis is global socialist institutions. It will not come about by itself and needs massive movements at the national and international levels. The problem, however, is that in the same manner that working class activism has always been weakest at the international level, global activism today is also the weak. Well, we can go to Spain and support a rally of Podemos, but it cannot solve the problems we are facing. Most people are active in the places they live, but I do think that there is a major change in consciousness. For example, in Sweden, many people in the Left have been following the election campaigns of Corbyn in Britain or Sanders in the USA. They know about Syriza or Podemos. They get ideas, and they learn to talk about other movements. I think culturally globalization has contributed to better understanding and consciousness.

Sam Gindin

SG: Before answering this question, I want to raise a point that is related to internationalization, focusing on labor. In the early 70s when I first came to the union, unions were very interested in globalization and in forming international unions to match the global trend in business. The problem with this, however, was that this direction was essentially extending the model of business unionism internationally. That is, in light of the state moving toward neo-liberalism, austerity, and free trade, the real question had become how to politicize workers and take on the state, and to do this, we needed not so much to look abroad as to develop solidarity across unions *in each of our own countries*. With unions not even cooperating nationally—for example, autoworkers competing with steel workers for members or public sector workers isolated from private sector workers—how could we expect any serious solidarity with Mexican workers?

The United Automobile Workers (UAW) was concerned to raise wages at Volkswagen (VW) and General Motors (GM) in Mexico so they wouldn't undermine US and Canadian workers, but the problem was that the workers of VW and GM plants in Mexico were already relatively well paid compared to *other* Mexican workers and the key question was solidarity within the Mexican working class.

On a visit to the VW plant in Pueblo in the 80s, we passed a slum of one to two million people for whom an auto job was an impossible dream. At the Pueblo plant, workers were working at a pace completely unimaginable to autoworkers in the USA or Canada. If they had worked at a slower and more reasonable pace, at least some of the slum dwellers could have entered the world of auto wages. We also noticed that the workers were remarkably young and in response to raising this, a manger told us that nobody older than 30 could possibly stand the pace and were let go. So to re-emphasize my point, the question was not how to raise the wages of Mexican autoworkers and isolate them even further from others but how they might create solidarity with other workers and the people in the slums. "International unionism" was in this context fragmenting the Mexican working class rather than bringing it together.

After that long detour, let me return to the question of socialism in one country. We cannot *complete* any revolution in one country alone. A revolution might be achieved and make gains, but it will necessarily be limited if confined to one country. Since we cannot just wait for this to fortuitously happen everywhere at the same time—that would be to essentially give up on social change—we can only do what we can wherever we are and cope with the limits. We can of course include an internationalist sensibility in our struggles, engaging in solidarity where possible, but our primary responsibility is to make whatever changes we can at home. Internationalizing the struggle begins at home. If, for example, we are fighting for change in Canada, we must assume that there are also other people who are simultaneously struggling elsewhere, and perhaps our struggles, like theirs, will inspire others or create more space for still others to expand their struggle. When we don't engage in struggle but accommodate to the pressures we face, the lower standards we accept undermine others struggling elsewhere. In the case of Greece, Syriza may form a government soon and have to confront hostile external pressures over and above internal ones. Sustaining the new government and progressive direction will need the support of movements in Europe, especially in Germany, even if it is just to limit what pressures these states place on Greece. The tragedy is not simply that such solidarity is not there but that the kinds of movements that might carry out such solidarity have not been built *within each of the European countries.*

SR: No doubt socialism should start somewhere and you cannot just wait for socialism to fall from the sky. But the problem is that if you do not have the right condition at the global level, it is impossible for any country nowadays to follow a socialist policy. Because of the predominance of global capital and its international organizations, as soon as a progressive government in a country decides to follow socialist policies, improving work conditions, higher wages, higher taxes, and so on, it will face capital flight, losing credit rating and other problems. I argue that since we are in a long haul in capitalism, we can push for progressive reforms with the aim of moving closer to socialism, but cannot follow socialist policies immediately.

SG: What you say has a number of implications. One, however, is that any government that comes to power committed to following a socialist path would have to be *more* rather than less radical. It would have to be prepared to develop a base for carrying out certain structural changes like imposing limits on the outflow of capital and controlling the allocation of the surplus by nationalizing the banking system. This is not to deny the reality of limits and the necessity of certain compromises; the question is how to do it in a way that retains your base and direction. This means constant information, education, and discussion of what compromises are happening and why. There is a great difference between a government telling the people who voted for it that there is nothing to do and selling austerity, and one that openly and honestly speaks to limits and addresses sacrifices that are part of transforming society as opposed to reinforcing the status quo. Central to raising class-consciousness is preparing our base for how difficult the project of moving to socialism will be and avoiding promises of immediate and sustained increases in material standards. Not an easy task.

SR: You are right, and this is exactly what I would like to emphasize that moving directly toward a socialist policy in a single country is not possible.

SG: These are difficult questions, especially for a small country like Greece that is not self-sufficient and has limited resources. If Syriza wins, the pressures will be great and certain sacrifices will be necessary. Part of the reason Syriza has had so much support is that people have already suffered so much from austerity, raising the possibility of them suffering *more* in the course of radical change may cost Syriza some support. I don't know of an option other than to address this honestly, use the power of the state to make it possible to see some concrete gains as corruption is overcome, tax avoidance eased, inequality addressed and commitments made to equality of sacrifice, and people are won over to the argument that previous sacrifices changed nothing and just led to more of the same, while now any sacrifices will be part of transforming society to build something better.

SR: It all depends on the situation of the country and the extent and depth of left movement. If you have really huge mass base support for your policies, and as you say, if the country has the resources, you can implement progressive policies incrementally. But even in such cases, you are faced with serious limitations, so far as international capital is so powerful, and the labor and left movements are weak at the global level.

SG: That is why the question of organization to build and maintain your base is so fundamental. But we should not assume that because of these limits, nothing can be done. If a mass class-conscious base has been built, there are possibilities of standing firm in confronting capital. Corporations might be played off against each other; in favorable circumstances, finance capital might be divided from manufacturers; past debts can be rejected (as, e.g., South Africa should have done but didn't with the apartheid debt when world opinion was sympathetic to the end of apartheid).

SR: Well, unfortunately, I don't think either case is a possibility now. In terms of GM and other MNCs in Canada, they can take the government to national and international courts if their licensing agreements are violated. And in the case of Greece default, it will not be able to exports even its feta cheese, and its ships will be confiscated in any harbor they land.

SG: These are conjunctural questions related to how strong we are at the time, what is happening elsewhere, the legitimacy of particular sections of capital and capital's own divisions, and so on. I don't want to underestimate these, but we must also refuse to let this paralyze us. You are quite right that a default might have led to all kinds of new problems, but these are risks that may be necessary to carry out real change and the key is preparing the base for such difficulties, not pretending they don't exist.

Peter Hudis

PH: First, the last point is easy to answer, and the answer is no. Socialism in one country has never been possible or conceivable, and that is even more true today than ever before. But that does not stop some people from wrongly speaking or claiming to have socialism in their country, like in Venezuela or Cuba. We should be honest and call things what they are, and not sow illusions. Some people have criticized Syriza in Greece for not promoting an explicitly socialist program. It is true that they don't have a socialist program, but this may reflect at least an implicit understanding that you cannot create socialism in one country. As matter of fact, you cannot create anti-austerity in one country.

What globalization means is that with a greatly integrated capitalist economy on a global scale, the possibilities of a socialist revolution or any kind of revolution become much more difficult in the immediate period. In today's globalized world, every worker is placed in a position of competition with every other worker. With the elimination of protectionism, US workers are competing with workers in China and elsewhere for who can produce more at the lowest wages. This creates tremendous problems and afflictions in terms of inequality and also in the breaking down of social solidarity. So in one sense, globalization has undermined the possibilities of revolutionary transformation. On a deeper level, however, there is something else, a counter current going on, and that is that it has never been easier for people involved in liberation struggles around the world to get in contact with each other, learn from each other, and adopt alternative means of struggle based on such intercommunication. For this, we can thank the globalization of capital and the globalization of technology and culture. We have a striking illustration of this with the Arab Spring, the Maidan movement in Ukraine, and the Occupy Movement, all of which occurred more or less at the same time and possessed striking similarities. Nobody planned it, nobody spelled it out theoretically ahead of time, and nobody envisioned it before it happened. But you notice that all these movements in different ways are all about reclaiming public space as a place for dialogue and political activism, by creating a forum for a discussion of radical ideas. That indicates while globalization initially creates greater obstacles to revolutionary transformation, on a deeper level, and under the surface, it also produces possibilities that run in the opposite direction. So we have to examine closely these contrary characteristics of globalization.

The only other thing I want to say here is that we should be careful talking about globalization and internationalization of all cycles of social capital. Not all cycles of social capital are yet globalized and internationalized. There are significant segments of capital that remain under national protection. Globalization is a process and tendency, it is not an accomplished result and there are many indications that there might be a reversal of aspects of globalization in light of the events of the past several years. If Russia pulls out of its connections with the rest of the world economy, or if it is followed in some respects by China or other places, the situation can dramatically change. Globalization in some respects is a rather fragile process. Also, we don't have a transnational capitalist class; we still have national bourgeoisies with national interests. We have an increasing globalized world but by no means a "flat world" as Friedman says, and we should not adopt the left-wing version or conception of a flat world.

SR: My understanding of the internationalization of all cycles of social capital is that all cycles of money, productive and commercial capital, have moved beyond national economies, and this does not necessarily mean that all categories of capital are internationalized. I emphasize big capital and not the medium and small capital that to different degrees have remained in the confines of their national boundaries, although heavily affected by the big international capital, mainly the so-called multinational corporations. No doubt, even big corporations are reliant on their national base and the support of their national state, but much of their surplus value is generated globally. Also, I would like to add that in sharp contrast to Friedman's "flat" world, there is no "global plain field", and the global field is dominated very unequally by the MNCs.

PH: I see your point, but we have to keep in mind that the national bourgeoisie never directly or completely realized the bulk of the surplus value that it extracted solely from its national confines. I give you an example. Once a student of mine referred to what the Belgians did in Congo in the 1800s and early 1900s and thought this contradicted or refuted Rosa Luxemburg's notion that imperial domination is greatly profitable for capitalism, since Belgium did not become the wealthiest country in Europe even though the Belgian national bourgeoisie ran up profit rates of 700 percent through its rape of the Congo. But the bourgeoisie of any country never realizes the entirety of the surplus value that it extracts from a given locale. The value that it extracts in a given local enters the three circuits of capital that Marx discusses in Volume 2 of *Capital* and is realized on the level of the world market. The value that the Belgians extracted from the Congo was invested throughout Western Europe and much of the world; the process of the realization of surplus value has never been directed by national entities. No individual capitalist realizes the entirety of the value of the surplus value that results from his or her actions in a given locale. But no, I do not agree that "all" cycles of productive and commercial capital have moved beyond national economies. Some have, some haven't; this is a matter that calls for specific, concrete, empirical analysis, not over-generalization.

Ursula Huws

SR: In responding to this question, I would like to ask if you link your response to what you have discussed in one of your books about the changing relationship between capital and labor: the four periods after the Second World War; 1945–1973, the so-called post war Keynesian welfare state; mid-70s oil crisis to the end of 80s; then 90s fall of Soviet system to mid-2000; and finally the present period since mid-2008. In all these periods, you explain how capital became stronger and labor weaker, and how the nature of work transformed.

UH: I am working on the hypothesis that there is an emerging new paradigm which even goes beyond those changes. But in the same manner that two things can work together to create a downward spiral, I think it might be possible to turn that logic on its head and come up with a more optimistic scenario, based on exploiting the clear contradictions that are present in the way that labor is now organized globally. Labor now is interconnected in an increasingly

complex way through elaborate global value chains. Workers do have common interests, and if they discover these common interests, they can take solidarity actions and they can support each other; they can in principle organize internationally. It is possible to organize along these value chains that give them a much greater power than whatever they have had in the past. But you cannot just do that by an act of will because workers live in specific territories with specific characteristics, and in those capacities, they have to organize locally. If you cannot organize locally, how can you organize at national and international levels? You organize with your neighbors against planning developments of the neighborhood, or you organize with other parents to have a safe school system and road crossing. People transfer their experience of organizing from one arena to another. If you are involved in community organizing, it is noticeable that if someone pops up with a good idea and suggestion, you can bet that he or she has been a shop steward in a factory, and vice versa. People who have political experience transfer that experience to other arenas. But there are many workers in different territories that have no rights, and they are not able to participate in such organized activities and international links. So we need to have a double-front approach. People organize where they are and where their strengths are, and then use their strength to reach out to others and help them organize. Usually, there are some abstract debates, as on what basis we should organize: Should workers be organized on the basis of crafts, or sectors, or companies, or region? As if we need to choose one or the other. This is rubbish. In whatever way the people want to organize, we should support them. It is the fact of organization that matters, not its specific form (although of course each form creates specific patterns of inclusion and exclusion that have to be addressed, case by case).
SR: This support should be within limits!
UH: Of course within limits, we have to recognize that people' propensity to organize is not necessarily progressive; they can also organize lynch mobs! If there is a factory that is successfully organized on the basis of company, we should support it, if there is another factory organized on a different basis, you work with them. I don't know whether you have heard of the Citizen London Campaign. This was a very interesting example of social unionism. It started with the demand of getting a living wage for very low-paid workers—cleaners, and mostly

migrant workers. Several trade unions got involved in it. What they did was very much against the traditional way unions were involved in it. They came to this decision that they should go wherever these people go. They went to mosques, to Polish churches, Catholic churches, Orthodox churches, Hindu temples, and community meetings. Wherever people came together, they went to spread their message. They formed a very broad coalition. Not around revolutionary ideas, but around what everybody could buy into, with a focus on wage demands and so on. They are now trying to take the campaign to the national level. This kind of approach which is not judgmental about what form of organization people should have is very important.

SR: Aside from opportunities, now we have additional obstacles for moving toward establishing socialism in one country. In addition to the growing powers of the multinational corporations and banks, all the major international financial organizations impose their neo-liberal policies, making it very hard for any government that wants to pursue a progressive policy.

UH: To start with the supra-national organizations, we see a real contradiction in the current phase of capitalism. In previous phases that you referred to earlier, nation states were reasonably strong vis-à-vis international capital, and most corporations had a clear national basis and were not as powerful and global as they are now. In those phases, to different degrees, nation states could exert some sort of control, and there were certain thing states could do vis-à-vis capital, like extracting taxes, breaking up monopolies, and implementing anti-trust laws. States did something to contain capital, but they can no longer do so. The terms of trade agreements are tipping the balance much more toward the corporations. Now we have effectively a series of global monopolies. So there is a regulatory vacuum, and a contradiction that is starting to come out. I don't know about North America, but in Europe, even the conservative Cameron government in the UK is trying to close down tax havens, because the behavior of global corporations is increasing out of control. Claude Serfati has written a brilliant article in a journal that I edit, *Work Organization, Labour and Globalization*, about how we cannot any longer distinguish industrial capital from financial capital because the industrial capitalists are also behaving like financial capitalists. They put their head offices in tax havens and behave like banks, they ship money around the world and avoid paying taxes, and they manage their affairs by shuffling money through the network of their subsidiary companies. That is why most of the largest corporations are not paying taxes. People are starting to see these contradictions and demand that states should do something about it. WTO is not doing that well, and that is why we are having so many extra bilateral trade agreements. WTO did a lot in the past in terms of forcing free movement of capital, but it did not do enough for capital. Capital is so greedy and needs to expand constantly so aggressively and on so fast. The contradictions are becoming more and more apparent. But there is a limit to what states can do to control it.

SR: It is true, and most of these governments to get reelected make sure that they do not antagonize these corporations as they rely on their support and money, and there is no mechanism to effectively control capital. That is why I believe any idea of socialism in one country is far more remote than the previous phases of capitalism. I would like to have your views on this matter and whether you think under present conditions socialism in one country could be a possibility.

UH: No, absolutely not, but aspiring toward socialism in one country produces relative advantages for the working class which help them to organize and feed into a kind of international organization. So it is necessary to struggle for it, even if you know you are never going to get it.

SR: You are absolutely right.

Michael Lebowitz

ML: Now, there are more opportunities as people in different parts of the world hear about different movements, about the common problems they have, and their common struggles. These are some characteristics that globalization has brought about. As for obstacles and difficulties, no doubt there are obstacles and there have always been difficulties for building socialism. There is problem of capital flight, brain drain, and so on. As for the possibility of socialism in one country, it depends what you mean by socialism. Do you mean the beginning, the inroads, or its full realization? As for inroads to socialism, of course it is possible. But for its full realization or what Chavez called the elementary triangle of socialism (social ownership of means of production, social production organized by workers, and satisfaction of communal needs), it is not possible because as long as we have enormous inequalities in the world, we cannot have a fully established socialist system. But we can start.

SR: I have no doubt that the process can and should start anywhere. Somewhere I think in your recent book you have a very interesting reference to a message Chavez had sent you through Marta Harnecker asking if, according to Meszaros, capitalism is an integrated organic system, then where can one start to change it. I add to this question, arguing not only capitalism is an integrated organic system, but also it is such an international and global system that makes the possibility of socialism in one country and its full realization exceedingly complicated. We have now international financial institutions like WTO, World Bank, IMF, and credit-rating agencies that regulate the dominance of capital at the global level and create serious problem for any progressive government that wants to implement pro-labor policies.

ML: Surely, this is the case. If Syriza had challenged the EU, the banks, and the IMF, that would have created problem for them, but at the same time, it would have stimulated Spain, Portugal, Ireland, and the peripheral countries of Europe. One country engaged in struggle could encourage others. But no doubt difficulties are there.

Leo Panitch

LP: This is something that troubles me very much. In one sense, one has to say that what Stalinism proved, after the failure of the German revolution that left the Soviet revolution all alone and encircled, was that socialism in one country was never possible. Today, where we have integrated global production, where we have such dependence on transnational finance, and many other features of global capitalism, I worry enormously about this, and what the costs would be for a people trying to carry through a socialist transformation. Take the case of Greece today, where Syriza once democratically elected to government found it impossible to carry through their promise to rescind the reactionary measures that have been taken to implement the memoranda of agreement imposed by the so-called troika of the EU, the European Central Bank (ECB), and IMF, in face of the danger is that Greece will be pushed out of the

Eurozone and even the EU, which would mean the Greek people would suffer even more. They would be subject to a massive inflation if they have to resort to go back to the Drachma and printing and distributing it to an enormous extent, they wouldn't be able to get imports of the kind that they desperately need, and many other economic problems. I said this publicly in Greece before Syriza's election, even though I was worried that the Right would use it against Syriza. On the other hand, should one endorse the appalling austerity that has been imposed on them? The real problem is that there needs to be a shift in the balance of forces in the state of northern Europe so that there is pressure on their governments to give the Syriza government breathing room, including allowing for capital controls and import controls. As this suggests, while I don't think socialism in one country is possible, I do think economic development at the national level is necessary.

SR: No doubt a radical progressive party should not surrender to capital, but at the same time, there are tough realities that socialists have to cope with them. In a recent panel on the Left, dealing with Syriza and Quebec Solidaire, and in response to a question on structural reform, I heard you saying that Quebec Solidaire and Syriza could not go for a full structural transformation now, because there are not the conditions for that at present. I compare this responsible position to a recent interview of Alan Woods about Syriza, criticizing that the closer Syriza gets to power the less radical it becomes, and recommending that the party has to get rid of the whole capitalist system and fight with the troika. It is easy to give radical slogans, but if Greece defaults on its debt, it would not be able to even export, and any Greek ship on foreign harbors can be confiscated.

LP: Of course we can't be purely voluntarist, and could not be relevant if we were. The main reason why one can't just offer such condemnations of Syriza or exhortations to Syriza to do such things is that the majority of people who were voting for them don't want to leave Europe and the party wouldn't have this percentage of the vote if they had said we want to pull out of euro. That said, the objective is indeed to take capital away from capital, and to take the Greek banking system and turn it into a public utility that is part of a democratic economic planning system. Now the question is how to keep that objective in mind, while understanding that the balance of forces does not allow you to do this yet. The danger is, and I think we have to be very honest about this, that when people get elected and they realize the balance of forces is against them, they then rationalize why they don't go the whole way and they demobilize people against the very goal of socialism. This has been the case with social democratic parties. I think it's very important that elected representatives continue to articulate socialist objectives. But I understand that by even doing so, they will be penalized for by the forces protecting the status quo. There are no easy options.

Catherine Samary

CS: I want to stress for the Greek and Spanish experience: there is a need for a European movement. There is a big debate among revolutionary currents in Europe right now. Some currents, including the organization I am involved with in France, argue that if we consider (and we all agree on that) that the EU is an anti-democratic and a bourgeois project, then we have to push for leaving it. This conclusion is not clear enough and convincing to me. Another view is that we need to resist and get rid of the existing treaties, which means a confrontation with the existing Union. There is a need to struggle for other treaties and institutions and another policy. It can be argued that the refusal of European policies imposed on Greece or Spain raises common issues for all other European countries. A progressive EU, based on the defense of social and democratic rights and of the environment— and not on market competition, dictatorship of non-elected bodies, and social austerity—could not only be of general interest to European people but also would challenge the US dominance. But the question is how to go in that direction?

We have to fight at the national and the transnational levels and within and outside the EU—toward a break with the existing institutions, providing alternatives to many aspects including the Troikas (European Commission, Central Bank, and IMF), the austerity Pacts, and work toward a new constitutional process and European democratic procedures. There is a need for counter institutions, and for European trade unions.

At the international level, the emergence of BRICS (Brezil, Russia, India, China, and South Africa) concretizes the end of an imperialist hegemonic "pole" and offers margin of alternative financing that challenge the IMF and World Bank. But as it stands now, this block represents neither a progressive alternative nor a consistent block.

Going back to the question of Socialism in one country, it is less possible as ever. But this does not mean that we should stop national resistance and waiting for others. We have to take into account the balance of forces, and this does not reduce the necessity of the fighting at national level, looking for national victories that could be a stimulant to fights elsewhere. In any case, we must prepare in advance, and during each phase of struggle, fight for platforms for collective international movement because any victory at a national level will be very fragile. One aspect of this is to confront the WTO, and also bilateral treaties that aim at strengthening the position of international capital. We also need to fight against the use of the debt issue by international capital and dominant actors to impose their rules: so we should support international networks such as CATDM (Committee for the Abolition of Third World Debts) and also fight for transformations of the functioning of the UN institutions (World Health Organization, UNESCO, etc.), and fight against the power of those who are instrumental in imposing generalized market competition and free finance, and against NATO and its "civilized" wars.

SR: No doubt all these international institutions need to be reformed or transformed, and some abolished, but the main issue is who would do it and how.

CHAPTER 6

Which Socialism?

In your view, what are the main characteristics and features of the "first phase" of post-capitalist society, socialism, and how are they different from what was experienced in the Soviet Union or China?

Gilbert Achcar

GA: This issue of two phases is also badly formulated. We must look at it differently. There is the utopia, which is the guiding principle, on one hand, and the actual and concrete program on the other. What Marx called "first phase", or socialism, is actually the concrete program, and what he called "higher phase", or communism, is the utopia, a guiding principle that inspires ongoing actual measures, but may need centuries to bring about in its full.

Let us recapitulate: the immediate goal of the socialist movement is to build counter-hegemony, to win the support of the popular majority and involve it in the political process. Winning this support is achieved by fighting for the betterment of the people's conditions of living and working. Then comes the question of the seizure of power and transformation of the state. You then enter in the long gradual process of transforming the economy, the rhythms of which depend on the national and international balance of forces. The better these conditions get, the more it will be possible to progress toward an economy free of private profit.

Socialization should be a gradual process. Even when banks are nationalized, you still need to keep the market as a regulator in conjunction with planning. The idea that planning can wholly substitute the market and that all the economy should be nationalized and centralized has become a bureaucratic nightmare. When you think of socialism as the free association of producers, you need forms of autonomous decisions of economic units, which would be workers collectives.

SR: While socialization and removal of private capital are goals, as you mentioned, these should be done gradually. The nationalization of every aspect of economic activities, including barbershops and taxi drivers, is meaningless. Do you envisage that in the first phase, while socialist policies are incrementally pursued, aspects of economy continue on market and capitalist principles?

GA: The goal is to get rid of an economy based on the pursuit of profit and the exploitation of labor, but as I mentioned earlier, this is a gradual and long process. This historical transition can take decades, if not centuries. Think of what we call the English Revolution or the French Revolution, which were much less radical in terms of transformation of society compared to a socialist transformation: you will then be able to envisage how protracted and complex this latter process can be. The bourgeois "great transformation" replaced one ruling class with another one that already possessed means of government and management. But for the working class and the socialist transformation, this is much less the case. That is why, as I emphasized earlier, in the revolutionary process, and before even the seizure of power, it is important not only to win the support of the popular majority, but also to attract the support of government personnel, in the bureaucracy and the armed forces.

SR: In the Introduction, I argue that there are no walls between the so-called phases of social development, and in the same manner that elements of the old system persist in the new, elements of the new system germinate in the old. That is why I talk of a phase during the capitalist era (Marx's phases deal with the post-capitalist era), a "preparatory phase" of transition from capitalism, during which efforts are made by socialists to implement socialist-oriented and social-democratic policies.

GA: This idea we can also find in Engels, when he says that the seeds of the future society build up already under capitalism. Think of the slogan of "from each according to their ability, to each according to their needs": anyone can see that in the major capitalist societies, there are already social security systems whereby huge numbers of people get subsidies from the state that are not based on their work, but on their individual and/or familial needs.

Aijaz Ahmad

AA: As mentioned earlier, I do not think of transition to socialism as a stage, or revolution as an event or a series of event, and think of all these as historical processes which have moments of condensation, which we may provisionary call revolution. However, I think there is a question of concrete issues, starting from the world as it exists. There are very particular issues like privatizations and financializations, and we have to build a movement against these and re-socialization, differentiating between nationalization and socialization. When we reflect upon the experiences of Russia and China, one important issue is this distinction. If all private property is abolished and turned into state property, then you have a collective capitalist, exploiting everybody, determining the condition of labor for everyone. You will get a monstrosity. What are the forms of transitions, there may be forms of private property whose functioning could be socialized much more than the state was socialized in Soviet Union, because that has to do with the condition of production. We have to rethink issues of socialization, political power, how political power is constructed; what would be the forms of social and political power, what would be the patterns of ownership, what would be the ideological structures, what would be modes of incorporating distinct revolutionary subjects in a united revolutionary project, and so on.

SR: Here, I would like if you elaborate on some specific issues on this process of transition, that I believe it goes through certain steps, whether we call if phase or not. For example, do you think that in the very early moments of post-capitalist society, abstract labor, wage labor could be eliminated?

AA: Transitions from one mode of production to another occur at a glacial pace. Capitalism is about 500 years old and is still growing. I can only hope that humanity gets to a post-capitalist society in half as long. These are not acts of will that you sit and decide upon such things as the value-form, and so on. That is why we have to start with what exists. How to rethink and how to start organizing around specific features of actually existing capitalism. Those quantitative changes will ultimately become qualitative. What happened in the past, what makes us unhappy about the experiences of the past in Soviet Union or China is that a break was made in forms of power at the highest level and they assumed that if you take power at the level of state, then you can make a quick transition to socialism. It was also assumed that capitalism was going to die soon. Neither of these assumptions proved to be correct. That is why I emphasize the question of processes, in which a sudden break may come, and you will learn. Every failure is a moment to learn. Let us take the case of Syriza. They now know that a peripheral country in Europe cannot move to socialism by itself. It is not the question of the subjective failure of this or that individual or organization. People of Greece did not want austerity, but at the same time, they did not want to leave the EU or the Eurozone. How can you educate a whole mass of people into the fact that the two things they want are irreconcilable? This deadlock in Greece has led to a great distortion in Portugal and in Spain. You are going to start all over again. This particular phase is also over, and yet, it has exacerbated the crisis of the Eurozone. Ten years from now, will there be a Eurozone or not? All these breaks, small or big, come and we learn from them.

SR: On the issue of socialization, while you rightly differentiate between socialization and nationalization, isn't it the case that a major component of any socialization involves some sort of state ownership and control? The anarchists, at least majority of them, would answer no to any state involvement and talk of self-management, direct democracy, and so on.

AA: Absolutely, state is the only political form modernity has. Any dissolution of the state is a post-socialist fact, not a starting point of building socialism. That extreme form of anarchism is just naïve.

Rob Albriton

RA: First of all, I have to say that I feel uncomfortable with the language of first phase and second phase because it is more a kind of flow. This question gets into the area that I am now doing research on and so my thoughts are not well developed yet. I feel that some Marxists think that markets are necessarily capitalist and I don't believe that. Obviously capitalist markets have many features that in a socialist society you want to get rid of. You certainly need to have some way of coming up with major decisions about what is going to be produced, how it is going to be produced, how it is going to be distributed, and so on. But you need to have markets. These markets would be organized not to maximize profits, but to advance human and environmental flourishing. Capitalist markets would become socialist markets as they would become increasingly constrained and shaped to advance the flourishing of society as a whole. Part of changing the whole economic and financial system is developing ways of democratic decision making, and in this case, the decision about what to do with total social surplus is made democratically. Of course, these are very large and important issues that ultimately need to be worked out at least to some extent through trial and error.

SR: So, in your view, there will be differentiated compensation in terms of wages, achievements, and competition.

RA: Yes, but eventually these differentials would be minimized. For example, I would aim toward a society in which the difference between the highest income and the lowest would not be very great, may be three to one or four to one. Efforts also should be made to reduce the sharp division between mental and manual labor characteristic of capitalism.

SR: My main question here relates to the notion that under socialism in the early periods should we end all differentiated inequalities, inequities, and should everything be decided through collective or state planning rather than market mechanisms of supply and demand?

RA: On the one hand, I think what you need is a certain mix of planning and market and you certainly want to get away from many kinds of attributes of capitalist markets. On the other hand, aspects of markets developed under capitalism can be useful in a socialist context, but they would no longer be capitalist markets. I am not advocating "market socialism". I am saying we qualitatively change markets to be a socialist markets.

Kevin Anderson

KA: Leaving aside horrifically negative examples like Pol Pot's Cambodia or North Korea, what these revolutionaries wanted and talked about was state control of the economy that would benefit the workers with social reforms and social services, at least from 1918–1919 onwards. But even in the USSR, in Lenin's time workers still worked for wages, and there was a very strong state, partly because they had to fight civil wars or foreign invaders. In any case, it turned out quite differently from what Marx had talked about. As you know, in the *Critique of the Gotha Program*, even in the first phase of communism, there are some kind of time chits that the working people receive, and thus the inequality among different occupations is abolished. But rather than equalizing wages, wages are supposed to be abolished altogether. Everyone who contributes some labor to society gets remuneration. Marx talks of the differing intensity of work, but that is the only kind of distinction. (The best recent discussion of these issues can be found in the writings of Peter Hudis.) Here, the issue is the overcoming of huge status and class differences that go back way before capitalism, like, for example, that between medical doctors and janitors. Both a surgeon and a cleaner who goes through sewage pipes, carry out intense work that is very exacting. Both provide crucial services to society. There is a huge status difference here and its defenders say the doctor preserves life, but also you endanger life without a good sewage system.

None of even the best examples of societies trying to overcome the rule of capital, including the Paris Commune or the early Russian Revolution, came very close to what was sketched by Marx in *Critique of the Gotha Program* as the "first phase" of communism, let alone the higher phase which is based on each according to her/his needs.

SR: No doubt there is a difference between what Marx said about post-capitalist phases and what Lenin and others formulated later. Marx wanted to end abstract labor even in the first phase, but maybe Lenin and German social democrats were more practical than Marx in this regard—and indeed it is extremely utopian to assume that any socialist transformation would be able to immediately equalize wages, let alone abolish the wage system altogether. In your example, a surgeon goes through at least over 20 years of education and learning as opposed to a janitor. This fact by no means should undermine the significance of a janitors work, and a sort of progressive job classification scheme can take into account the difficulties of a janitor's work or hazardous environment of an occupation and accordingly determine the differentiated remuneration. I believe we are very far from even a wage-based post-capitalist first phase. That is why I believe in a preparatory phase within capitalism to prepare for radical transformation.

KA: No doubt this is a very tricky issue. Marx at one point was critically supporting Abraham Lincoln as a representative of the northern capitalist class against the southern slave owners. In the *Communist Manifesto*, he and Engels call for free public school systems and other measures that are simply a normal part of life in liberal democracies under capitalism today.

SR: You are absolutely right. Actually the 10 "measures" of the Manifesto are radical reforms.

KA: Marx's final goal was obviously communism and he articulated this goal in many of his writings. How do these two link up together? We cannot just talk about refining the concept of socialism, and we have to engage in living struggles. For example, in the USA, there are two very important living struggles right now; one is "Black lives matter", that we see in schools, in neighborhoods, and streets. It is a mass movement and compared to the much larger anti-war movement over Iraq, it has had greater intensity. The second one demands raising the minimum wages to $15 an hour, with demonstrations in front of MacDonald's and places like that, with some success, as recently in a $15 minimum wage law passed in Los Angeles. We need to insert ourselves into those movements, try to engage discussions with them about what capitalism does to the working people. Obviously, I cannot say I am against a $15 minimum wage because I am against the wage system, but I can say this is necessary but insufficient.

Barbara Epstein

BE: There are two questions here: what I would like, and what will actually happen. I can envision the "first phase of post-capitalist society" as a form of social organization that is not yet quite socialism but that has nevertheless moved beyond the neoliberal version of capitalism. In such a society private property, including small and maybe medium sized businesses would still exist, but through taxation and other forms of redistribution the wealth gap that we now experience would be greatly reduced. The priority of the society would be the welfare of all, not private gain. Social planning would be extensive, and labor unions and other popular organizations would play a major role in it. The responsibilities, and power, of local governments would be enhanced. The fostering of individual growth, creativity, and dissent and the protection of human rights would be a priority. War would not be seen as a viable solution to international conflicts and military spending would be vastly reduced.

In the USA, or in Western Europe, a shift from neoliberal capitalism to a more egalitarian society, leading toward socialism, would require the strong support of the majority. It would have to be democratic and it would have to respect human rights, because otherwise it would lack the support that its continued existence would require.

Whether things will move in this direction is anyone's guess. If the problems of environmental degradation, the massive extinction of non-human species, and the exploding human population on the planet are not addressed effectively things could easily move in the opposite direction, with increased competition for declining resources and a widening division between those with access to resources and those without. The socialist left should pay more attention to the environmental crisis. If the environmental crisis and the loss of species are not reversed, it is difficult to imagine a positive future for human society.

Aron Etzler

AE: I think first of all we know very few people want to go back to the experience of Soviet Union or China. I can say that the Left in Sweden or Europe are set for a multi-party parliamentarian system. We see many deficiencies in the existing democracies, but no one sees a non-democratic or dictatorial system as an alternative. The idea that state should own as much as it did in the Soviet Union and operate through central planning system, is not believed to be the solution either. In Sweden, we have many public institutions but they are managed in a very different way. In Soviet Union, for example, factories also used to run child care system, but in Sweden, we manage it differently, through a public sector that is separated from production, paid for and enjoyed by all. A dual system, if you want. Ownership of means of production is very important aspect of a Marxian vision, but is not the only thing that defines socialism. In the past, it was the only thing that defined socialism. Taking over the factories were the line between socialism and capitalism was drawn. Here, the Left has wisely adopted a more loose understanding of a different system based on public institutions, public ownership of schools, hospitals, and what is traditionally called the public sector, setting the rule for the labor market, taxes, defining social welfare, and social rights. Many of these elements are intrinsically socialist, and what it lacks is having clear political leadership at the state levels, and to have economic projects that are socialist and put people's interests first and market functions second. The Russian Socialist and Marxist intellectual, Boris Kagarlitsky made two very valid statements about the differences between the Russian and Scandinavian socialists. He said that the Scandinavian socialists came much further than the Russians. Second, he argued that as society develops, the factory is not the only place or even may not be the most natural place for starting socialist development, pointing to a much broader range of public spheres other than factories. And you can see the same phenomenon in the ongoing Latin American socialist wave. As I am talking to you, I am thinking that we have to move away from ideas that were prevalent in 50 or 100 years ago about socialism, and what we should do is to have a much clearer view of what we need today.

SR: That is true. Also there are other questions that we need to resolve, when talking about socialism. For example, would there be wage differentiations, let alone wage work in the early stages, and so on.

AE: Yes, we need that, and we adhere to the motto "from each according to his/her abilities to his/her needs". People contribute differently to society and in the earlier stage, they should be compensated differently.

Sam Gindin

SG: I am hesitant and even uncomfortable with speculating on these "later" questions because of how far we are in Canada, the USA, and in most countries from even getting socialism on the agenda, never mind the details of what it will look like. Our movements include so few socialists and nothing close to a mass socialist organization is yet on the horizon. So I feel preoccupied with the question of how to simply get the socialist project *started*. In a very real sense, we are virtually starting over. Yet your question is valid because when fundamental societal alternatives are raised, most workers want to immediately know what socialism would look like.

A good part of the answer is, I think, philosophical. It involves asserting that capitalism cannot be the ultimate of what humans society can ever strive for, that we need to believe that something different *is* possible and that we have confidence that humans can, though struggles, experiments, and learning, figure out how to run our lives in a richer way. When I have tried to give people a detailed vision of what socialism would look like, a typical response is "but you're assuming that people will not be like they are today—greedy, individualistic, etc". That is, they see the contradiction of imaging another society with people as they are today. So the task is to convince people that humans can change, that in the process of struggling for socialism, popular consciousness can change in all kinds of ways. And, of course, even if we get beyond this point and people *can* imagine a different world, we still need to confront the lack of confidence in actually being able to get there, given the power of capitalism.

SR: This is true, but if you were to envisage the type of socialism you have in mind, the ideal one, even at the philosophical level, what would be its major features? Would everything be socialized? Competition exists or not? Wage differentiation, etc.?

SG: While we should be careful not to try to envisage a detailed plan about everything, I can say that finance would have to be socialized. We would need to replace finance as it currently exists with a democratic way of allocating capital according to social priorities. If we're not ready to end the power of finance, we're not serious about changing the world. Our natural resources should also be socialized, and strategically it is easier—though there will of course be problems—in taking over resources and find markets for them. This would also give us control over a significant part of society's surplus. The question of taking over manufacturing companies that are integrated would be something that would completely depend on how strong they are, their local content, and what technical capacities we have or can build at that time. Obviously, if all you have an assembly plant and you take it over, without access to research, design, and components, you may end up with very little of use. There are many other issues that go into imagining an alternative society, for example, the environment and the need for conversion of many polluting plants. Then you have the familiar issues of adequate social programs that aren't reduced to fitting into a market economy and public education geared to developing the widest range of student potentials. On the other hand, I'd assume that certain spaces for the private sector would remain. I wouldn't want to close down shops and restaurants on Bloor Street or Queen Street (in Toronto), for example, but we would need to have standards for health, safety, minimum wages, and working conditions.

Let me also raise the issue of taxes as an immediate issue. There is a need for a fair tax system and that especially includes going beyond thinking we can finance everything by soaking the rich and avoiding the question of general taxation. We've got to tell people, as part of the kind of cultural change socialists believe in, that if you want a particular kind of society, it will mean higher taxes *and it will be worth it*. Another issue that needs emphasizing is that of individual consumerism and reassessing what we consider important in life. And finally—since my answer here is getting rather long—we must, all think deeply about what it means to "transform the state" so that democracy isn't reduced to periodic voting but includes imaging the kind of state that is adapting and developing structures through which popular capacities to participate in decisions about their lives are constantly strengthened.

Peter Hudis

PH: First of all, it is important to underline that Marx never made a distinction of socialism and communism, and there is no notion that a socialist phase precedes a communist phase. In the *Critique of the Gotha Program*, he explicitly talks of the "first" phase and "final" phase of communist society, and he does not make a distinction between socialism and communism.

SR: You are right, it was Lenin and others who made this distinction.

PH: Well, Lenin is a different story. Of course, I should add that if Marx says something it does not mean that he is necessarily right. We are not Biblical scholars! But given who Marx was, we have to take seriously why he does or does not make a certain distinction. This is a very important point, because a conceptual slippage occurs when we assume that a socialist society is followed by a communist society. I believe this is one of the biggest mistakes that the radical movements have made and it got them into lots of trouble. It was not just Lenin who made this distinction between socialist and communist "societies"; some of the German Social Democrats made this distinction before Lenin wrote his *State and Revolution*. He was misreading and misrepresenting Marx in claiming that there is a distinction between a socialist and communist society.

Now, it is important to understand why Marx talks about the first phase of a socialist/communist society in terms of the abolition of value production. The Abolition of value means there would be no dual character of labor, no division between concrete and abstract labor; there will be no alienated labor; labor will not take a value-form embodied in products that have independent exchange value, and human relations would not be governed by relations between things, either as mediated by the market or the state. According to Marx, all of this will cease to exist not only in the higher phase of communism, but also in the lower phase. The main argument I make in my book is that Marx theorized a much more radical break between capitalism and the most initial phase of socialism/communism than Marxists after him have appreciated. In his discussion of the lower phase, Marx already talks about indirect social labor being replaced by direct social labor as the governing medium of social interrelationships. Indirect social labor is what we have under capitalism, where relationships between workers and their products of labor are established through an indirect medium, in our case, exchange value, money or a value-form of mediation. Already in the initial phase, Marx says that this no longer applies and we now have communal associations that directly organize production and distribution according to the needs and abilities of the freely-associated members. There is no value-form of mediation in socialism or communism. He even goes so far as saying that in this initial phase of communism, there is no exchange of products, but instead an exchange of activities, because there will be no abstract labor—and hence, no exchange value, since abstract labor is the substance of value.

So why does he speak of an initial phase of communism at all? It is because he is a realist. Even though he has such a radical and visionary conception of a break between capitalism and the initial phase of communism, he understands that you cannot immediately reach a phase in which social relations are not based on a quid pro quo. By quid pro quo, I mean that you give something to society in order to get back something else in return, in some form of equivalent. In the higher phase of communism, there is no such quid pro quo; there is no longer any need for a social equivalent. But that is not going to be able to emerge shortly after the revolution or immediately upon the emergence of a communist society. Those societies would still be marred by the birthmarks of capitalism; the old society will be still attached to us in some, however limited, way, and we will not have progressed economically, culturally, and intellectually to be able to yet practice "from each according to his abilities to each according to his needs". Still, in this lower phase, none of the fundamental principles of capitalism any longer exist. However, what does exist in the initial or lower phase of communism—BUT NOT IN ANY SORT OF CAPITALISTIC FORM—is the notion that I should get from society an equivalent of what I put into it. Marx calls this a bourgeois right—I give to the extent that I get. Marx is realistic to know that a quid pro quo would still exist, so he outlines a different form of remuneration based upon a very concrete equivalent, not a social average; the equivalent is simply quantums of actual labor time. This means: each member of the community obtains a given quantum of goods and services that corresponds to the actual amount of labor time that the member gives to the community. Please note that the "equivalent" here, if it is even proper to use such a term, is not an abstract average; it has nothing to do with socially necessary labor time. Remuneration is instead based on actual labor time, which is totally different than abstract universal labor time.

My main point is that the biggest problem of state-capitalist societies that called themselves socialist, and virtually of all Marxists with a very few exceptions, is that they assumed that there should be a transitional society between capitalism and communism in which wage labor still operates, with the difference being that wage labor is controlled by a state plan instead of the market. The notion that a state plan using wage labor can produce a movement toward a communist society is a myth. If you have value production, it does not matter how good intentioned are the leaders of revolutions—that society will regress to "normal" free-market capitalism—sooner or later. We have vivid proof of this from every single so-called socialist society or regime that has ever come to power

SR: Here, of course, we have a big problem, and my question of how we can move toward socialism becomes far more complicated.

I have no argument with your very accurate depiction of Marx's views of the first phase, but I find the original idea too idealistic and utopian. You rightly said we are not Biblical scholars and do not need to agree with whatever Marx has said. I believe, not considering a period of transition would mean expecting a jump from one stage to another. Maybe the reason why German Social Democrats, Bolsheviks and others opted for a separate transition period—putting aside their mistakes—was because the practical realities necessitated preparing for such major economic, social, and cultural changes. I even believe that we need an additional preparatory phase within the capitalist system to prepare for a conscious majority to fight for a post-capitalist society.

PH: Well this is a difficult question. You call it jumping, but I would use a different word. Marx does talk of a transition to communism, but he says that the transitional society to socialism is capitalism. Capitalism is a transitional form that, he thinks, leads to a communist future. The material conditions prepare us for these non-capitalistic forms through a revolutionary process. So it is a jump, but it is not a jump into the dark. The leap to a new society utilizes elements within existing society in such a way as to transform it in a direction contrary to the value-form of mediation. That is the question that I am going to discuss in more detail in a follow-through to my Marx book. What are the actual material conditions within capitalism today that can be utilized to turn a revolutionary process against the value-form of mediation, so that a radical breach between capitalism and a new society can be effectuated as soon as possible? That is the key question. If we do not answer this, nothing prevents a revolution that does occur from regressing back to the old society. Capitalism is a very powerful system, ideologically as well as economically. In the same manner that a little bit of poison destroys the entire well, a little bit of value production destroys an entire society. If you do not eliminate the foundation of value production, then that society will become increasingly capitalistic, even if you name it socialism, even if you give it any name you want.

So how can society be fundamentally transformed? First of all, it needs a transformation of the labor process. We have a hierarchical system of social domination in which people are governed by socially necessary labor time. We are dictated by time as an abstract universal measure that we have no way of determining, and it determines us. The real thing that dominates us in capitalist society is not the capitalist. We are subjected most of all to the domination of a certain modality of time, abstract universal labor time. This abstract form of time, governs what is produced, how fast it is produced, how it is produced, when it is produced. It is based on a globalized social average determined by the law of value. If we can break from this domination of abstract universal labor time, then we can turn society away from value production. This means there has to be a different modality of work, a different kind of labor process in which producers have control over their enterprises, effectuate democratic control over the work process, and experiment with different forms by which they meet their desires without having to listen to the dictates of the socially necessary labor time. This begins with the labor process, but of course, it extends throughout society beyond the labor process. It does not matter if 80 percent of the society or 8 percent of the society is proletariat. What matters is that the value-form of mediation that is rooted in the productive system is challenged in the revolution itself. If it is not challenged during an actual revolutionary process and is left for a later period when revolutionaries have come to state power, it will not work.

SR: I understand this if we are talking about the ideal final goal or the so-called higher phase, which I think of it as a utopia that we should constantly strive for without necessarily achieving all aspects of it. But if it is for the immediate aim of socialism, it is really hard for me to understand how one hour of any labor could be considered equal. As you well know, doing an hour of work in some jobs requires over 20 years of education and experience, while some other jobs, would need half an hour of job training. There are many other issues that unfortunately we may not have enough time to discuss in this short interview.

Ursula Huws

UH: This is difficult to answer. Last year, I wrote a piece about the "Social Division of Labour in Utopias"; I went through all utopias from Thomas More, Fourier, William Morris, and so on to see what division of labor they proposed. If we were historical materialists, we would understand that all things are dialectical and there is never going to be a perfect stage, and if you find a perfect stage, soon you discover that it will be imperfect. Because human society has contradictions, developments, and scientific discoveries will not stop, and each new development sets in motion new sets of contradictions. One of the problems with the written utopias is that they always look in terms of the existing technical division of labor, and they don't see beyond it. For example, in 70s, Ivan Illich and Andre Gorz and others, were saying that societies need X amount of production and if we rationalize production, we won't need to work more than six hours or four hours a week, and the rest of the time will be leisure. Oh bullshit! What is this leisure? Writing symphonies? Who is going to take care of children? Who is doing the cooking, and so on? In their analysis, the older divisions of unpaid household labor were completely rendered invisible. As soon as you introduce social reproduction into the picture, you get a completely different picture. There has been this terrible blind spot. In Stalinist Russia or China, social reproduction tasks were taken care of by the state, but not for the benefit of the children [or women], but for the benefit of the economy. They were designed in a very instrumental way. We have to take very seriously the whole social reproduction sphere and also to understand the way the technical division of labor is constantly changing. Under capitalism, new commodities are being introduced and affect the division of labor, both paid and unpaid. There is currently a movement that lots of people are talking about to promote peer-to-peer production, and it is sometimes imagined that this is how the transition to post-capitalist society can take place. They give the example of 3D printers, [assuming everyone would have one of them and produce what they want!]. Of course, they don't take into consideration that these printers need raw material, have environmental impact, have health hazards, and then there is the question of economy of scale, and so on. Imagine getting rid of economy of scale! They mean well, but they are so disconnected from the real world in every way, imaginatively, politically, and in terms of ever meeting workers. I find some of these arguments very amusing. In any case, in discussing post-capitalist society, the key concept is de-commodification. But we should be careful that de-commodification would not end up with a re-commodification. We have so many cases of this. For example, the land nationalization policy of Yugoslavia under Tito, and what eventually happened to it later in Croatia in the 90s, when the corrupt government sold much of the nationalized assets to foreign banks. Or, we see the same thing in the waves of public sector commodification and out-sourcing of government services.

Michael Lebowitz

SR: I am aware of your views and reading of *The Critique of the Gotha Programme* and your rejection of any concept of stage or phase of socialism, and your belief that socialists should move toward the final goal of communism from the outset. But would like to have further discussion of it here.

ML: Well, as you know, I completely reject the idea of the "first" or "lower" stage or phase of the post-capitalist society known as socialism and the "higher" stage known as communism. I think this reflected a particular interpretation of Marx's critique of the Gotha Program that Lenin made before the revolution and under the circumstances in which he was functioning. Bolsheviks were being attacked as utopian dreamers on the grounds of wanting to introduce into society the demand of "to each according to his needs" right from the outset. Lenin argued that we understand that we cannot do it immediately and there are two stages, and in the first stage, we are going it build up productive forces immensely in order to make the transition to the higher stage that is full of abundance and can satisfy everyone according to their needs. I understand why he did that. But the Bolsheviks and later communists in different parts of the world took this as the word of god. If we read the Critique carefully, we see that Marx was not making such a distinction, a distinction based on recognizing the right of inequality, where someone who is stronger or has more skills should earn more than someone who does not have these qualifications. He stresses that from the outset we have to provide for everyone's need.

SR: But in the Critique, Marx makes such distinction based on ability and needs in the two phases. We can argue that regardless of who has said this, such distinction perpetuates inequality even in the post-capitalist system. That is not my concern. My main concern is again how could it be possible for any socialist force to move from the outset toward satisfying everyone according to her/his needs. Doesn't this seem to be too idealistic?

ML: First of all, the concept of abundance is a flawed bourgeois concept. Marx said we don't talk about wealth and poverty like bourgeois economists, but we talk of rich human beings and poor human beings, and rich human needs and poor human needs. The rich human being has many capacities and many needs. In the *Grundrisse*, he talks about multi-sided people with all their capacities. If we start from the perspective of human development, the response to your question of "how" is by developing people's capacities. The argument that we need a certain level of development of productive forces, the position that Lenin developed, is a distortion of Marx's point. Let me give you an example. If we look at what Marx's had to say about the possibility of revolution in Russia in his response to Vera Zasulich, you will see Marx not as saying that the possibility is based on a foreign revolution. He explicitly says that the village commune, the *mir*, does not need to go through the inevitable process of capitalist production experienced in Western Europe, and he talks about the possibility of building on the basis of the commune. This was a perspective focusing on social relations first and only subsequently upon productive forces; and this was something that Lenin finally understood, when he wrote "On Cooperation". He said when we followed the New Economic Policy (NEP), we made a mistake by not focusing on cooperatives. If all of Soviet Union were based on cooperatives, he insisted, we would have been on the threshold of socialism right now. Therefore, we have to encourage people to move to cooperatives and we will provide them with the help they need. So this is the question of building social relations first, and it is precisely the perspective of the Critique of the Gotha Program.

SR: I have no problem at all focusing on relations of production, particularly that now much of the world including my country Iran is fully capitalist. The main concern is transition and preparation for it. We have the very sad experience of the Iranian Revolution that was taken over by reactionary religious populists and decades of struggle by left and progressive forces were lost and the country is now far more backward than it was. The human development that you rightly emphasize needs massive and lengthy organizational and educational mobilization. You yourself talk of transition, and it was interesting for me to see that during the transition you even see the possibility of some capitalist corporations, or private sector, whose technologies or knowhow might be needed, continue to operate, but being regulated.

My other question here deals with another point that you strongly discuss in most of your works, and that is self-management, something that socialists of the twentieth century, whether revolutionaries or reformists did not pay serious attention to. My question deals with the limits of this very important concept. Full workers' control can only be limited to small local firms, and cannot be applied to large national corporations and institutions. Instead of workers' control, the workers of these large strategic organizations should be involved in different forms of workers' participation. For example, workers of a national transport system cannot by themselves decide to change their hours of operation, as it has an immediate impact on the economy, on people commuting, and the operation of other industries.

ML: I have focused on the question of worker-management for many years. Certain things should be said in this regard. Without worker-management, you cannot develop people's capacities. Once people break down the distinction between thinking and doing, they can develop their capacities and put an end to what Marx called the capitalist division of labor. This is the good side of worker-management and we could see this in Yugoslavia and in Venezuela. The bad side of it is the extent to which people who have grown in capitalist society focus on self-interest. This self-interest generates enormous negative tendencies even in self-managed industries. This was true in Yugoslavia. The nature of the struggle is two-fold. On the one hand, you want to ensure there is as much development of people's capacities within workplace to allow them to understand more and more. On the other hand, you need to fight against the tendency toward self-interest.

SR: You are right about fighting self-interest, but my question deals with an organizational issue that makes it impossible for large industries and institutions to be solely controlled by their respective workers. I gave the example of a national railway system. It is also true for oil industry workers, where amount of production per day or price of a barrel of oil cannot solely be determined by the oil workers. Same is the case with steel, petrochemical, and other industries, where different stakeholders, to different degrees, need to be involved in the decision-making process. There is another organizational issue. As you know well, today's large industries, like auto, are no more operating as a sort of continuous Fordist plant in a single location, and are scattered through clusters of smaller units in different locations, each producing sections or parts of the total product. I don't think post-capitalist institutions would necessarily change such structures. Decision making in each of these affiliate firms cannot be solely made by their respective workers, as there is a chain link among the whole process, and instead of self-management in its absolute sense, we can have high level of participation in all decisions-making bodies with representation of workers from different related units and stakeholders. Organization theory and design is very well advanced in this area, and if we remove the capitalist control and domination, we can use some of these models for self-management and workers' participation.

ML: Implicit in your perspective is the suggestion that workers are self-oriented and will not take into account the larger picture. I give you an example. One of the best unions in Venezuela is the Union of the Electrical Workers Federation, which I worked closely with. This Federation, while having the interests of its members in mind, was concerned about the industry and the country, and was aware of how bad the electrical distribution system was and constantly pushed the government to improve the situation.

SR: Again, my point is that workers of each integrated unit while they have knowledge of their own firm, they cannot possibly have the knowledge and information about other units and need to have the workers representatives of other related units. I am sure you don't mind if I also refer to Marta Harnecker, who in her new book, *The World to Build*, rightly talks about limits of direct democracy and that it cannot possibly be applied in large institutions, like a large municipality, and other forms of democratic participation should be followed. For factories, she rightly says in addition to workers' council in each workshop, there must be councils in each factory and each branch of industry.

ML: Obviously, you have to have a larger bringing together of workers from different sectors to develop the concept of the whole picture. No doubt about that. But the question is how to get to that. I give you another example from Venezuela. There was an important process that was encouraged by Chavez. It was in an industrial [zone] called Guyana where there was a steel plant, aluminum, and other state-owned heavy industries. They started to introduce worker-management in an aluminum company in the industrial zone but it failed. This was in large part because the state bureaucrats were against it. In 2009, though, there was a major struggle in a steel company that had been privatized. The workers were engaged in a major battle with the corporate owners on safety, wage, and other issues, and since these were not resolved, they called for renationalization of the company. Ultimately, Chavez responded and nationalized the company. As soon as this happened, the workers in steel industry began to organize to work with the workers in other companies in the area and began a process that was endorsed by Chavez, called a "Socialist Plan for Guyana". The workers got together to coordinate their activities. They created workers' tables that transcended the particular sector and had representatives from different sectors, to see how their production could be rationalized, where the output of one company becomes the input of another. This was an incredible process from below that bureaucrats fought against it, but Chavez endorsed it. So you need coordination that you are describing but you need the consciousness of the workers involved in it.

Leo Panitch

LP: My mentor, Ralph Miliband once said to me after he came back from a trip to Soviet Union, said to me: "You know why they don't have cafés there? Because cafes are where revolutions are planned". Obviously one wants lively cafes in a socialist society. One wants autonomous enterprises as arenas of goods and service production, and there may be arenas of distribution that can be market-based. There could be, for example, a system of barbershops that is or isn't based on the market. But I would not want to have a press determined by the market, as opposed to the ability for the people to take initiatives to apply for the means of media production and run them as media outlets with workers' participation, and so on. I don't think we need to pretend to be all-knowing about this. Nationalization is a terrible term that we have been stuck with, because it implies that the "nationalized" institutions are going to be taken into the existing public sector and state. The existing public sector and state is bureaucratic in part because it is capitalist, so the whole idea is to transform the state in such a way that encourages decentralization, initiative, and so on. What I do think is a priority for structural reform—although I don't know how long of a period it would take to get even this far—is that under the contemporary conditions of capitalism, it is absolutely crucial that financial institutions be public. Syriza in its platform used the notion of socialization, but made it clear that this involves common ownership; yet the position they are in now has them recapitalizing the banks under the aegis of European Cenrtral Bank (ECB).

SR: But in any case, state remains a main institution of socialization, despite what anarchists claim.

LP: I am referring to public institutions of democratic representation and democratic administration; As Marx once said to Bakunin if you want to reject even that as a state, so be it. The point is we do want to transform the state and not just to inherit it, on the one hand, or pretend we can smash it and do without such public institutions on the other. I agree we need to begin with bringing the banks into the public sector and we need to have a goal of taking the major industrial and resource corporations in to the public sector. It is too easy to say we need workers' control so that workers in each enterprise decide what is to be done in their units. We also need to conceive of forms of community control and a degree of representation that allows for decision making above and beyond those enterprises. In this sense, the workers of enterprises are not the sole arbiters of what is to be done with the resources of society. And how to do this is far more complex than what Marx imagined and what he wrote on the Paris Commune.

SR: I am glad you mention this. Talking of workers' councils, as you know during and a while after the 1979 Iranian Revolution, we established Showras in almost all major factories and institutions, and we were in control of everything. In our Union of IDRO Councils, representing over 100 major industries, I remember moving from one council to another, appointing new CEOs and strengthening the workers' councils. We had lots of illusions, but soon learned that this is short-lived, not only just because of the suppressive nature of the new regime, or internal weaknesses of the Showras, but because of the nature of councils and workers' control itself. You can have full workers control in small local units, but in the strategic national or regional industries like oil or steel company, or services such as public transportation or public utilities, not all decisions can be left to the workers and employees of that particular enterprise. Many talk of self-management without explicitly saying what exactly they mean by that.

LP: Yes, I read your article on this. We also need to learn the lessons of the problems of the Yugoslavia in this respect.

Catherine Samary

CS: First, I would not make "classical" distinctions between socialism and communism (the so-called two-phase presentation of the classical texts). I think the communist aims (to each according to his/her needs) should be there from the very beginning (and at whatever level of development), and that before and after the revolution, we should fight against all relations of domination, to prevent their crystallization. No doubt there will be limits, and of course conflicts will occur. But the communist aims must be explicit from the very beginning, as much as the satisfaction of as many fundamental needs are possible, and in the broadest possible sense. Some products and services should be distributed even in a poor society with collective share of the costs at the national level, through specific funds, based on redistributive taxation and democratic planning. This is a key factor to consolidate a revolution against foreign and internal enemies, because of the popular support it will have.

Another point against the classical division of phases, that defines the communist phase as that of "abundance" of resources, is the reality of resource scarcity. We need today to fully take into account the ecological issue and the scarcity of natural resources.

Moreover, we should distinguish between "real socialism/communism" or historical concrete experiences, and socialism/communism as a utopian and non-existing, but a possible project of emancipation. The key issue is the concrete and historical analysis and interpretation of the gaps between the experience and the ideal. What was experienced should not be a model for us to follow. Of course, we can learn from it: I have studied the Yugoslav experience with that purpose and against all attempts to reduce the past revolutions to their failures or to the Gulag camps and to Stalinization.

SR: Now the question about socialism becomes even more complicated if we were to follow communist aims from the very beginning—goals that I believe are very utopian and are ideals that we should strive toward them without necessarily expecting to achieve their full extent. The focus of my question is what exactly do we mean by socialism. Does it involve socialization of all aspects of economic life, and will there be private ownership of any sort? Will there be competition, differentiated wages, and so on? What are the features of the future society you have in mind? And of course, the main issue is how all these demands can be achieved.

CS: First, I don't believe that socialization of everything is the goal of socialism. The goal is satisfaction of needs, in a very broad sense. The other goal is "emancipation" which would be impossible to attain through totalitarian planning.

Second, we have to differentiate between socialization (let us say a process of "social control", which is never perfect, and without simple answer about how to implement it) and etatization or state control that was experienced in the Soviet Union or elsewhere, along with bureaucratization of the planning system. We have had also other experiences such as Yugoslav self-management system. Marxists put a theoretical emphasis on the fight against alienation. But there are two sources of alienations that the Yugoslav Marxists stressed: alienation of human choices by market and alienations by state. The emphasis must be put on the process of socialization through deep democratic content and control both of market mechanisms (which can still exist even if labor market and capital market have to be suppressed), and of planning. The aim of socialism is the elimination of relations of domination and not just removing private ownership. First, there are different types of private ownership, and second, we can imagine different forms of socialization (social control). In all of these forms, there should be the right of self-management.

SR: In many of your writings, you put a very strong emphasis on the concept of self-management. As you know, during the Iranian Revolution, we had the experience of Showras (councils) in almost all factories and major public and private institutions. But the Showras failed for a variety of reasons. Can self-management be a universal form of organization or are there some limits for its implementation? For example, can it be implemented in small and medium local institutions only? And how can it be applied to large strategic industries or service institutions that have a national impact and need national coordination? Of course, we can have democratic administration and participation at all levels, through different methods.

CS: I believe we need to clarify the meaning we give to self-management. First, we should not identify self-management only with one "model" or concept (similar to the anarchist one and to one phase of the Yugoslav experience—"market socialism" between 1965 and 1971) based on atomized (decentralized) factories linked to the market. Even in the Yugoslav experience, there were different combination of plan, market, and self-management.

Second, I want to distinguish between self-management *rights* (or status for human being) and self-management *as a system* (with its institutions). When we talk of the rights to self-management, it points to an aim that should be universal and implemented in relation to all citizens, as consumers and all "workers"—all those who contribute through their work to the creation of material and non-material wealth. This includes men and women, whatever their field of work, in countryside or industry, as employers or manual workers, qualified ones or not. They all should have the right to manage their work, through individual and collective procedures, and to be involved in the process of decision making as users of services and products. Of course that raises all the issues of the means (institutions) to implement those rights in an efficient way. The idea is that the rights should be constant and "constitutional". But the means should be regularly evaluated and change according to their capacity to satisfy the needs—which themselves have to be established through democratic procedures. The "fundamental needs" must be selected as those that should be satisfied for all, through the planning system, while other kinds of needs should be satisfied through more flexible and decentralized procedures, permitting individual choices. Different forms of social and individual, cooperative ownerships and local planning can give a capacity to the whole system to stimulate initiatives and permit variety of choices within collective rules and control.

SR: You define self-management very broadly. I believe we can have democratic participation at all levels but not self-management that I equate with "workers' control" and which I believe remains limited to a single unit owned and controlled by its workers and employees. National institutions cannot be owned and controlled only by their employees.

CS: The concept of self-management (rights and system) integrates the micro and macro levels. In the Yugoslav system, it changed according to different phases and conflicts.

The first phase of introduction of self-management (1950–1965) maintained planning through social funds under the control of the party/state, while self-management was introduced for short-term choices and local management of factories: the dominant part of their "surplus" (after payment of wages and productive costs) was channeled to central funds. The demand for more decentralization "against the state planning" was coming both from liberal economists in favor of "socialist market" and rich republics (resisting redistribution of their wealth toward poorest one through funds and planning), and by anarchist kind of currents (fighting for more power of decision making at the local level against central planning and state).

The second system, ("market socialism" 1965–1971), accepted the suppression of planning and increased the decentralized rights of decision making at the level of factories—with the market and a banking system as the mechanism of coordination and determination of choices of investments. Banks were to support investment by their credits according to market criteria of profitability. This increased inequalities and unemployment with trends of private accumulations. The Yugoslav Marxists proposed a third system at the end of the 60s: self-management was to be established at local and national levels and to act against market and state domination. Self-management planning, chambers for self-management, and "self-managed communities of interest" (linking users, workers, and public actors for the management of different productions) were to articulate different views of the users and workers, at local and national levels. At the same time, the process needed to transform the party and the state authorities that could have been a form of withering away of the state. But in a congress of self-management, instead of a democratic approach and discussion of these proposals, the communist leaders decided to repress all criticisms. They introduced new reforms from above in a climate of increasing strikes and conflicts between republican powers and also of several significant international crises (Soviet tanks in Prague after the spring of 68s, crisis of profitability and of imperialist domination in the capitalist world-system, the dollar's crisis and the oil's crisis in the 70s). The attempt of the Yugoslav regime to resist domination from both sides (through "non-alignment") could not provide a stable system. It is important to understand and explain the crisis of the Yugoslav experience and take into account both its strengths and weaknesses. I have done this elsewhere The Yugoslav crisis in the 80s and 90s must not prevent us from learning the very rich ideas and proposals made from within the system at the end of the 60s by social movements and intellectual Marxist currents. Their historical importance is that, on the basis of a unique experience, they could reject both "state socialism" and "market socialism", putting emphasis on processes and means of "socializing" (putting under social pluralist control) both market and state. The democratic issue is at the core of that concept and is so important for the future.

SR: No doubt the Yugoslav case is very significant and we definitely need to learn more about it. For now, the big question remains whether self-management in this sense can be implemented at all levels, or instead, we can have incremental participative democracy.

CHAPTER 7

Social Classes

Which social class(es) would be the driving force for a socialist revolution? The focus has obviously been on the working class, what constitutes the working class, and does it include the white-collar workers and the new middle classes or not?

Gilbert Achcar

GA: It depends on what you mean by "new middle classes". If this refers to salaried workers, I don't consider them as "middle class". If we define the class by the relations of production, not by status or level of income as in the Weberian typology, but by the location in the production process and the relations of production, and if we consider the basic definition of workers as those who sell their labor force, then salaried workers are part of the working class. Only those managers, who are involved in the management of capital as salaried managers, must be excluded from this category; in any event, with stock-options and the like, they are increasingly full members of the capitalist class as shareholders.

SR: You use working class in a very broad sense. But if this is the case, we deal with a class that is much diversified in terms of status, income, roles, aspirations, and so on, and this has major implications for mobilization and organization.

GA: Those who get high wages because of their skills should not be considered as enemies, as no modern economy can survive without such skills. This is a complex issue that is also related to the point we discussed about the impossibility of building socialism in one country. Take Cuba, for example. The Cubans have great health and education systems. If they were to open their border, many of their skilled people whose incomes are less than those of cigar workers, would leave the country. The Cuban state tells them: "We provided you with education and training, and you must therefore serve the people". But in order to implement this, they have created a fortress, which many Cubans resent as a jail. It boils down again to the balance of forces. Either you manage to win over enough of such skilled people dedicated and ready to sacrifice material benefits for the cause of serving their people, and this certainly sounds utopian, or, as long as the conditions are not met at the global level, you need to grant them some material privileges because you need their skills. (Needless to say, those who wish to forgo these privileges out of idealism and socialist commitment are welcome to do so.) In the same way, you will need for a long time to keep in the economy capitalists who operate only for the sake of profit.

SA: No doubt that no economy can work without highly skilled people. But the question is that since you have such very diversified strata of working people, socialists cannot follow very radical policies that would push the upper echelons of skilled people to the side of capital.

GA: As you mentioned earlier, there is no wall between phases of social transformation. The socialist transformation means that you have to increase more and more what is available to all society. There should be a viable minimum universal wage, free education, health, transportation, and many other services, which lead progressively to more equalization of the society. Some will enjoy privileges compared to the rest, but these differences will be gradually reduced. Such a very profound change of society cannot happen overnight.

Aijaz Ahmad

AA: Our conception of working class needs a lot of fine-tuning. Let us see what is the gender of this working class. According to the World Bank, some 65 percent or more of the productive labor in the world is done by women—and we are not even speaking of reproductive work which is additional. They were not the central part of the working class in Marxist conception. Or what we called the peasantry is now mostly wage labor. In much of the world, peasantry in the historic sense no longer exists. In countries where rural areas predominate demographically, most of the countryside is either inhabited by wage laborers or landless peasants who work part of the time, or who may live in villages but work in towns. In all the great cities of Asia and Africa, most workers work in the informal sector not in the formal industrial sector of great concentration of workers in huge factories, with their trade unions, and so on. The very nature of the working class is now changing. So the historical Marxist prejudice against the so-called lumpen proletariat has to be revisited. Lumpen-capitalism only creates lumpen proletariat. Capitalism has become lumpenized in the industrial centers even in the USA. The high bourgeois culture of the nineteenth century and early twentieth century has actually collapsed and no longer exists. Finance capital with post-modernism as its cultural form has destroyed not only proletarian culture, but also high bourgeois culture. We also have lumpenized middle classes.

It is a completely teleological question what role the so-called blue- or white-collar workers will play. They will choose. When the fight is on, they will choose. What we do know is that the centrality of multi-class alliances has grown even more than in the time when Lenin spoke of the worker–peasant alliance and the revolutionary potential of de-classed petty bourgeois. Historically the dissident middle classes, the dissident intelligentsia, broadly speaking, have played a central role in all revolutionary movements. We don't know what their social weight in the socialist movements of the future will be.

SR: The question is that the industrial working class at the time of Marx or Lenin was large and homogeneous and worked in large factories. But now as you rightly mentioned, it is heterogeneous and fragmented. Now it is much harder to organize and mobilize this diversified class.

AA: When Marx wrote the Communist Manifesto, most of Europe did not have much industrial production and therefore the organized working class was in fact very small. The extraordinary fact about the Manifesto is that it did not reflect its own time. It reflects the future. So I even go beyond what you said. The working class at that time was homogeneous not only in relation to capital, but was very much rooted in national traditions, so that every national working class was culturally, religiously, socially, and even racially homogeneous, and very distinct from the culture of the petty-bourgeoisie. They were few in number and belonged to few churches, and so on. So the point is taken. But my emphasis, like in other questions we discussed, is that we need to start not from the good old days, but from the bad new days. Yes the industrial working class remains smaller but plays a very important role, and yes most workers work in the informal sector and are very scattered. Now, we have immense amount of household labor. Household is a unit of labor in Bombay and accounts for a high percentage of simple manufacture. So how do you organize this and around what? So may be major historical form of organization should not be around the place of work where employment is available only to a small proportion of the working class, and the work itself is often of a transient nature. Perhaps the political organization of the working class should increasing take into account the place of residence—the slum alongside the factory, so to speak. In terms of your question of how to conceive the working class, yes, the very idea of the working class has to be reconceived.

Rob Albriton

RA: Well, I have a rather unorthodox view here that is basically we, and by we, I mean Marxists, have at times gone overboard in wanting the working class to be *the* agent of change, and have assumed that if the working class comes to power, all of our problems are solved. I don't buy this. I would say that capitalism hurts everybody, obviously it hurts some people more than others, and most of the people that it hurts the most are the ones that are most mobilizable. Even capitalists are hurt, now they paper over the hurt with dollar bills and with high status purchases that give them status and satisfaction. I wouldn't necessarily go after mobilizing these people because one of your aims is a fairly massive redistribution of wealth and they're probably not going to support it. I wouldn't exclude any particular group off the top and I would be open to somebody who would support a socialist movement even though they're quite wealthy. You know, there are some extremely wealthy people who give money for economic development. As for the middle classes, all of them are hurt by capitalism. The working class to some extent is in a fairly strategic position because workers can strike, can organize general strikes, and so on. But the problem is that they are less and less unionized, and in some countries like Latin America, 80 percent of the jobs created there in the last ten years have been in the informal sector, which is hard to organize. In many countries, workers don't have the full right to organize and get unionized. Peasants' lives are also getting damaged by capitalism, and peasants can get radicalized. In short, we need to think about more than class. For example, religious fundamentalists are not likely to be socialist even if they are working class, and liberation theologians in the Catholic Church were among the strongest supporters of socialism during a whole phase of history in Latin America.

SR: I would particularly like to know your views on the new middle class, the salaried. While sections and strata of the salaried, particularly the higher echelons are definitely on the side of capital, and are against socialism, but at the same time, the vast majority of socialists, social democrats, feminists, peace activists, and pro-labor activists come from this same class.

RA: No doubt you have to be a student of some sort to be able to better understand and analyze the global character of social problems. Peasants and workers may be unhappy about their working conditions and a whole lot of things, but they don't necessarily have a clear understanding of what's going on in the world in a kind of large picture and how they are getting particularly screwed because of their position within the system.

SR: That's why I believe that in confronting capital, it is absolutely necessary to build bridges between the working class and the new middle class and mobilize them to push for change.

RA: Absolutely. I think that in all industrial countries, mobilizing the vast majority of working people, and even those that are not part of the working class or middle class, as, for example, young people who have never had a job and cannot find one, is most crucial in bringing about meaningful changes. In other words, all the people that are being hurt by capitalism and are mobilizable in a socialist movement should be the target of mobilization. I just want to say that it takes forming initially broad coalitions to work on broad fronts to make changes that can be made and that will really move the struggle ahead. Obviously it is hard to generalize, and forms of mobilization and issues will vary from one country to another.

Kevin Anderson

KA: There are several dimensions to this question. One relates which class creates value, or debates about the social consciousness of which groups or social classes, and so on. We can talk about this not just in terms of classes and by looking at social groups, which is the way I like to do. In the tradition I come from, the Marxist–Humanist tradition whose origins go back to C.L.R. James and above all Raya Dunayevskaya, the notion is one of multiple forces of revolution. In addition to the working class, there are new social movements, women, oppressed racial or ethnic minorities (such as Blacks in the USA, Kurds in Iran, and elsewhere), and youth.

SR: You discuss this in your piece, "Karl Marx and Intersectionality".

KA: Yes. All those groups outside the industrial working class have at least some middle class members. The politically active youth are mostly students and are usually from the slightly more privileged part of the society. So you have a multi-class movement. The Black movement could range from the top echelons of society to the most impoverished. Police stop Black millionaires driving a luxury car, and even US Attorney General Eric Holder once could not get a cab in the middle of Manhattan. There are many movements that have radical or revolutionary potential, movements that cut across social classes. We also have the diminution of the working classes in the more industrially developed countries. Virtually everything we are wearing is produced in China or India, or in other low-wage countries. The industrial working class of the world is no longer centered in the West and Japan. In the latter, the so-called white-collar workers that you mentioned or the service workers are also an important part of working people, and many of them are women or minorities. In the Marxian tradition, we distinguish between the working class and the working people, which is broader and includes peasants, white-collar workers, and so on. We have a new middle class in the West and Japan, and it has some radical potential. Even in some of the more traditional middle classes—in professions like professors, doctors, and lawyers—there are some junctures around which people can become radicalized.

SR: The problem is that for much of the left that is solely fixated with industrial workers, there has been no recognition of the importance of this class. No doubt they are in an ambiguous and contradictory position, and a section of them is on the side of the capital, but, at the same time, others who are on the side of labor, progressive social movements, feminists, anti-racist, and so on come from this class.

KA: Let us look at it for a moment in terms of the contradictions we face as leftists approaching such groups. Many of the white-collar and managerial workers were seen by Andre Gorz and others as a new working class. These people are alienated and exploited in the sense that their companies benefit from their inventions, and although they get bonuses, they do not own the means of production. They are in a certain class position. The white-collar workers such as bank clerks get almost minimum wages and yet it is hard to unionize these workers. In Germany going back at least to the 20s, there were attempts to organize the bank clerks. Here, the status position of mental versus manual labor—as emphasized by Max Weber—becomes important in terms of explaining the difficulties such groups have in reaching a revolutionary anti-capitalist consciousness. But there are also countervailing possibilities. In France 68, we see many members of these groups coming to the streets and more significantly, occupying their workplaces just as industrial workers were occupying the factories. No doubt there are even greater potentials for radicalization of service workers, whose status and economic position is generally lower.

SR: Definitely, because most of them to different degrees are suffering under capitalism, and there are many similarities among these groups. But the main question is how to mobilize these diverse groups. Organizing them is far more complicated than that of the industrial workers in the so-called proletarian fortresses of the past, when such large and labor-intensive factories did exist.

KA: I think trade unions have not been as effective here as they might have been. Many of the service workers are female and their grievances include sexual harassments on the job, and so on. Until the last couple of decades, trade unions had difficulties addressing these questions. (I remember, in 70s, in New York, a woman clerical worker told me a male union organizer approached them but was wearing some type of emblem associated with the soft pornography of Playboy magazine.) Especially in the more developed countries, we have such a small industrial working class, and we have to look into other groups and we have to understand their problems. We also need to look at the new middle classes in terms of gender and race.

Barbara Epstein

BE: As you suggest, the definition of the working class is not as clear as it once was: do we include highly paid workers, such as technical workers in the electronics industry, or not? But it is clear that the definition of the working class must be expanded beyond industrial workers to include white-collar and service workers. There are also other sectors of society that tend to support progressive politics and from which many left activists are drawn: racial minorities, women, middle class young people, intellectuals, those in the helping professions. People of all of these groups would presumably be part of a post-capitalist, proto-socialist coalition.

SR: No doubt in addition to the element of class, we need to include all these other movements and many other theories including intersectionality also emphasize this. But isn't it true that class remains such a significant factor in the analyses of all these movements.

BE: Yes, class remains fundamental, and unfortunately in the USA, the category of class has tended to drop out, leading many people to forget that the support of the working class is crucial to any progressive or socialist transformation of society. Also, it is easier to understand the weaknesses of some movements if one looks at them through the lens of class. For example, the women's movement had the most significant impact on the lives of professional women and more generally women of the middle class; this is no doubt related to the fact that the majority of young feminist activists of the 60s and beyond were drawn from the middle class; the women's movement opened the professions to women. The civil rights movement of the 60s consisted of young blacks of the rural South, of the working class, and of what was then a quite small black middle class. One consequence of the civil rights movement was to expand the black professional and middle class, and to integrate it to a considerable degree into mainstream white society, and thus to draw blacks who might have provided leadership for the black community as a whole out of that community. In the absence of an awareness of class, in the 80s and 90s movements fragmented along lines of race and gender and were weakened by lack of a sense of common purpose. The influence of post-modernism and post-structuralism, which celebrated fragmentation and sought to subvert unity, also played a large role in the weakening of the left in those decades.

Aron Etzler

AE: Well, I think this has lot more to do with the formation of class than class in itself. Socialist movements in several countries see many of the white-collar workers as the main backers of their projects. In some other countries, we see antagonistic strife and struggles between the strata of the broader working population. It is in the interest of our socialist project to have a broad base in the population. And, it seems much of the actual political struggle is about whether the middle strata are leaning toward the working class or not. One of the biggest differences during the neo-liberal epoch in Sweden has been the change in housing market. While before housing was almost a social right, in a sense that very few people did not have a place to live, today it has become a commodity, object of speculation, and this has particularly impacted the difference between the white- and blue-collar workers.

It means that whole areas of inner cities tend to be inhabited by middle strata, while the working class gets pushed to the corners of the cities, or smaller towns, also impacting education, work and democracy. Working class and the middle strata now live in very different circumstances, developing quite diverse views, maybe not even understanding each other. This tends to make one of the biggest political differences to be between larger cities on one hand, small towns and countryside on the other. To me, it seems to be one of the biggest obstacles for the left today—the difficulty in forming a unity of working class and middle strata, instead of this landscape shaped by a polarization by ethnicity and cultural difference.

SR: This is the reality, and I agree that we need a broader sense of the working class, and we should recognize that the vast majority of socialists in any country come from the so-called white-collar or new middle classes. But the problem is that when we use this broad category of the working class, we deal with a highly differentiated and segmented class, and it would be harder to find a political party that could represent all different strata of this class.

AE: You are right, it is a classical problem and I think Gramsci was among the first to deal with this issue. In modern time, Marta

Harnecker from Chile has written a lot about it. I think one of the perspectives is that when you form your socialist project, it has to be inclusive. When you look at the successful parties of Podemos or Syriza, we see that it is possible to form an inclusive left party. You also have to see that the process is much longer than one election cycle. Social democracy in Sweden was successful when they consciously made an alliance between the working class and the middle class, and they used all policy tools to do this, and all the necessary concessions on both sides. We need to be attractive not only to white-collar workers but also to blue-collar workers, and peoples of different creeds and religion, and then to shape society with policies that make it natural for people of different strata of working class and middle class to work and live together.

Sam Gindin

SG: The narrow definition of workers as the industrial working class has always been problematic. It led to strategic errors in terms of dealing with government employees, postal workers and others. The "working class" references those who don't have private assets to live off and therefore have to work for wage and salary, and people who don't control the labor power of others. But defining it broadly doesn't mean that the working class is homogenous. For example, teachers sometimes see themselves as professionals and look down on janitors in the school yet other times they can be very militant and solidaristic. The mistake lies in assigning workers to fixed categories and not linking this to questions of organizing, education, and struggle.

Consider an example involving nurses. Jane McAlevey, a brilliant American organizer, was trying to build a union at a number of hospitals in Nevada, a right to work state. She began with a principle she had learned from her communist mentors—when you organize, you organize the class. She refused to organize the nurses into a separate nurses union, as is the common practice in the USA and elsewhere, and had to win the nurses over to wall to wall organizing—that is, all workers in the hospital belonging to the same union and bargaining together. She argued that what happens in any section of the hospital affects all the workers there; every group of workers is part of one team. If, for example, the janitors who clean the floors are excluded and this leads to a health issue no one is left unaffected. She was not only able to win the nurses and lab technicians over to one over-riding union and joint bargaining, but able to establish some of the best collective agreements in hospitals anywhere—even though Nevada is a so-called right-to-work state.

SR: Did she want to organize the whole hospital into a house union? If so, you may agree with me that house unions compared to industrial unions have got their own problems. I am particularly surprised in the case of Canada with a strong legacy of industrial unions. I agree and I have argued that in many less developed countries, where workers do not have industrial unions, they should start with house unions.

SG: This isn't a matter of one union per hospital. Each hospital is still part of a larger union, the distinction being that in other hospitals, the workers were fragmented into different unions—nurses in a nurses union, food workers, and janitors in another. It was the unity within the workplace, as part of a larger national union that McAlevey was arguing for—essentially the industrial union model in which skilled and unskilled workers belong to the same union—and this wasn't just a question of convincing nurses, but even the leadership of the union she was working for (SEIU). Note that such fragmentation is common. In Toronto, elementary teachers, high school teachers, and janitors (along with secretaries) are in different unions. My experience has been that as the discussion shifts to dealing with the attack on education and mobilizing the community to our side, it becomes more possible to bring the fragments together.

SR: This is a very important topic and a big organizational issue. There is no argument that we need to define the working class very broadly. But differentiation in terms of wages and income, in terms of taste, living standards, and other things, makes organizing more difficult. The section of working class identified as the new middle class is playing an increasingly important role in today's politics, but in a highly contradictory way. Many of them, particularly in the higher echelons, are pro-capital, but at the same time, all progressive and pro-socialist people belong to this category. It seems to me that the left everywhere has neglected the new middle class, and by doing that has pushed them toward liberals and the right.

SG: There are of course innumerable barriers to making working people broadly defined into a class that is united and has both the interest in, and capacities for, building a socialist society. One very significant barrier is, as you say, public sector workers self-identifying as "middle class". I would offer three points of optimism. First, as neo-liberalism advances privatization, commercializes the operation of social services, and attacks the wages and conditions of public sector workers, it erodes the special status these workers thought they had—it essentially "proletarianizes" these workers and highlights their common status as *workers*. Second, because these workers aren't just dealing with particular departments but a coherent state with an antagonistic agenda, there is an opening to emphasize that resistance is only possible through coordinated action alongside other public sector workers whether they are teachers, nurses, sanitation workers, street cleaners, or childcare workers. Third, workers aren't "just workers" but have lives in the community and it is becoming ever clearer that the time it takes to get to work on public transit, the erosion of health care and quality education, threats to the environment and so on are at the same time intimately related to the jobs and conditions of others—the fight for social services and the conditions of work are part of the same *class* battle. That this will be translated in a new social force rooted in the working class is obviously not inevitable, but it is—with a radical emphasis on defending and expanding social needs and organization—possible.

Consider the Chicago Teachers Union. In a city with a very large black and Latino population, the authorities kept on increasing class size, starving schools of resources, and attacking the conditions of teachers. They even changed the law so that in order to have a legal strike the union had to have 75 percent of the members voting in favor of strike. And this was led by a Mayor who had recently moved from being President Obama's Chief of Staff and was a dominant figure in the Democratic Party. So the deck was stacked against the union. A core of radical teachers, who had been organizing for a number of years, managed to take over the union in 2010 and decided that the key for success was integrating the mobilization of their members with intensive organizing at the community level and countering the state propaganda blaming the teachers and their union as the barriers to good education. This core happened to include a good number of socialists committed to mobilization in and beyond the workplace. They knew they couldn't limit themselves to sympathetic teachers and needed to win over those that leaned in a conservative direction. Organizing committees were established in each school and the union booked teachers off to act as full-time organizers coordinating these committees. What was formerly a traditional union was now organizing at the community level and "fighting city hall". They won because they addressed not just their work relationship but the larger question of the quality of education and built an organization that operated at various scales, included people of different politics and ideologies, and acted creatively.

Peter Hudis

P.H: I have two responses to this. Yes, people have education, training, and so on that prepares them for their particular forms of employment. But I have never understood why I as a professor should earn higher wages than a manual worker who has also undergone a process of training and preparation to perform her job. One hour of labor counting for one hour of labor does not mean all get the same level of remuneration; some may choose to work more than others. It only means that there is no wage labor. And if there is no wage labor, there is no capital.

On the question of classes, the answer is to a certain degree we don't know, and we cannot know before we know. A lot depends on the situation of a society and the nature of the society we are living in, and the situation at the moment of a revolutionary experience. It is going to be different for different countries and for different moments. So in certain contexts, it may well be that the working class will be the driving force of the revolution, in other contexts, it may not be the working class. We have to keep in mind that different forces move at different times and we cannot anticipate in advance which social force will be in the vanguard. But we can know which are likely to be in the vanguard given particular societies in question. In my view, the social force that is the vanguard in any social transformation in the USA is the Black populace. The nature of US history and society makes this plain, I believe. But that is not the same as positing a universal theory of who or what is the driving force of revolution everywhere in the world. A second part of my response, however, is that the working class is too often thought of as the industrial working class.

Marx viewed the industrial working class as the vanguard of the working class movement. But we should note that at no time and in no country has the industrial working class formed the majority of the working class. In his draft of 1861–63 of *Capital*, he puts forward a very interesting discussion of how one third of the working class in Britain constituted service workers at the time, mainly domestic women workers employed in cleaning households and domestic labor. He considered them part of the working class, obviously not part of the industrial working class. He did not dismiss the role of these women in potential revolutionary transformation. And as you are well aware, some of these same non-productive workers were women who played a pivotal role in the Paris Commune; in fact, they started it. So probably there has never been a society with more than 35 to 40 percent of the population involved in the industrial production in the nineteenth century, let alone today. The whole drive of capitalist society is to reduce the amount of labor time relative to output and that is why the law of value dictates that you must shorten the amount of living labor involved in producing a commodity, and thereby increase the quantity of commodity output in order to achieve the goal of the maximization of profit. So the logic of capitalism ultimately is to shrink this productive sector and we have to expect this trend to continue. In the USA, the number of people involved in industrial production is down to 7 percent of the population.

SR: You mean the manual labor, because if you include workers involved in the process of information and not material, the figure is much higher.

PH: Yes, that is right. They may not be considered part of the industrial proletariat, but they are part of the working class. I should add that at the same time that capitalism reduces the relative share of productive labor in the total working population, it also turns a growing number of the population into a working class in so far as they are subjected to alienated conditions of labor. This includes both mental and manual workers, and gives a much more precarious existence to the lives of the people who are involved in the service sector, and so on. This is why the category of middle class becomes a very slippery concept particularly in the USA, where almost everybody thinks they are part of the middle class—when it fact most who use this term are working class

SR: Right, but I am not using middle class in a sense used in the USA, where anybody above poverty line and below the very rich categories is considered a middle class. In other cases, as you know, for example, Africa, the African Development Bank considers as middle class anyone who spends equivalent of two US dollars and above, up to $20 a day. I use the term "new middle classes" to refer mainly to the salariat, professionals, artists, and so on.

PH: Yes, you are talking of the service sector. There is no question that this sector is for the most part a section of the working class, and there is no question that this part of the working class is more insecure and less certain of its future, and less politically organized than the traditional industrial working class, although in some countries, they have relatively strong unions in the government sector. This is of course a major problem if we think of Marxism purely as a theory of class struggle in the narrow sense of the term. But if we view the matter more broadly, we see that today the working class is largely composed of racial minorities, immigrants, women, and young people who may not respond necessarily to the traditional class slogans and demands, but who are at times politically conscious and potentially rebellious.

I don't underestimate the difficulties that this transformation of capitalism presents us with. It is not as clear today who are the revolutionary forces as 100 years ago. Nor is it clear how we can get from capitalism to socialism. But we are far ahead of where people were 50 or 100 years ago, because we have a clearer understanding of what socialism is not. So we need to engage in careful study and analysis of each particular society we are part of in order to determine who are the potential revolutionary forces, what are their demands, and how can a vision of an alternative to capitalism be worked out with them. I want to argue against a reductive class analysis that forgets the fact that there are multiple forces of liberation, sometimes expressed in classes, but sometimes across class lines, or even outside of class categories. I don't think saying this makes me less of a Marxist. It only makes me a less of a Marxist if Marxism was simply defined as being a theory of class struggle. My position is, as mentioned earlier, is that Marxism is a philosophy of liberation; it is a body of ideas that elucidates the necessity for social transformation from the contingent struggles and conditions of life that people are experiencing. In that sense, I think we have our work cut out for us.

Ursula Huws

SR: In your works, you have elaborated the complexities of class under globalization, and I would like to ask if you would refer to the model you developed for class analysis.

UH: We have to think of class in two ways, there is objective class position and there is subjective class consciousness, and these two things are often very much at variance with each other. This is very important to take into consideration. I differ from theorists who are passionate about including public sector workers as part of the working class. From the 60s to the 80s, many of them fiercely insisted that public sector workers were part of the working class. And there was a sense in which, if we speak of subjective class consciousness, they were right. Many of them came from working class families and they entered the public sector labor force with the attitudes of class-conscious working class people—expecting to negotiate with the employer and not part with their labor power too freely. Objectively, of course, they were not part of the working class in that their labor was not producing surplus value for capitalists. Now that the public sector is increasingly commodified this is no longer the case. Capitalist relations have penetrated deep into the public sector through privatization and outsourcing. So now such workers are not working simply to produce use values for service users but to produce profits for capitalists. So you could say that the wish of these leftists working in the public sector has been granted. They have now genuinely become part of the working class. But rather few of them are actively building on this to forge links with other parts of the working class. Partly because the older generation is approaching retirement, or has already retired, and it is new generations who are most affected by these changes. And partly because working conditions are much, much worse in the new commodified public services where they work directly for capitalists. Like other workers in this era of neo-liberal globalization, they are fragmented and exhausted by the sheer pressure of work and have less energy for organizing than they did in the period when public sector work was to some extent protected from the full savagery of the market.

SR: The main issue is that if we consider public sector, service workers, or the so-called white collar as part of the working class, we have an extremely diversified and segmented working class because of different objective conditions. And if we don't include them, the working class would not form the majority of the working people. It all depends how we define working class. You have very elaborately questioned the conventional class analysis and distinctions such as "productive" versus "unproductive", "paid" versus "unpaid", and so on. Would be good if you briefly discuss your model.

UH: First, I believe that the working class has expanded objectively, but has shrunk subjectively. As for the categorization of class, I came up with a model in my piece, "The Underpinning of Class in the Digital Age: Living, Labour and Value", in the 2014 *Socialist Register*, and here I just refer to some aspects of the model. It is based on a matrix, cross-tabulating "paid labour" and "unpaid labour" with two categories that I call "Reproductive" (productive for society and capitalism), and "Directly Productive" (for individual capitalist enterprises) labor. The Reproductive/Paid labor (quadrant A) includes public administration and service work, and individually provided private service. The Reproductive/Unpaid labor (quadrant B) includes domestic labor, childcare, household, and non-marker cultural activities, and so on. The Direct Productive/Paid labor (quadrant C) includes commodity production and distribution. And Directly Productive/Unpaid labor (quadrant D) includes "consumption work", which is part of the tasks that were previously paid but now transferred to customers to handle.

Of the four categories, Quadrant C is what I call labor "inside the knot". This means that only in this category is labor carried out directly for a capitalist employer by a worker who is dependent on this labor for subsistence, and is therefore a front-line adversary in the struggle between capital and labor. This does not mean to exclude workers such as those in the public sector and some service workers, and to consider them as unproductive. Actually, many of their tasks are essential for the reproduction of labor, but their exposure to the coercive logic of capitalism is somewhat mitigated.

It is important to note that there are movements among the different quadrants. For example, as we face the increasing commodification of the public sector, we witness movement from Quadrant A to Quadrant C. Also, increasing commodification of consumer goods and services involves shifts from Quadrant B to Quadrant D. With capitalists reducing their labor costs, there are also shifts from Quadrant C to Quadrant D. Austerity measures have also created shifts from Quadrant A to Quadrant B. In all these movements, we witness how Quadrant C or commodity producers are being enlarged, not only by physical and material production, but also by immaterial production.

SR: The model is very useful for today's class analysis and very clearly shows the dynamics of class mobility in global capitalism. But maybe we need a third dimension of skill level which also is a major determinant of wage and salary, as the situation of high-skill and low-skill workers for all these quadrants are very different. Hence, a tri-dimensional matrix

UH: I would not be in favor of this. All work requires skill and knowledge and the extent to which that skill and knowledge is formally acknowledged, certified (and rewarded) is something that is socially constructed. It is the result of past contests between capital and labor as well as between different groups of workers. The more a group of workers can successfully organize to restrict access to their specialized "skills" the greater their bargaining power. Capital of course has an interest in having a skilled workforce. It also, under conditions of globalization has an interest in having these skills standardized, measurable, and certified so that workers can be interchanged with each other across the world as seamlessly as possible. So it wants the skills but it also wants cheap labor. To resolve this contradiction, the state steps in and offers universal education, which generalizes the skills across the population, thus reducing the bargaining power of specific groups of workers. But of course this too is contradictory because providing the workforce with generic skills also provides them with the means to understand and develop critiques of what capital is up to. The development of education systems aiming to provide universal numeracy and literacy in the nineteenth century are a clear historical example of these contradictions: it was necessary for capitalism in that stage of development to have a numerate and literate workforce; but a numerate and literate population also started to demand such things as universal franchise.

SR: It is also very important that your model takes into consideration areas neglected in much of earlier Marxist analyses, particularly the area of social reproductive labor.

UH: I make a distinction between reproductive and productive labor, using Marx's definition, but include in the category of productive labor, the labor involved in distribution. I am sure if Marx were alive today, he would have included distribution workers as part of productive workers. It is ludicrous that, as some suggest, when a worker moves the boxes in a warehouse this is productive work, but when s/he puts them onto the shelf of a supermarket, the work is unproductive! I include the whole value chain up to the point of the final consumer, [as productive].

This model and the movements among different Quadrants show the objective situation of the working class and its enlargement, but as for the subjective aspect, as mentioned earlier, unfortunately this class is very poor.

SR: Earlier, you mentioned that the Quadrant C is being populated by producers of physical and material, as well as immaterial commodities. This is a very important point, but some sort of distinction is also needed between material producers and immaterial producers, as their overall situation are somewhat different. As well, in terms of number and size, those who process information now are larger than those who process material. Is there a reason you do not make a distinction between wage and salary earners, or the so-called new middle classes?

UH: I am not sure how useful the distinction between material and immaterial labor really is. The dynamics of change are enormous and the Quadrant C (the sphere of labor that is directly productive for capital) is expanding very fast indeed. We don't have just the public sector workers being transformed into private sector workers. We also have an enormous class of people belonging to the informal sector; private servants, drivers, cleaners, childcare workers, and many others, who are being mopped up by new companies (especially in the "crowdsourcing" sector, by companies like Uber, Taskrabbit, Helpling, and so on) and brought into the formal economy under very tight capitalist control. People usually identify the informal economy with precariousness. But much of the formal economy is also becoming precarious. In other words, the work has been formalized in a precarious way. The formalization of precariousness is now characteristics even in jobs previously seen as part of the primary labor market, right up to middle management.

SR: You coined the term "cybertariat". No doubt, this growing trend in labor market at the global level has weakened workers and trade unions. But, has it also created new opportunities?

UH: I coined the term to be provocative. Partly because some were implying that those who worked online are all privileged, autonomous knowledge workers, and were suggesting that the old-fashioned idea of the working class is gone. I argued that many of these jobs are terrible, heavily Taylorized and controlled. Call-centers are a good example. Many of these have now been moved to developing countries but it is important to realize that the effects of this so-called offshore outsourcing are mainly qualitative rather than quantitative. The main effect is to discipline labor. Let us imagine that there is a company with 50 call centers in the USA, and one of these is transferred to India. All those workers in the other 49 call centers that have remained in the USA are now under constant pressure and threat that they could be moved to India. This is the classic reserve labor army effect. It is brought into play in two distinct ways. One is through migrant workers and the other through outsourcing to offshore locations. The traditional Marxist conception of the reserve army was bounded within national borders. Now, the reserve army could be outside the border, either it is brought in or deployed elsewhere. We need to further develop the concept of the reserve army. I think this is the Marxist way of understanding this phenomenon.

Michael Lebowitz

ML: As I have discussed elsewhere, when I talk about the working class, I talk about all those who have to sell their ability to work in order to survive. Regardless of how they sell it, performing activity within a factory or an organization, whether selling in a store or in the street as part of capitalist circulation selling capitalist commodities, I view them as working class. It is not the stereotype, it is not a male industrial worker, and it includes everyone working and selling her or his work. I don't exclude anyone as middle class or because they are workers in circulation.

SR: You also include in the category of the working class, all those who are excluded and not exploited.

ML: exactly.

SR: In this sense, we have the broadest definition of the working class, and in a sense makes the concept of class equivalent to *popolo* or people. If so, do we need to come up with a new theory of class, as it is no more just based on the relation of production and value creation, but also includes all those who are somehow directly or indirectly affected by the capitalist system?

ML: Yes, I have no difficulty of including the exploited and those who would love to be exploited in this category. I don't see why any group of working people or the unemployed should not be included in this class.

SR: It is true that the vast majority of people who are affected and suffer under capitalism have many things in common. My main concern is how such a hugely heterogeneous and segmented class can be organized. Working class at the time of Marx or Lenin was much less heterogeneous and more concentrated in large factories or the "proletarian fortresses".

ML: Marx said trade unions are the main instrument of the working class. Now, we know that there are also other instruments. With all the changes you mentioned, the end of Fordism and others, we have to have a different way of organizing them. Rather than just going to factories for organizing, we can look in other places. In Venezuela, communal councils were created to reach workers in their communities. Trade unions' success has been related to their work in the communities. You organize one ethnic group and it spreads to others in the same ethnic group. You are right about the heterogeneous nature of the working class, people with different interests and focus, and that is why I believe that we need a socialist party. In the absence of a party that could bring all these diverse groups of people together and focus on what is common to them all, what I call the right of all people to the full development of their potential, we will end up with spontaneous processes which cannot challenge and confront capital

Leo Panitch

LP: Well we always have to define the constituency for socialism as a very broad and very diverse working class, which should never have been conceived as only industrial workers, even though this was sometimes the limited conception of traditional socialist parties. The sole focus on industrial workers, which were always a minority and not including, say teachers, let alone service workers—even barbers—was a mistake. If those parities had a broader view of what their responsibility was in terms of who they politically educated, who they mobilized, and so on, this could have made them stronger. But that would have involved trying to convince teachers and others that whatever the difference in education, they are part of the working class. This is of course not easy, as teachers often identify themselves as having a higher status, or barbers see themselves as entrepreneurs. So it involves changing people's conceptions about this, which I think is possible. But obviously not everybody can be included in the working class, let alone managers and CEOs. You need a class map but you need a much broader class map than just the industrial workers. Also, it was a wrong assumption to think that all the industrial workers would be revolutionary. Industrial workers can also identify with being Catholics, with being Islamists, let alone with being nationalists of all sorts, and so on. So it is a matter of a balance between objective positions in social relations and all kinds of subjective possibilities, some of which can be oriented to socialism, because people do see themselves as exploited, marginalized, dominated, and so on although never only that.

SR: It is true, but the main question is the need for new theories of class analysis particularly in relation to the new middle class, the salaried employees. On the one hand, now, we have a shrinking working class in its tradition sense, and on the other hand, massive increase of mental workers and employees. While both groups have similar position in the production relations, they are different in terms of income, status, demands, tastes, and aspirations.

LP: Yes, that's because so much more of life has been commodified and so much labor goes into those aspects of life which are commodified. As Doug Henwood often points out, it is an absurd notion that the only thing that is a commodity is something that is so heavy that if it is dropped on your foot it hurts. All of the "non-material" products we get from the new telecommunication media today (which are brought to us through a vast material infrastructure) are commodities; and many education and health services have been turned into commodities. The people producing them need to be seen as part of our constituency. As their numbers have increased, they have been subjected to proletarianization, at least in the sense of an increased loss of authority in the work place. It used to be that an accountant, an engineer, a university teacher, had an enormous amount of authority in the workplace and control over the labor process. Insofar as this is now being diminished, the difference between knowledge workers and even manual service workers such as cleaners, as well as industrial production workers, diminishes. All I can say is that there is a greater opportunity, objectively, for creating a sense of common interest in overcoming capitalist social relations.

SR: I have no argument with that. My point is that with this highly differentiated class, the socialists need to recognize these diversities and formulate their policies in a way that could attract and represent a wide constituency. We know that sections of the new middle class are ideologically on the side of the working class—most intellectuals, socialist, and so on, but a significant number are either on the side of capital, or can easily be absorbed by them. We need policies to attract these, and if we only focus on the demands of the workers, we may end up in a situation like present Venezuela.

LP: I am not sure if that is true of Venezuela, and would like to look at who actually was supportive of the Venezuelan revolution. But again I don't know that one should see this as a middle class separated from the working class. I think increasingly we have working classes that are also composed of service and knowledge workers, and we should not treat the latter as a middle class, which is separated from them. Obviously no revolutions are made without class alliances, but as those who have had access to mass higher education, find themselves in or out of work in positions of precarity and subordination there is an enormous opportunity for such people to be convinced that it is in their interest to support a socialist project.

Catherine Samary

CS: All experiences show that any vision of the working class that limits it to male, white, and industrial workers is wrong. Of course there is extreme cultural, sexual, racial, ethnic, and professional diversity among the proletariat. Also, in the existing capitalist system, there are a large number of those who have no employment, or are in very precarious employment. This diversity obviously affects the consistency of the resistance of the organized working class. The way multinational companies have organized their process of production (outsourcing, de-localization) has also negatively impacted the labor's organizing power. Membership in trade unions, in countries that workers are allowed to have unions, have often radically decreased or have been "integrated" in class collaboration. Moreover, besides sexism, there is the unfortunate existence of extensive racism that divides workers within each nation and between them. In France, for example, Front National is the number one organization attracting workers. So we see that the working class is highly differentiated and heterogeneous. The issue is to overcome those divisions.

SR: And this makes the project of socialism even much more difficult.

CS: Yes more difficult, but deeper as it combines the fight against different forms of oppression. In any case, the very narrow definition of working class is not correct. Parts of intellectuals and of the so-called middle classes should be included in the working class. However, concrete analysis must take into consideration both their material condition of life, and concrete and subjective behavior. New features of increased precarious work, loss of employment as a result of outsourcing by the multinational firms, feminization of the working class, along with massive immigration, and increased exploitation of unprotected workers, have produced dramatic changes in societies and have created serious difficulties for the old workers movement to organize and to fight against racism, sexism, and so on. Inequalities and work differentiations are on the rise and class interests divide intellectuals, employees, private entrepreneurs, and wage earners.

The building of "organic intellectuals" coming from new social movements and their integration within a "collective intellectual" or new socio-political organization, are part of the rallying together of new "actors" of the transformation, men and women from different strata. They must respect autonomy and self-organization of different actors, resisting different kinds of oppressions and relations of domination; and they must altogether permit an egalitarian collaboration within a general fight for common goals. To fight against capitalism, we need to take into account all kinds of oppressions and establish an ideological counter hegemony against the dominant one at different levels, from local to global. As a global system, capitalism imposes its rules along with social and environmental destructions. The resistance must create counter powers at all those levels before being able to create a new world order. No doubt, it is a very difficult task, and with no guarantee of success. But if we don't try, there is a guarantee of barbarism.

CHAPTER 8

Practical Steps

What are the practical steps for the proponents of socialism to move closer to the desired alternative to the present global capitalist system?

Gilbert Achcar

GA: Since you are speaking of an alternative to the *global* capitalist system, we must therefore define what it is in the first place. We have discussed the social-economic contours of gradual transition. I think that the political framework of a global alternative should combine maximum decentralization—which is an indispensable condition of direct democracy—with an international federation of social republics run by a dual representation of citizens (a house of representatives) and national republics (a senate), the latter on a historical transitory basis. This federation ought to be ruled according to the principle of subsidiarity observed by the European Union, whereby problems are dealt with at the most immediate level consistent with their solution. Such an alternative can only be built gradually with the birth and multiplication of social republics. The most important practical step in that direction is the building of a new international workers' association on the political model of the nineteenth century's International Workingmen's Association. This was regarded as obsolete and replaced with the Second International, in 1889. However, the initial model is more in conformity with the state of the socialist movement and the needs of the socialist struggle nowadays in my view, not to mention the historical lesson of the need for ideological pluralism.

Such an international association should organize coordinated and synchronized international actions—on social, economic, political, and ecological issues—such as those its ancestors did organize, and such as the present Global Justice movement also did in its heyday.

Aijaz Ahmad

AA: One thing that I have already mentioned is precisely reconceiving the class and finding out a way that this vast majority of the working people emerge as a collective political agent, instead of a dispersed and fragmented army of workers and the unemployed. The other thing is the issue of culture and ideology that has been transformed in such a degree in our time to new forms of ideological coercion. Manipulation of the mind, and colonization of how you see. For example, take the case of the terrorist actions in Paris. Similar incidents had happened in Beirut, Baghdad, and elsewhere, and no one had paid any attention to them. Why? Partly because the way ideological structures and information structures are controlled by the corporate elite.

A most important question is, how do you create an informed citizenry in this age of global disinformation so that they actually think about the kind of issues that you are talking about? It is astonishing that so many hundreds of thousands of activists around the world keep the mobilization and the raising of consciousness going, and this is an immense achievement in the face of this ideological offensive. But the question is how to create a counter state, how can you create a different alternative public sphere. Some activities are going on, but its reach is extremely limited. In India, for example, you have a situation that most of the progressive editors have been thrown out and replaced by right-wing editors. The majority of the journalists are left-wingers, and they have to work in these newspapers and struggle hard to somehow smuggle few progressive sentences within the pieces they write. They work in these newspapers because there are no alternative public sphere created by the left, and in which they would be able to play a useful role. There are immense numbers of people who would love to read progressive pieces if there were some organizational forms within which the left journalists could work. But there are objective limitations. The amount of capital it takes to organize an ideological sphere of that kind is enormous and the left cannot provide it. But there is a historic task. People are thinking and they are vulnerable to indoctrination. The instruments of indoctrination are in everyone's home. Television serves as a party school, a study circle of the bourgeoisie. It always propagates its ideology. How can we create an alternative of the left is an organizational question and an intellectual question. Combating the ideological triumph of corporate capital and its machineries of disinformation is, I believe, as important as inventing appropriate organizational forms for the greatly changed character of the working class in our time.

Rob Albriton

RA: Such a large question is difficult to answer briefly, but I shall try by focusing on two very large steps: (1) Breaking with the capitalist focus on profit maximization, particularly when such maximization has huge social costs or destructive "externalities"; (2) Build a strong international movement against capitalism and for human and environmental flourishing.

First, we need to find ways of rewarding economic activities that advance long-term flourishing, particularly when they replace economic practices that are socially or environmentally costly in the short term or long term. For example, adding sugar to processed foods may increase profits because many people like sugar nearly to the point of addiction. The result, however, is likely to be increased obesity and poor health, along with a shorter life span. Furthermore, most of the sugar used to sweeten foods comes from sugar cane or corn syrup, with the result that these crops take up more and more of the earth's arable land and fresh water that could be used to grow healthy foods. If we had a transparent financial system, we could tax away all profits and redistribute them as needed to advance those economic activities that most advance human and environmental well-being. Finally, markets are not self-governing institutions, and in a democratic socialist society, they need to be treated as nothing but instruments of planning.

Second, while local anti-capitalist struggles can make gains, at the most basic level, the most serious crises we face in the long-run are global—global warming; exhaustion of resources; pollution; degradation of land, water, and air; the globalization of capital in order to exploit the cheapest labor and exploit the environment where protections are weakest and corruption is strongest; refugees and immigrants trying to escape poverty and violence; the sale of arms that fuel wars or are used to maintain authoritarian regimes. One can go on and on, but the point I want to make is that the closest thing to global government is the UN, but despite the many just minded people who work for the UN, it generally serves the interests of the most powerful capitalist states and would need some radical changes in order to even pretend to be at all democratic. In light of these brief comments, I think it is obvious that we need to build an international movement with real strength, and we need to either radically reform the UN or replace it with more democratic and politically effective institutions, although at this point in time, the UN is better than nothing, for it along with some NGOs and other international organizations do push progressive causes internationally.

These two steps—the redistribution of profits and a powerful international movement—may seem impractical and utopian in the world as currently constituted. However, practical steps in the short term often cannot be made unless they are informed by long-term goals, possibilities, and visions based on ideals that can mobilize masses of people to fight, even if it is a long hard fight.

Kevin Anderson

KA: I think we are in a better position compared to 15 or 20 years ago when socialism was very discredited. I remember Richard Rorty, a left wing philosopher and declared socialist, wrote in 1992 that entrepreneurs are necessary for any society and most unfortunately the example he chose was Donald Trump! (You can find the quote in my Lenin book.) Social consciousness has now advanced compared to that period and the word socialism is not as discredited as during that time. Yeltsin's rule did not turn that well, or even Vaclav Havel's more attractive model in what became the Czech Republic did not deliver the hoped for free market utopia. Right-of-center people had this utopian dream of the so-called free market system, with some of their left-of-center allies speaking of a social market system.

Philosophical and political clarification of our actual aims is very important. We have many younger people coming to the so-called alter-globalization or global justice movement, but they do not have the knowledge of past attempts at socialism or the necessary theoretical education and we have to develop that. We should not skip over the experience of statist communism in the USSR and Maoist China, but come to terms with it. The more democratic statist models, where they tried to force the state to be social democratic and to create a stable welfare state under capitalism, also turned out to be illusory, as capital cannot be controlled on such a basis over the long term.

Some kind of articulation of what communism is in Marx's own terms and those of some of the more astute people in Marxian tradition, like Rosa Luxemburg, has to be theorized further for today. Second, we need to conceptualize the various social forces and groups with revolutionary potential, as we discussed in the previous question. The left has carried out—and rightly so—a lot of analysis of the global capitalist system, its controversies, the causes of recession so forth, but what we lack is enough hard-nosed analysis of social groups and forces of the capitalist society in the twenty-first century, what their revolutionary potentials are, and how issues like class and globalization relate to what is sometimes called identity politics, around issues such as gender, race, sexuality, age, disability, indigenous status, religious minority status, ethnicity, and so forth.

We are still in a phase where the more identitarian politics have the upper hand in the social movements in the USA, and while the critique of capital has reasserted itself, I don't think it is as present as needs to be. Thus, in the USA, in light of the Black Lives Matter movement, people are speaking of the need to change the racist system from top to bottom. But there is less discussion of the relationship of racism to capitalism. I don't mean in a reductionist sense of course, but in the sense that the successive forms of racial subordination that have characterized US history were connected to different phases of US capitalism, as I argued in a recent piece building on the Marxist–Humanist tradition. I wrote that in discussing race in America, we have to talk about various historical regimes, various forms of capitalism and the forms of racism and racial subordination connected to them: (1) Black slave labor in the plantations of the South, when the USA was not yet really industrializing and was an agricultural dependency of Britain; (2) after the Civil War, semi-free Black agricultural labor, often sharecropping, in the South, policed by Ku Klux Klan (KKK) and other forms of violent terrorism, and over time with mass migrations to the industrial North, with formally free Black industrial or service labor under racially unequal conditions, this during the era of the USA as the world's paramount industrial capitalist nation; (3) since around 1975, with the global downturn of capitalism that we are still experiencing, mass Black unemployment as a result of deindustrialization, followed by mass imprisonment of a considerable portion of this large relative surplus population, and at the same time, the emergence of a small relatively affluent Black middle class of which Obama and Holder are among the most successful examples.

And at each of these junctures, there have been efforts—with mixed success—to unite Black and white labor across the lines of these racial barriers. One of the most effective of these was during the Great Depression of the 1930s, when interracial industrial labor unions gained headway in mass production industries like automobile, steel, and so on. Racism did not disappear of course, then or now, and Black workers struggled, sometimes in alliance with radical white workers, against both the new union bureaucracy and continuing forms of racial subordination. Today's Black Lives Matter movement is another example of solidarity across racial lines, as this movement has involved Black youth from some of our economically most downtrodden communities, as well as Black and white youth from some of our top universities. As I mentioned earlier, however, the anti-capitalist dimension of this struggle is in need of development, both theoretically and practically. But can racism be abolished without uprooting capitalism? That is the kind of question that needs to be addressed more today.

In other parts of the world, we have similar problems. Look at France, for example, with the *Charlie Hebdo* killing, carried out by disaffected French Muslims of North African descent who grew up in conditions similar to those of the Black ghettoes of the USA. In the past, the Communist Party had a big influence in the Arab neighborhoods, but not anymore, in no small part because of its insensitivity to ethno-religious differences. These communities are not composed of Islamic fundamentalists, even if the perpetrators of the Charlie Hebdo massacre were themselves fundamentalists.

These communities do have a social and ethnic consciousness that can move them in a leftward direction, although there are many conservative religious influences as well. What will be decisive is the attitude of French white progressives. If they continue with their free speech absolutism, dismissing concerns over how caricatures of the Prophet in the dominant media are perceived in these marginalized communities, as ethno-religious insults, then the prospects are dire: more support for fundamentalism and continued growth of the reactionary National Front Party. Some forces on the Left are trying to create solidarity across these barriers, among them the Marxist publisher Editions Syllepse, who has translated a lot of material from English on race, ethnicity, and revolution, among these my own *Marx at the Margins*. They publish not only theoretical works, but also hard-hitting books about French racism and police repression of minorities.

We have to be present in all these movements. I am a big supporter of grassroots movements, but I believe we should be aware of and openly opposed to reactionary elements among these movements. One litmus test to help determine whether a movement is essentially conservative is its attitude toward women's rights. But it is necessary to study each of these situations concretely, historically, and dialectically.

SR: This is a very important point that you raise and it is what we are confronted with in the case of Iran and much of the Middle East. Islamism along with other religious fundamentalisms are on the rise not only in the Middle East, but also in the western world and it has become harder and harder to confront these reactionary forces. Unfortunately, some on the left do not recognize this threat, like when some were supporting Ahmadinejad and I wrote a piece criticizing them including James Petras, and some in MRZine and other journals.

KA: One could add to your list those who support Putin's enclave in eastern Ukraine and his takeover of Crimea. Putin is gaining support not only from some of the less critical parts of the international Left, but also from outright reactionaries like the French National Front. This takes us back to where we began our conversation. If we focus on what type of society we want to build, on a positive vision of the future, on socialist humanism, then we can avoid the trap of getting sucked into failure to critique or even support for reactionary forms of anti-imperialism. Moreover, if so-called socialists are supporting or failing to critique the likes of Ahmadinejad and Putin, it raises serious questions about what type of new society they have in mind. Would it just be a twenty-first century version of Stalinism? That's why I think that as part of figuring out what socialism is, we have to assess more carefully what it is not, going back again through the whole experience of the twentieth century, especially the origins and nature of Stalin's Russia. Doing so would place us in the tradition of Marx, who spilled a lot of ink critiquing forms of socialism of his era that did not measure up to the needs of the time.

Barbara Epstein

BE: The first step is to form a broad organization of the left intended to attract the participation of organizations, movements, individuals that share the intention of moving toward an egalitarian society, protecting the natural environment and other species, and rebuilding the public arena. Without an organization in which discussion of goals, strategy, and tactics can take place, we will remain trapped in cycles of short-lived upsurges of protest that lead to no concrete results. This organization, which I envision as less than a party but more than an umbrella, would engage in electoral politics, educational campaigns, direct action, and any other forms of activity that might seem appropriate, hopefully without sectarian bickering over which is best. The aim would be to bring together those who see the urgent need for a society governed by the common good, and the good of the planet. Socialists would participate along with others, but would put aside the view that as socialists they are automatically more advanced than others and more deserving of leadership. There are clear limits to the degree to which equality can be achieved short of socialism. Many socialists, including myself, are convinced that a harmonious relationship between humanity and the rest of the planet is not possible under capitalism. But we cannot separate ourselves from non-socialists who are working toward equality and environmental sustainability on grounds that they are not convinced of the necessity of socialism, or do not share our conception of socialism. An organization of the left would be an arena for discussions of this question along with questions of tactics and strategy.

We need to rebuild unity on the left without losing sight of diversity. This means overcoming the barrier between our generation, of the 1960s and 1970s, and younger generations of radical activists. It also means creating bridges between the various sectors of the left: on the whole, white leftists know little about left movements among people of color, academic leftists know little about the labor movement left, and so forth. It means creating organizations and institutions of the left, on a national and perhaps also an international scale. It also means dropping the traditional conception that reform and revolution stand in opposition to one another, and the effort to create a pure revolutionary politics, untainted by reform. But the left, and the power of ordinary people, is built by demanding and winning reforms, while at the same time pointing out that these problems are embedded in a capitalist social structure and that while reforms may make people's lives a little easier, they can only be partial solutions. The organizations that are built and the concessions that are won in this process strengthen the left and help to create confidence that further change is possible.

Aron Etzler

AE: I think a key strategic goal is to make the public sector a strong instrument for the needs of the population. In this process, our party clearly has the role to spearhead the debate. And, after we win it, we will make it reality together with the Social Democrats. They are not hostile, just a bit wavering.

I give you one example, after 30 years of privatization in Sweden, we challenged the policy in the election, trying to get rid of the profit seekers in the public sector. It was successful, but we still do not know whether it will pass through the parliament. If this goes through, it will be the biggest de-privatization program in Europe, and a major strategic shift. It shuts capital off from a substantial portion of the Swedish economy. A huge chunk of the economy, the tax money which is a huge amount, goes to schools, hospitals, and other public sector institutions. They will be either under public ownership for most part, or some kinds of cooperative, and other forms of ownership that we can democratize them more and attune them to the people's needs. This could be a huge step forward.

Another step that we are taking now is to challenge the government tax policies, which unfortunately brings in too little money to the public sector and to satisfy needs of the people. These are just two examples, but they are aimed at the roots of the neoliberal program.

I think one should not neglect the fact that in general, the last 30 years have been a backlash for us. This does not mean that we cannot move forward on some issues. When you move forward on many issues, it means that you have broken the backlash, and it can be done. I was studying the case of Norway from 2005 onwards and its third biggest city of Trondheim. A right-wing government for 14 years had ruled the city, until the left found a way to fight back and win in 2003. Last week the left, and in a sense, a traditional social democracy in its best sense of the word, won the election again for the fourth time and that means they will have ruled this town for the 16 years. They've followed a program of democratization, and have made it the most equity-based cities of Norway. They did it as trade unions radicalized. These unions through their members they asked what kind of policies they would like to be followed, and then put forward them as demands to different parties. This process was also followed at the national level in 2005, leading to the most progressive government in Europe. Democracy was at the core of their political strategy.

SR: One point I wanted to ask regarding de-privatization that you mentioned. Would these institutions become part of the government, or they would be managed differently. As you know, there is the issue of bureaucratization that we have seen historically.

AE: We don't say that everything should go back to state. We allow schools, hospitals, and other service organization be run by NGOs, community, or religious organization, as well as companies, but we say in these activities, you cannot make profit above something like 5 or 6 percent. Companies seeking profit will have no interest in investing in these activities. All money should go to the things they were meant for. It is a de-marketization of one of the biggest parts of our economy.

Sam Gindin

SR: In your article, "Rethinking Unions, Registering Socialism" in *Socialist Register, Question of Strategy,* you end your argument somewhat philosophically, which I found most interesting. You talk, with a reference to Daniel Bensaid, of "the existential choice to live our lives as *if* working class potentials to create a new world can in fact be realized".

SG: To begin with, I would re-emphasize the *methodological* point that history is contingent and has to be understood as contingent. There is no teleological principle that says that workers will become revolutionary and that socialism will necessarily come. But it is also a *philosophical* point because there is nothing in our experience that suggests we can win. This is not a matter of being pessimistic but of being confronted with a choice. Even if the chances of socialism being possible are very slim, and even if a convincing argument is made that there is no chance of socialism coming in our lifetime, or even in 100 years, what else can we do with our lives? For some of us, pursuing the socialist dream is the most meaningful thing to do with whatever time we have.

Peter Hudis

PH: The most important practical step we need to take is to have collective discussions about what is a genuine alternative to capitalism that avoids the failures of what it called itself socialism or communism over the last 120 years. We need a debate about it. We need organizations, committees, academics, activists, and others to be engaged in a vibrant debate about what is socialism for the twenty-first century and explore it with new eyes.

SR: And also the question of how to move toward it.

PH: Yes, but it is less important to discuss the transition to the final goal than the final goal itself. Not that the former is not needed. It's that the former is already known. The transition must be based on decentralized, democratic, rank-and-file forms of association, and organization that breaks down the hierarchy of leaders and led and thinkers and doers in the course of the struggle itself. We know from history that this is the proper form of transition. What is lacking is an adequate understanding of what we are supposed to be transitioning to. If we cannot articulate the ultimate goal, we cannot expect that even if massive struggles do arise they will move in a socialist direction. So, I think we are facing the opposite position of Marx in his era. Marx felt that the first task is to advance the working class movements, and second to articulate the alternative to capitalism from that. We are in a reverse position today because we have an experience that Marx did not, namely Stalinism and other forms of pseudo-socialism. We have to work out a philosophically grounded concept of the alternative to capitalism, and from that, we can expect necessary and important struggles to emerge and grow. This means breaking with the habit that the entire left has inherited in the last 150 years of thinking that envisioning the future is somehow less practical than organizing a strike or a demonstration.

Second, we need to redefine the role of organization. We should stop imagining that we need to create a party that will seize political power and somehow figure out what to do with that power when we get there. There is no point to forming an organization or party unless these organizations are involved in the process of developing a philosophically grounded alternative to capitalism. Because if we don't and we get lucky enough, like Syriza in Greece, to come to power, we will not have a clue as what to do with that power. I think that we have to realize that the old idea that the role of a Marxist organization is simply to seize political power and lead the working class to the political domination of the state does not make any sense in an era when the alternative to capitalism is so vague and un-discussed.

Ursula Huws

UH: There are two fronts; one is in the labor movement in the workplace to try to bring a better match—earlier I talked about the mismatch between objective class position and subjective class-consciousness. That means to do the sort of consciousness raising work in the workplaces that produces series of "kerching!" moments (moments of realizing that the result of your labor is being appropriated by a capitalist). To make that happen in the heads of all those people who are objectively part of the working class, but not subjectively. This is a huge task. But once it has happened, you can use that to develop organization along the value chain. The other strand is organizing locally in a particular territory, not within the workplaces, [but within neighborhoods and other places]. If we think of the value chain in the work place as a kind of vertical linear thing, the line of organization at the local level is horizontal, and involves everybody else who is in that territory. Working with whatever organization exists on that territory, be it a community organization, political parties, and so on. Miners living in a mining town, workers in their housing estates and communities [can mobilize and organize]. So it is always a double front. The vertical and the horizontal have to be connected at multiple points so that where there is a conflict one can come to the support of the other.

SR: Also, as you mentioned earlier, we need mobilization at the national and global levels. Moreover, in your earlier works, you have discussed the need and complexities of working with different movements, such as collaboration between socialists and environmentalists, the so-called red and green.

UH: Yes, as for the national and global levels, absolutely this is what we need. In principle, it is possible and there can be many solidarity actions of various sorts internationally. Historically over the centuries, workers have taken many solidarity actions. The classic cases have been the logistics workers, such as dock workers and transport workers. You can draw a line from the factories in China to the Amazon warehouses, and along that chain, all workers involved in the production, transportation, and distribution can be involved. Or you can take it back [upstream] to the mines and provision of raw materials. In another way, this can be done along the whole linear value chains; also, horizontally, there can be collaboration among other movements and organizations, including with other movements, feminist, environmentalist, anti-war, and so on.

Michael Lebowitz

ML: We have to learn to walk on two legs. We should have a party and that party must walk on the leg of taking the existing state away from capital; struggling and pointing out to the people how the capitalist state is an instrument of capital. This is one side of the struggle: we have to show the irrationality of capitalist ownership of the means of production in the context of the destruction of the environment and human beings. The other leg is to build peoples' capacities by struggling for creating new forms of organization, and new institutions, and so on. I stress communal councils, workers' councils, and local organizations.

Another thing that I want to add is the absolute importance of the struggle for transparency. I was looking recently at the policies of the New Democratic Party of Canada in my province of British Columbia, where I was the policy chairman in the mid-1970s, and I was showing to Marta Harnecker the part of the policy on which the party ran and got elected. It was under the heading "Open the Books" of the companies and institutions. Open the Books is very important offensive demand that puts capital, the corporations, and the bureaucrats on the defensive. When they say we cannot open the books, we can say what are you hiding from the people, from the workers, and from the state?

Leo Panitch

SR: In the introduction of *The Question of Strategy*, in *Socialist Register* (2013), you and your colleagues emphasized among other factors, the great significance of organization. The question is what type of organization?

LP: I think everywhere one needs to begin where Marx began; with socialist education and association. Partly because of the failures of the past, there is no longer much of a socialist culture left. It is a tragedy that communist and socialist and labor parties have given up that role. As I said earlier, my father was a worker, he worked in factories as a cutter and sewer for fur coats. He only had a grade four education. But he knew more about politics, including Roberts Rules of Order than do my fourth-year students at university. He learned that in the trade union movement and in the socialist movement. It is not just a matter of vanguards coming along with Leninist ideas and imposing them upon people. It is about people developing their capacities that are otherwise being stifled in a capitalist society. Socialists of course need to get people's attention by articulating a set of relevant and attractive demands upon the state and upon capital, and a lot of this can be around de-commodification. It can be around de-commodification of transport, of education, of health, and not just about working conditions and income. I think that increasingly makes sense to people. It also involves being honest with people. I am very critical of the tendencies in social democratic parties to compete with the neoliberal parties by being anti-tax. If we just go around saying "make the rich pay" in the sense that we only need to tax the wealthy, we don't help working people understand that in order to have de-commodified social services they also need to pay taxes. If you play the anti-tax game with them, you're only undermining the process of political education through which people can alter the current situation and prepare themselves to be able to make socialist change. As Marx once said this needs to be seen in terms of a long 15, 20, and even 50 processes; if you tell people that the revolution must come right now, when people know there aren't the conditions for it, they will more likely take to their beds—or hide under them. I am very suspicious of catastrophists of the type who always predict the final crisis of capitalism is coming soon, having already predicted some 15 such capitalist crises before now. Similarly, you have some ecologists now who are constantly speaking in terms of us only have five or ten years left before the ecological catastrophe is upon us. I am not challenging the seriousness of our ecological crisis today, but these people are not doing anybody a service with this kind of talk. I think they are creating basis for fatalism. We need enough time to be able to build the capacity to change the world and if you give people the impression that there is no time left, then what is the point of engaging them in this process? In that sense, like you, I believe we have to have long-run strategic perspective not a short-run strategic perspective.

SR: That's why I argue, while we should not leave aside the grand ideal of socialism, we have to be practical in coping with the challenges of confronting global capital. And since, unfortunately, we are in a long haul in capitalism, we need to strategize what is to be done during the capitalist era, in order to move to post-capitalist phases. That is why I came up with the suggestion of a preparatory phase.

LP: I understand, but I think we should never limit ourselves to the responsibility for making capitalism better in any country since socialism is not on the cards today. We need to have a long-term socialist perspective, not the kind of long perspective that says I will leave that to others while I meanwhile take responsibility for making a better capitalism instead.

SR: It is very true. The aim is not to make better capitalism, but to radically prepare the ground for transition from capitalism.

Catherine Samary

CS: We are obliged to think and act from the local to the global. Capitalism has become, more than ever, globalized. We need to contribute to the emergence of an "alternative hegemonic bloc" against dominant neoliberal and xenophobic ideologies. This should be anchored in local/national/regional/global realities, linked with existing networks and associations fighting against the destruction of fundamental rights, human dignity, and the environment. Intellectual and militant resistances must invent counterpowers to the dominant forces; they must be radically democratic, encouraging self-organization of all the oppressed, discriminated and dispossessed people. How to transform scattered resistances of the 99 percent into new collective rights against the powerful 1 percent is a key strategic question that must find articulated answers at different territorial levels. Those answers should take into account the richest experiences of the past and present struggles and draw collective balance sheets of failures in order to learn from them. More than ever, "don't mourn, Organize!" should be concretized with a radical humanist and internationalist content against any gender, racist, or other kinds of discriminations.

Index

A
Achcar, Gilbert, xi, 27, 53, 87, 109, 135, 163, 189
Ahmad, Aijaz, xi, 29, 56, 88, 110, 137, 164, 190, 191
Albriton, Rob, xi, 31, 61, 89, 112, 138, 166, 191
Alexander III, 68
Algeria, 74
Allende, 7, 87, 97, 105
Al-Qaeda, 8
Alter-mondialism, 2
American Civil War, 90, 97
Anderson, Kevin, xii, 33, 62, 90, 114, 139, 168, 192
Arbenz, 7
Austrian Social Democratic Party, 12
Autonomist Marxists, 75
Aziz al-Azmeh, 30

B
Bakunin, 9, 15, 24n22, **25**, 66, 156
Bernstein, Henry, 45

Bismarck, 11, 31
Black Lives Matter, 141
Blanquist revolution, 53, 61
Bolsheviks, 3, 28, 41–3, 52, 55, 59, 79, 80, 83, 110, 148, 151
Bonapartist, 33, 62
Brazil, 59, 96, 103
Bretton Woods, 38
BRICS, 132

C
capitalism, xi, xii, xiii, 1–24, **26**, 45, 57, 98, 119, 137, 148, 165, 203
Charlie Hebdo, 194
Chicago Teachers Union, 174
Chinese revolution, 65
CIA, 87, 90
COMECON, 30
Communist Manifesto, 9, 10, 22n1, **25**, 57, 78, 141, 165
communists, 4, 95
consciousness, xii, 77
Croatia, 150

Note: Page numbers followed by "n" denote notes

Cuban Communist Party, 51
Cuban revolution, 51
CUPE, 94
Cybertariat, xiii

D
democracy, xiv, 7, 22n6, 23n20, **25,** **26,** 198
Denmark, 99
Die-Linke, 98
Dunayevskaya, Raya, 42, 168

E
education, xiv
English Revolution, 136
Epstein, Baraba, xii, 34, 65, 91, 116, 141, 170, 196
Etzler, Aron, xii, 36, 68, 93, 117, 142, 171, 197

F
FBI, 90
First International, 9, 15, 82
flat world, 125
Fordist, 154
Fourier, 149
French revolution, 51, 59, 62
Friedman, 125

G
Galiev, 42
German revolution, 32, 130
Gindin, Sam, xii, xiii, 39, 69, 93, 120, 143, 172, 198
globalization, xi, 109, 116, 118, 125, 128
Great Depression, 194
Gulag, 157

H
Harnecker, Marta, **25**
Hegel, 22n2, **25,** 33, 41, 43
helpling, 181
Hezbollah, 60, 96
Holland, 9
Hudis, Peter, xii, 40, 72, 96, 124, 140, 145, 175, 199
Human Development Index (HDI), 6
Huws, Ursula, xii, 44, 77, 98, 126, 149, 178, 200
Hyndman, Henry, 9

I
IMF, 20, 110, 112, 113, 116, 118, 130, 132, 133
India, 30, 59, 111, 168, 182, 190
Indignatos, 107
ISIS, 8
Islam, 60

J
Jacobins, 33
Jihadists, 60

K
Kaiser, 80
Kautsky, 2, 4, 54, 62, 110
Keynesian, 110, 126
KKK, 194
Kurds, 115, 168

L
Latin America, 59, 93, 100, 119, 143, 167
Lebowitz, Michael A., xiii, 23n9, 45, 78, 99, 129, 151, 182, 201

Lenin, 12, 13, 28, 33, 41–3, 48, 50, 57, 58, 65, 76, 82, 83, 88, 110, 139, 140, 145, 151, 152, 165, 192
Leninist party, 44
Lukacs, 40, 74
Luxemburg, Rosa, xii, 41, 42, 52, 80, 83, 126, 193

M
Maduro, 7, 101
manufacturing capital, 59
Maoism, 65
Marxian social revolution, 22, 53, 77
Marxist Humanists, 75
Marxist institutional analysis, 104
Meszaros, Istvan, **25**
Middle East, xi, xiii, 4, 7, 64, 84, 195
Moody, 118
Morales, 7
MRZine, 195

N
Napoleon, 33, 51
Narodnaya Volya, 68
nationalization, 155
NATO, 111, 133
neoliberalism, 30
New Deal, 34
New Economic Policy (NEP), 3
Nigeria, 74
Nove, Alec, **25**

O
Occupy Wall Street, 57
October revolution, 42
OECD, 6, **26**, 111
Ontario Council of Hospital Unions, 94
Ordoliberalism, 105

P
paid labour, 179
Panitch, Leo, xii, xiii, 22n1, **25**, 49, 79, 102, 130, 155, 183, 202
Paris Commune, 9, 10, 28, 29, 53, 56, 59, 82, 87, 97, 140, 156, 176
Parti-Ouvrier, 10
Plekhanov, 43
Podemos, v, 6, 37, 98, 120, 172
Pol Pot's Cambodia, 139
proletarianization, 111

Q
Quebec Solidaire, 131

R
racism, 17, 194
radical social democracy, 21
Rahnema, Saeed, xiii, 24n20, **25**
reform, 2–9
reformist, 5
Russian revolution, 27, 50, 52, 68

S
Samary, Catherine, xiii, 52, 82, 105, 132, 157, 185, 203
Sandinistas, 54
Seattle, 77
SEIU, 173
self-management, 160
Social Darwinism, 41
social democracy, xiii, 22n3, **25**, 42
Social Forum, 2, 111–13
socialism in one country, 109, 110, 124, 133
Socialist Party of England, 9
socialization, 136
Soltanzadeh, 42
South Africa, 96, 123
StingRay, 91

Sweden, v, xii, 6, 36–8, 64, 68, 118, 120, 142, 171, 172, 197
Swedish social democracy, 37, 50
Syriza, v, 6, 7, 37, 45, 61, 98, 106, 120, 121, 123, 124, 130, 131, 138, 156, 172, 200

T
Taliban, 8
Taskrabbit, 181
third world, 34, 65, 133
Troika, 3, 132
Tsarist Russia, 34, 65

U
UAW, 121
UNESCO, 133
United Socialist Party of Venezuela (PSUV), 7
United States, v, 9, 30, 31, 34, 61, 64, 74, 76, 90, 96, 99, 102, 111, 141, 142, 165, 176
unpaid labour, 179

V
Venezuela, xiii, 7, 48, 76, 94, 97, 101, 114, 124, 153, 154, 183, 185
Vietnam War, 35
violence, 65, 88, 92

W
Wahhabism, 60
Weberian typology, 163
working class, 171, 183
World Bank, 20, 110, 113, 118, 130, 133, 164
World Health Organization (WTO), 20, 110, 113, 118, 129, 130, 133

Y
Yeltsin, 192
Yemen, 8

The manufacturer's authorised representative in the EU is Springer Nature Customer Service Centre GmbH, Europaplatz 3, 69115 Heidelberg, Germany. If you have any concerns regarding our products, please contact ProductSafety@springernature.com

Printed and bound by CPI Group (UK) Ltd, Croydon, CR0 4YY

23/03/2026

02076662-0003